Current Issues in International Business

To our colleagues in the School of International Business, Griffith University, Brisbane, Australia.

Current Issues in
International Business

Edited by

Iyanatul Islam and William Shepherd

Edward Elgar
Cheltenham, UK • Lyme, US

Published by
Edward Elgar Publishing Limited
8 Lansdown Place
Cheltenham
Glos GL50 2HU
UK

Edward Elgar Publishing, Inc.
1 Pinnacle Hill Road
Lyme
NH 03768
US

A catalogue record for this book
is available from the British Library

Library of Congress Cataloguing-in-Publication Data

Current issues in international business / edited by Iyanatul Islam
    and William Shepherd.
        (New horizons in international business)
        Includes bibliographical references.
        1. International business enterprises. 2. Competition,
    International. I. Islam, Iyanatul, 1953– . II. Shepherd,
    William F. III. Series.
    HD2755.5.C87 1997
    658'.049—dc21   97-5355
                                                             CIP

ISBN 1 85898 292 8

Printed and bound in Great Britain by
Biddles Limited, Guildford and King's Lynn

Contents

PART THREE: CURRENT ISSUES AND CONTROVERSIES

PART FOUR: FUTURE DIRECTIONS IN IB EDUCATION AND
RESEARCH

Figures and Tables

About the Editors

Associate Professor Iyanatul ('Yan') Islam was a member of a pioneering group that implemented Australia's first undergraduate programme in International Business at Griffith University. He has written extensively on the role of public policy and politics in the internationalisation of East Asian economies. He is one of the founding editors of Journal of Asia-Pacific Economy (Routledge) and is a member of the editorial board of Journal of Asian Business (University of Michigan).

Associate Professor Bill Shepherd led a group at Griffith University that designed and established Australia's first undergraduate programme in International Business. He has written on financial integration and is involved in a collaborative research project that is aimed at developing innovative data-analytic techniques for international productivity comparisons. He is currently Dean, Faculty of Asian and International Studies, Griffith University.

Contributors

Nancy Adler – McGill University

Christopher Bartlett – Harvard University

Thomas Brewer – Georgetown University

Peter Buckley – University of Leeds

Mark Casson – University of Reading

Farok Contractor – Rutgers University

John Dunning – Rutgers University

Sumantra Ghoshal – London Business School

Dafna Izraeli – Bar-Ilan University

Ray Loveridge – Aston University

Stefan Robock – Columbia University

Alan Rugman – University of Toronto

Kenneth Simmonds – London Business School

Satwinder Singh – University of Reading

Brian Toyne – St Mary's University

Alain Verbeke – University of Brussels

George Yip – UCLA

Stephen Young – University of Strathclyde

Preface

This edited volume is a collection of commissioned essays that deal with a wide range of topics in International Business (IB): its historical evolution, its inter-disciplinary roots, some current issues and controversies and future directions in IB education and research. Written by leading scholars in the field, the book represents the forging of an intellectual partnership between this distinguished group and a young and enthusiastic institution (School of International Business, Griffith University).

The publication of this book needs to be set against recent developments. In 1994, when the Journal of International Business Studies (JIBS), the official journal of the Academy of International Business (AIB), reached its 25th anniversary, it decided to engage in a massive stock-taking exercise. It aimed to achieve this through

- Commissioned articles on trends in IB research
- Compilation of a 25-year index of JIBS
- A series of autobiographical essays by pioneers in the field.

An initial attempt was made to design a book project along the lines of JIBS in 1992, but the idea was temporarily set aside because of resource and personnel (as well as personal) constraints. The project was revived in 1993 when it was scaled down to a small collection of commissioned essays by leading IB scholars, some of whom are pioneers in the field. The current volume represents the fruits of that long and dogged effort. Readers will find that the essays represent a very timely, thoughtful and honest appraisal of what IB is all about and what it ought to be about.

Acknowledgements

In designing and developing this book, we have inevitably incurred debts to many. Acknowledgments certainly need to be made — and we do so with a great deal of pleasure.

First and foremost, we would like to thank all the authors who responded to our invitation and have written in this volume. Despite their stature and onerous commitments, they strongly endorsed the publication of this book and ensured that deviations from deadlines were kept within tolerable limits. Without such support and co-operation, the book could not have materialised.

The Faculty of Asian and International Studies of Griffith University funded overseas trips of both editors that were crucial in initiating and launching the book project. Bill Shepherd went to the UK in 1993 and held preliminary discussions with Ken Simmonds, Stephen Young and Peter Buckley. This was followed up by a very productive visit to the 1994 AIB Conference where discussions were held with Stefan Robock (Columbia Business School), Brian Toyne (St Mary's University), John Dunning (Rutgers), Christopher Bartlett (Harvard), Alan Rugman (University of Toronto), Nancy Adler (McGill University), Farok Contractor (Rutgers). Don Lecraw (University of Western Ontario) and Raj Aggarwal (John Carrol) were most helpful on that occasion. Bill Shepherd also undertook a second visit to the UK in early 1996 for final discussions with Ken Simmonds and Stephen Young. Iyanatul Islam made an extended trip (as part of his sabbatical) to the USA and Canada in 1995. Farok Contractor, Sam Beldona, Sankaran Raghunathan (Rutgers) Ben Kedia (Center for International Business Education and Research, Memphis), Raj Aggarwal, Thomas Brewer (Georgetown) and Alan Rugman turned out be wonderful hosts and freely shared ideas.

Managing a book project that entailed the collaboration of scholars stretching across Australia, UK and US proved to be a daunting task. Jennilyn Mann ensured that such a task was smoothly accomplished. Jennilyn demonstrated her incomparable technical skills when she managed to ensure that the draft chapters — which arrived in various shapes and sizes — met the exacting specifications of the publisher. There was also the onerous task of following up editorial queries with different authors which she did with customary efficiency. Without the technical support and assistance so spontaneously offered by Jennilyn, it is most unlikely that much progress would have been made. Of course, we bear responsibility for any remaining errors and omissions.

In editing this book, we had to spend many hours away from our families. They bore the burden of isolation with grace and dignity and allowed us to complete our tasks. Nothing could have been accomplished without such wonderful support.

Introduction

Iyanatul Islam and William Shepherd

THE CONTEXT

International Business — henceforth IB — is both old and new. Transactions in goods and assets as well as movement of people and ideas across national boundaries stretch back centuries. It is, of course, fashionable to rediscover such cross-border transactions with a great deal of vigour and dub them as 'globalisation'. While we may not yet be in a 'borderless' world, changes in communication technology, public policy (most notably economic liberalisation) and a host of other factors are, on balance, leading to a closer integration of nations with different historical, cultural and political backgrounds.

While the phenomenon of cross-border transactions has an ancient pedigree, its study as a distinct academic enterprise is of comparatively recent origin. One could argue that a formal formulation of theories designed to understand a subset of such transactions — namely, international trade — started with David Ricardo in the last century. IB, however, is much more than just international trade — or even international economics. The Ricardian perspective focused on countries as units of analysis. It is probably banal to observe that it is ultimately organisations (both public and private) — and not countries *per se* — that engage in international transactions. Hence, understanding what motivates organisations to seek goods, assets and human resources across national boundaries remains a central question of interest. IB theorists have turned to the economics of organisations, rather than the traditional domain of trade theory, but even such an approach is inadequate. After all, one needs a knowledge of organisation specific and country specific variables and the complex interplay of history, culture, politics and economics that shape such variables. Inevitably, a single discipline will not be adequate in dealing with such issues. Hence, the need for IB as a distinct academic enterprise that spans across disciplinary boundaries.

1

While it is relatively easy to establish the distinctiveness of IB *vis-à-vis* more traditional disciplines, the pioneers in the field and the leading scholars of today (many of whom are represented in this edited volume of essays), continue to express a sense of anxiety about its identity as well as its future as a dedicated area of academic inquiry. This is a reflection of its youth (IB as a field of study is a post-Second World War phenomenon), the stranglehold of disciplinary specialisation on the academic world and the inherent difficulty of shaping a coherent paradigm for intellectual endeavours that deal with diffuse and disparate topics. Nevertheless, the quest for a distinct field of study that approaches and appreciates cross-border transactions from a blending of different paradigms remains highly pertinent. It is this sense of mission that has driven the editors — disciplinary specialists by training, but multi-disciplinary by temperament — to compile a set of essays by pioneers and leading scholars in the field of IB. These commissioned essays are, in most cases, original, but inevitably contributors have drawn — in some cases heavily — from their previous research and publications. These essays are both reflective and forward-looking: they look at the past, discuss the present and make projections about the future.

A READER'S GUIDE

This volume follows a thematic structure in which a sense of 'history' is injected in Part One (two chapters), the conceptual frontiers of IB are discussed in Part Two (three chapters), some current issues and controversies are surveyed in Part Three (five chapters), and future directions in the field of IB are delineated in Part Four (two chapters). A final chapter rounds up this volume with a summary and synthesis.

The Historical Evolution of IB as an Academic Discipline

As noted, the two chapters in Part One offer a historical perspective on IB. Kenneth Simmonds (Professor, London Business School) (Chapter 1) observes that IB (defined to mean cross-border transactions) is not new and goes back to 2500 BC. Although one can identify a prototype IB school at Oxford University (known as 'school of estate management') that operated for some 400 years since the twelfth century, it is only since 1960 that one can discern a move to give IB organisational identity within universities. Ever since then, IB has been subject to the perennial question: is it an academic discipline? To this Simmonds offers a cogent and compelling response. Judged in terms of the ubiquity of cross-border transactions, student demand,

and the simple but effective criteria of a body of knowledge that can be taught, IB can be regarded as a discipline. Simmonds emphasises that IB should continue its quest for general understanding of disparate and difficult issues and should avoid vocationalising itself, particularly along the lines of a conventional MBA. The author is confident that, over time, IB will build on its own special discipline and rigour.

Stefan Robock (Professor, Columbia University) (Chapter 2) also revisits the early days of internationalising the business curriculum and sets the appropriate historical context for identifying the obstacles such an effort faces and the strategies that need to be adopted for a flourishing field of IB. He highlights several historical events: the adding of an IB curriculum to conventional business programs at Columbia University (1956), Indiana University (1959), Harvard University (1961) and New York University (1961); the establishment of the Association for Education in International Business (AEIB) — the forerunner to the Academy of International Business (AIB) — and the establishment of *Journal of International Business Studies* (JIBS) in 1970. Robock provides a fascinating account of the early days of IB in terms of paucity of teaching materials, the lack of publication outlets and the opposition from unsympathetic disciplinary specialists. The author acknowledges the important role that pioneering professors played (particularly those 'internationalised' through the First World War military service and the Peace Corps) and the assistance received from such United States-based initiatives as the Fulbright Scholars program. While the struggling and fledging phase of IB is over, Robock concludes that sustaining IB as a field of study requires a change in recruitment, promotion and tenure rules as well as in ensuring that IB programmes are adequately funded.

IB as an Interdisciplinary Field of Study

Part Two of this volume focuses on the question of the interdisciplinary foundations and frontiers of IB. In Chapter 3, Brian Toyne (Professor, St Mary's University) delineates the conceptual contours of IB. The author recognises that the field is a 'fragmented adhocracy' as he surveys the major paradigms that have guided the field for the last 40 years. The chapter proceeds to highlight two dominant paradigms: the 'extension paradigm' and the 'cross-border' management paradigm. In the case of the former, international business is simply seen as an extension of a firm's nation-bound activities. Theories, metaphors and methodologies developed to study a nation-bound firm can also be readily adapted and applied to international business activities. In the case of the latter, the emphasis is headquarters-subsidiary interaction (in terms of monitoring, co-ordinating and integrating) in diverse environmental circumstances that are typically engendered by the movement of goods and services across national boundaries. The author highlights the need to consolidate an evolving 'interaction' paradigm that stems form their 'social' process approach to IB. This makes the IB boundaries rather less well-defined since it encourages a multi-disciplinary approach and the need to understand how international organisations, governments, firms, and individuals 'accommodate their persistently changing cultural, social and political differences through an ongoing process of reconciliation'.

John Dunning (Professor, Rutgers University), in Chapter 4, reflects on the contribution that the economic theory of the firm has made to the development of a 'core' theory of international production. He makes a distinction between the 'internalisation' paradigm and his own 'eclectic' paradigm. The emphasis of both is on international production — defined to mean production financed by foreign direct investment (FDI) and undertaken by multinational enterprises (MNEs). The author notes that the internalisation paradigm is primarily concerned with analysing why firms 'supplant cross-border intermediate product markets by administrative fiat and why ... they choose to locate these value-added activities in a foreign, rather than a domestic location'. Dunning argues that the eclectic paradigm extends the scope of inquiry by seeking to 'identify and evaluate the advantages or assets which enables the investing firms to out-compete their foreign rivals in the first place'. The author contends that both paradigms proved very effective in dealing with IB issues in the 1970s and 1980s, but the 1990s pose fresh challenges to any theory purporting to be a 'core' theory of international production. He draws attention to the emergence of 'alliance capitalism' in an innovation-driven, globalising economy characterised by both inter-firm cooperation and competition. This means that extant, firm-theoretic approaches will have to move away from its focus on hierarchies and markets to a study of more pluralistic combinations of hierarchies, inter-firm alliances, networks and markets as well as the role that national governments play in such a process. This inevitably means a holistic approach that draws on different strands of economic theory and business disciplines as well as the recognition of the central fact that political, cultural, strategic goals and aspirations of firms and governments impinge on, and shape, purely economic motives.

Thomas Brewer (Associate Professor, Georgetown University) (Chapter 5) explores the potential synergy that exists between IB and international political economy (IPE). The author maintains that the traditional concern of both the IB and IPE literature is with the power and strategies of MNEs. Brewer maintains that there is now an increasingly important concern, namely the interaction of international public policy regime change and MNEs' strategies. The author documents a number of significant changes in FDI public policy regimes at various levels (national, bilateral, regional, multilateral) since the early 1980s. Thus, there has been significant liberalising tendencies with respect to FDI in both industrial and industrialising countries; there has been a big increase in bilateral investment treaties (BITs); regional initiatives, such as NAFTA (North American Free Trade Agreement) and APEC (Asia-Pacific Economic Co-operation) have consolidated; a series of international agreements have spawned a new multilateral FDI regime centred on the World Trade Organisation (WTO). Brewer believes that the net effect of such changes is to create a new era in the public policy environment of MNEs. The author concludes that IPE literature on international regime changes offers a rich array of concepts and approaches that could be incorporated in the conventional IB literature to yield insightful interdisciplinary studies of public policy regime change and MNEs' strategies.

Some Current Issues and Controversies

While Parts One and Two of this volume focus on tracing the historical evolution of IB and exploring its interdisciplinary terrain, Part Three uses such a context to introduce the reader to a sample of current issues and controversies. George Yip (Adjunct Professor, UCLA), in Chapter 6, launches Part Three by re-visiting the much-cited notion of a 'borderless' world and its impact on MNEs' strategies. The author observes that in a truly 'borderless' world, the standard prescription is that MNEs should have a global strategy. This inspires him to evaluate the standard prescription. Yip finds that global strategy is multi-dimensional concept encompassing market participation, product standardisation, marketing, and competitive moves. He points out that a multiplicity of variables — organisation structure, human resources practices, corporate culture — influence the propensity to adopt a global strategy. Nationality matters too and one can observe variations across US, Japanese and European MNEs. An exhaustive survey of published research allows him to conclude that the 'effective use of global strategy involves a flexible approach that globally integrates or standardises some activities or functions while localising others'. The author concludes that in order to advance to the next frontier of research on global strategy, a more rigorous theoretical construct would need to be devised that can trace the multiple variables that determine MNE strategy under diverse circumstances.

Christopher Bartlett (Professor, Harvard University) and Sumantra Ghoshal (Associate Professor, London Business School) re-visit their much noted work on the 'evolution of the transnational' in Chapter 7. Their conceptualisation of the transnational company is inspired by case-study type work on a range of well-known US, European and Japanese companies (e.g. 3m, ABB, Kao, Intel). Eschewing the traditional approach that perceives companies in terms of a formal organisational structure, they focus on three core processes that characterise the management paradigm of the future — the entrepreneurial process, the integration process and the renewal process. In the case of the first, the focus is on the ability of organisations to 'open markets and create new businesses'; in the second, the emphasis is on the integration of 'world-wide resources and capabilities to build a successful company'; finally, the renewal process entails the ability to revitalise an organisation by challenging extant beliefs and practices in order to develop a durable institution. Bartlett and Ghoshal, through carefully selected and documented cases, show that the implementation of these core processes entails a radical re-thinking of conventional roles of different layers of management. Thus, front-line managers should become 'aggressive entrepreneurs' rather than 'operational implementors'; middle managers should transform their conventional role of 'administrative controller' to 'that of inspiring coach'. The most challenging role is for top management who must 'create the necessary infrastructures and contexts for others to play the new roles demanded of them'. Organisations that are able to carry out these transformations at different levels of management will be the 'winners in the game of global competition'.

The issue of global strategy is once again the subject of Chapter 8. The authors, Alan Rugman (Professor, University of Toronto) and Alain Verbeke (Professor, University of Brussels), take the work of Michael Porter as their starting point. They conclude that Porter's well-known three generic strategies (cost leadership, product differentiation and focus) are '30 years out of date when applied to the analysis of MNEs'. Such a critique enables them to develop a new framework of global strategies. The core concept pertains to firm-specific advantages (FSAs) which can, in turn, be location-bound (LB-FSA) or non-location bound (NLB-FSA). The authors note that strategies can in turn be either 'efficiency-based' or 'shelter-based'. In the case of the former, firms seek government protection (through tariffs, for example) to sustain business operations in the face of both domestic and international competition. Efficiency-based strategies, on the other hand, exploit both LB-FSAs and NLB-FSAs. Depending on the nature of FSAs, MNEs can either use multiple home bases or a single home base in carrying out their strategies — where a home base is defined in Porter's sense to mean the nation where the firm 'retains effective strategic, creative and technical control'. The framework developed by Rugman and Verbeke can accommodate different strands in the IB literature on global strategy, such as Bartlett and Ghoshal's 'transnational solution' and the notion of transnational networks.

In Chapter 9, Nancy Adler (Professor, McGill University) and Dafna Izraeli (Professor, Bar-Ilan University) reflect on gender issues in IB. The authors lament the fact that companies worldwide draw from a highly restricted pool of potential managers: women are grossly under-represented in international assignments. Drawing on a multi-country study, Adler and Izraeli rigorously examine some popular beliefs — or 'myths' — about women managers in international operations. First, there is the widely held perception that women do not want to be international managers; second, companies refuse to send women abroad; third, 'foreigners are so prejudiced against women that they could not succeed as international managers'. The authors find that both the first and third perceptions are false and hence myths. The second is true: 'firms are hesitant, if not outright resistant, to sending female managers abroad'. This leads them to conclude that the solution for rectifying gender imbalance — and outright discrimination — in human resource systems that undergird international operations lie with companies themselves. The authors conclude that the subject of women as international managers is no longer a strictly equity concern. It has become a central business issue given that global competition need top quality managers. Some leading MNEs have recognised this reality and are acting accordingly.

While Chapter 9 focuses on human resource management (HRM) issues from a specific, but crucial, perspective, Chapter 10 by Mark Casson (Professor, University of Reading), Ray Loveridge (Professor, Aston University) and Satwinder Singh (University of Reading) examine the theme of HRM in a broader context. They draw on a large-scale, multi-country survey (200 affiliates, 50 parent companies plus follow-up in-situ interviews with 47 firms spread across thirteen parent countries and twelve host countries) 'to explore the relationship between HRM practice and the stances adopted by senior management towards other strategic issues'. Respondents in the survey were asked to articulate their position on job security and career, business objectives, the inculcation of a corporate culture and headquarters-subsidiary relations. In some cases, national archetypes are confirmed, such as the greater concern for job security among Japanese parent companies and affiliates, the lesser weight attached to short-term profitability in Japanese firms relative to their US counterparts. In other cases, similarities emerge, such as the general perception that 'headquarters determine long-term strategy and affiliates determine short-term tactics' and 'regular visits' as the most common mode of communication between headquarters and subsidiaries. Many firms within the sample were beset with cross-cultural problems of communication that impaired headquarters-subsidiary relations, while the development of global managers were disappointingly small. The authors conclude that 'the redesign of management structures and accompanying career structures to ensure better local representation might improve the development of MNEs' core competencies in the long run'.

Future Directions in IB Education and Research

Part Four of this volume provides the opportunity to explore future directions in IB education and research. Farok Contractor (Professor, Rutgers University), in Chapter 11, asks: What are the traditional approaches to the training and education of the 'compleat executive'? What needs to be done? Contractor reminds the reader that progress in internationalising business education in the United States (but not so much in Europe) is still disappointingly modest. This reflects a host of factors: the dominance of specialists in the education system, the enduring perception among some specialists that IB is not an intellectually rigorous field, limited academic positions (despite rapid growth in recent years) of IB doctorates and so forth. Despite such constraints, Contractor is confident that there are niche areas in which IB education can flourish, even in the United States. These include: 'specialised certificate programs, IB 'finishing schools' and IB programs designed from the perspective of managers in emerging and developing countries'. The author also provides a comprehensive review of current modes of delivery in IB education (specialised IB departments, IB centres, 'infusion' of IB curriculum in traditional departments, etc). All modes have both strengths and limitations. The new niches described above thus hold a great deal of promise. Ultimately, one has to recognise that in a rapidly changing and globalising world, traditional business education is far from adequate. IB, as a field of inquiry, has developed distinct concepts, approaches and paradigms and will continue to remain highly relevant in the training and education of the 'compleat executive' of the future.

Peter Buckley (Professor, University of Leeds), in Chapter 12, examines trends in IB research and reflects on its future. He highlights the role that economics has played in shaping IB theory. The field has matured to the point where 'it has fed back concepts into the core disciplines rather than being a mere borrower of basic concepts'. Buckley recognises that international management theory, stemming from the work of Porter, Bartlett and Ghoshal and Doz, Hamel and Prahalad, has also enriched IB theory, but the influence of certain fields — such as international political economy and social anthropology — has been under-rated and under-exploited. The chapter delineates several issues — globalisation, international alliances among MNEs and the social and cultural context of IB — that are going to impinge on the evolution of research paradigms in the field in the next 25 years. The author notes that these issues have already bred a range of novel concepts —

such as commitment and reciprocity, signalling and business culture. Still, a lot needs to be done. The integration of a range of related fields (noted above) will have to occur to a much greater extent than has been the case so far. The fluidity and volatility of the international business environment and the way MNEs are responding to such developments will occupy the energy and attention of future researchers.

CONCLUDING ASSESSMENT

Stephen Young (Professor, University of Strathclyde) (Chapter 13) provides a summary and synthesis of the writings in the volume. Young believes that one has reached an 'appropriate moment to review the state of international business as an academic subject and to ponder on the future'. He appreciates the need by the writers of the volume to clearly delineate the conceptual boundaries of the field and the multiple channels through which challenges to MNE management are being transmitted by a rapidly changing international business environment. Unlike some contributors, Young believes that the contribution of economics to the development of IB theory, while clearly significant, can be easily over-rated. More importantly, the future of the field needs a genuinely multidisciplinary approach. The author contends that 'the time is ripe for international business journals and conferences to encourage contributions of a review nature which specifically seek to explore the international dimensions of related subjects. This will both further promote interdisciplinary research and highlight more clearly the boundaries of international business'. Young warns that unless international business studies 'get(s) closer to practitioners and the writings of managers and consultants', IB research runs the risk of becoming 'isolated from the work of the international executive'.

PART ONE

The Evolution of IB as an Academic Discipline
— The Institutional and Regional Context

1. International Business as an Academic Discipline

Kenneth Simmonds

INTRODUCTION

International Business is not new. Sumerian merchants as early as 2500 BC found that they needed to station men abroad to receive, store and sell their goods (Wilkins 1970: 3). Nor is the teaching of International Business new. When Manchester Business School was formed in 1965, Sir William Mansfield Cooper, Vice-Chancellor of Manchester University, acknowledged that the first British business school was a school of estate management at Oxford University. It ran for some 400 years from the late twelfth century, and almost certainly dealt with the export and merchandising of wool to the Continent.

International Business has also funded universities for centuries. For their 150 years, the oldest American universities were British universities often funded by merchant venturers. The early Spanish universities in the New World were funded in a similar way.

What we have seen since 1960, however, is a move to give International Business organisational identity within universities. Such moves have not been universally applauded. For every case advanced in favour of International Business as an academic discipline, another criterion is advanced for questioning its right to exist. Yes, Dorothy, there are sceptics.

Some of the arguments against International Business seem unnecessarily pedantic. Yet International Business holds up well even when the viewpoint adopted is itself questionable. International Business can meet the same criteria as any other business subject and can even hold its own against such an established university subject as history.

SIGNIFICANCE AS JUSTIFICATION

To a few, the simple existence of International Business is enough to justify its place in a university. International Business is there, and therefore worthy

13

of study. This view is consistent with the concept of a university as a group of scholars who may pursue their enquiries in any direction in which they feel human understanding might be furthered. Such a viewpoint of course, raises the question as to whether any subject needs organisational identity within the university. Real freedom of enquiry would require that any organisational unit be no more than a loose grouping of scholars currently interested in that field.

Others base their acceptance of International Business on the significance of the phenomena. International Business is undoubtedly huge and ubiquitous. It is economically important. It shapes our economic world and has a long history of doing so. Modern economics virtually began with Adam Smith's concern for explaining the wealth of nations. Real national wealth and value added can move one country to country just as significantly today as in Adam Smith's time. One has only to compare successive issues of the *World Bank Atlas* to see how major the fluctuations in GNP per capita of single countries can be. Argentina for example, which for 50 years followed the United States and Canada as third in the world, was 30th by 1973, 54th by 1983 and back to 33rd by 1993. The Gulf States, in turn, boomed to importance after 1983. What *have* changed since Adam Smith's time are the strategies of multinational firms in switching the investment and activity between countries, and the strategies of the competing countries. Understanding of how multinational firms formulate their strategies and react to changes in country strategies is of crucial importance to any country concerned with improving its lot. By any standard, International Business passes the significance test.

THE MARKET TEST

Perhaps the strongest case that can be made for separating any subject within the university is that students want to study it As Cardinal Newman pointed out so eloquently (Newman 1852), freedom within the university is essential if academic integrity is to be maintained. If students want to study and think about International Business, they should be permitted, even encouraged, to do so. This overrides any idea that more advanced scholars know best and that academic tradition should dominate.

A belief in the academic freedom of the student, of course, raises major questions about attempts to plan academic offerings centrally. There are so many who mouth the concept of freedom and abhor central planning above them, yet who believe in planning the levels below them. The rigid MBA design of the American Association of Collegiate Schools of Business, which for many years held Business Schools away from International Business verged towards this orientation. At the very least, it infringed upon the responsibility of individual universities to determine their own future as self-governing communities of scholars. And freedom to choose the actual focus of study reduces the possibility of rigid teaching or of the number of student places being based upon the existing status of any area.

There is some evidence, moreover, that student demand is rational. Many students want to study what is not well known, what has scarcity value and what will challenge them. Conversely, the study and memorisation of others' patterns of thought that is less likely to be as valuable is limited to smaller numbers. In effect, economic value lies behind the choices students make. The large and growing demand for International Business courses is thus *prima facie* evidence of expected value in use.

ACADEMIC OR VOCATIONAL

The term 'academic' derives from Plato's concept of an academy whose members are concerned with general and liberal understanding rather than technical or vocational learning. Is International Business concerned with general understanding, or with understanding for a particular decision purpose?

At the extreme, there are some who argue that International Business should cover training in how to fill in a bill of exchange or clear goods through customs. A little more broadly, others assert that international firms are the customers for International Business education and that training should be for the current needs of these customers. Such an assertion ignores the fact that all education must reside with individuals, not with statutory entities. Thankfully, though, these are not majority views. If organisational needs as perceived by some with power in organisations were to become the guidelines for the subject, any striving for general understanding by teacher or student would quickly die.

A more widely accepted view, even within universities, is that International Business as a subject exists to develop abilities to take decisions in business or affecting business, with cross-national implications. While adoption of such a decision orientation should limit the subject in some ways, it would not necessarily eliminate it from classification as an academic discipline. The cross-over into a vocational subject would occur only if the subject were structured to focus the scholar, whether teacher or learner, away from general inquiry. Tied to a vocational curriculum, the subject could quickly become static, without the continual questioning needed to provide further insight.

In seeking broader understanding rather than vocational inculcation, International Business has a clear advantage over business subjects for which there are functional posts with similar titles within organisations. An International Business academic defining the subject as what international businesses do, could still maintain academic integrity because of the definition's very wide scope. It would be much more narrowing for a marketing academic if marketing were to be defined as what marketers do.

International Business also has an academic advantage over business subjects that have allowed their training to degenerate into basic platitudes. Approaches which advance trite ideas such as three generic strategies, four Ps, or five forces, as a basis for evaluating complex situations, can position a subject as a collection of vocational mantras. Allan Bloom (1987: 369–70) has some justification for his criticism of American MBA training:

> Moreover, a great disaster has occurred. It is the establishment during the last decade or so of the MBA as the moral equivalent of the MD or the law degree, meaning a way of insuring a lucrative living by the mere fact of a diploma that is not a mark of scholarly achievement.

International Business has luckily avoided these pitfalls. It incorporates the study of so many different issues, accommodates so many different paradigms, and has changed so frequently that it could not be classified as forsaking the quest for general understanding.

IS INTERNATIONAL BUSINESS A DISCIPLINE?

The loosest definition of a discipline is any body of knowledge that can be taught. Measured by this definition, International Business is certainly a discipline. It is a branch of knowledge. But how does the subject measure up against a tighter definition of a discipline as teaching that requires mental self-control in mastering a coherent body of knowledge?

Few subjects outside the natural sciences, mathematics and philosophy follow very far the rigour of applying existing theory to arrive at predictions that fit the details of particular situations. Economists working within the International Business field have tried more than most to apply their own pattern of rigour to the field. The limitation they have confronted, however, is that their approach is to work outward from generalisation, while International Business requires the rigour of particularisation. In the first place, International Business is multinational, rather than binational, and requires the continual identification of how specific actions will impact upon different consumers, different competitors and different county interests that are continually changing. Longitudinal understanding rather than cross-sectional understanding is also required in order to allow for the time from the introduction of any change through to reaction by first one country and then subsequent reaction by others.

In these respects, International Business seems to produce greater understanding when the skills of the historian are harnessed in preference to those of the economist. The skill of the outstanding historian is to examine complexity over time and synthesise a simple model that best describes the inputs and the outcome. It requires a diagnostic rigour of the situation. Economists tend to apply pre-chosen minimalist models and examine the situation against the model. As one would expect, the economists' explanations are limited to the variables of the pre-chosen models. For this reason alone, International Business academics should be wary of over-reliance on economics paradigms.

The vitality of International Business stems from its flexibility in adopting not only the reductionist approach of the historian and the generalisation-based approach of the economist but also a range of paradigms from anthropology, political science, sociology, finance and other fields. The field is certainly eclectic. It is, however, more than the application of concepts from other fields. Concepts specific to International Business can already be identified and more will certainly emerge as future research targets the extensive aspects of International Business in which little research has been recorded.

International Business will never be a science with set of defined and consistently related propositions, which have been tested in predicting and explaining real-world phenomena. There is not enough repetition for that. The field, however, does have its own phenomena in which important variables have been clearly defined and relationships established. Some lawlike relationships are even beginning to appear. For example, it could be postulated that a country will not over time impose costs on international firms that reduce the country's achievement of its own collective objectives. Minorities within countries would either yield to the majority or find ways of taxing the higher benefit. Similarly, at the level of the firm, it might be postulated that a firm's allocation or reallocation of activities among countries reflects predictions of countries their controls so as to maximise achievement of their national objectives.

All this, however, does not mean that, without its own theory, International Business could have no identity as an independent discipline. The application of concepts and paradigms from existing fields to International Business phenomena lying outside those fields provides sufficient justification on its own for identifying a field as a separate discipline. It encompasses phenomena that other subjects do not cover and could not cover with any coherence. In this respect, the quite common suggestion among business academics that, all that is needed for understanding International Business is to 'internationalise' existing subjects within business schools, is a dream that could never be achieved.

Multi-country Transfers

At the core of International Business as a subject are business activities that cross country boundaries. These may involve transfers of physical items including goods, capital, people and information; transfers of intangibles such as ownership; voting power; training; or the exercise of managerial or governmental influence across country boundaries. The subject also includes actions that will affect boundary-crossing activities, although not themselves actually crossing the boundaries. Hence government regulation of the local operation of multinationals is very much part of the subject.

Boundary-crossing activities are perpetually changing. Individual firms can change dramatically the attention they devote to geographical markets, their location of funds, their employee nationality and location, supplier sourcing, and location of research and development. These changes, moreover, are more often multinational than binational. A firm may, for example, place a new plant in one country that involves closing production in several others and changing the entire global supply and distribution pattern. Even a simple pricing strategy may involve differential adjustment by country, perhaps to lower revenue levels where a competitor is strong and to hold revenues where the firm needs to record profits rather than market share growth.

To understand how and why changes come about in boundary-crossing activities, and the moves taken by the interested governments to control the changes, requires a subject that analyses cross-boundary changes in an integrated way. The partial approach of other business subjects would add little understanding. A subject is also needed that looks at the micro-level and not national aggregation alone. Real understanding of why changes occur will only come from examination at the micro level.

Country Conflict

While business firms are the entities primarily performing the switching of wealth and activity from country to country, the net effect after allowing for marginal gains from International Business is that some countries gain and some countries lose. Country interests do conflict. What countries do to protect their interests in effect amount to longitudinal strategies against country competitors, acknowledging firms as the intermediaries. Countries develop strategies for influencing the international strategies of firms. And these country strategies usually consider ahead of time the reactions of competing countries.

These country strategies are a large part of the environmental risks facing multinationals. As such, the strategies need to be understood and projected. No field of business other than International Business adequately copes with this.

Nationality and Country Allegiance

The whole area of national identity of both firms and individuals raises a range of interesting research issues that lie within the domain of International Business.

Nationality is used as a basis for recruitment, pay and promotion within firms, often with significant discrimination between nationalities. The wisdom and ethics of discriminating on the basis of nationality have not yet been investigated very deeply. Few firms adopt policies of worldwide recruitment at the cheapest possible location, even allowing for productivity differences and the difficulties in overcoming immigration barriers. The alternative of individuals changing nationality in order to benefit has largely been left to the individual rather than adopted as a regular practice by firms. Universities seem to have been more creative in this respect.

How far do firms move away from value maximisation in avoiding cheaper sourcing? At any one time, for example, advantage in recruitment may lie from recruiting all systems or accounting staff in India. Even for firms that do recognise where lower costs arise, they seem more prepared to move tasks to the employees than employees to tasks.

Firms have been even more reticent to change their own corporate nationality (i.e. their country of corporate registration) when they face discrimination based on corporate nationality. The success of the few exceptions of changed nationality seems to show that other have forgone value maximisation. They have been prepared to shoulder a nationality cost.

Corporate allegiance to a country also shows in other ways. It is evidenced when a firm tailors any of its actions to benefit a country, at a cost to its own performance. In doing so, it disadvantages itself against competitors who do not have that allegiance. Ultimately such allegiance, however, may disbenefit a country because its firms fail competitively. This raises interesting research questions for International Business. Should countries encourage allegiance, and to what extent? Do countries that describe their legislation on the basis of corporate nationality actually gain?

Allegiance issues also arise when managers are faced with putting the interests of their own country before that of their firm — or vice-versa. Measurement of how employees handle firm-country conflict is in its infancy. At a very basic level, the conflict occurs daily within the multinational as internal transfer prices are set. Some managers seem to feel that taxation minimisation through the legal use of tax haven arrangements is unacceptable and argue for profits and taxation in their own countries.

Cultural Assessment

The crossing of country boundaries inevitably requires an understanding of comparative cultures. Whether the boundary crossing involves physical things or persons or intangible rights and actions, the impact will be different on the receiving side than on the sending side. Things, people rights and actions all have different cultural positionings and meanings.

Because of the holistic nature of any culture, it would be inefficient to attempt to understand differences for specific parts of a culture only. It would be inefficient, for example, to study how management actions might impact on employees in a different culture and as entirely separate exercises assess how suppliers and customers might behave in the same culture. The study of the business significance of cultural variation between different countries is better integrated under International Business than under any subject with primary concern for some part of business only.

The Development Impact of International Business

International firms are change agents to the extent that they transfer new things, ideas and practices into a country from outside its boundaries. It is not unusual for extensive culture change to be brought about by firms — in some cases unwittingly.

To date, very little has been done by business academics to understand the impacts, roll-on effects and total value of innovations introduced by firms. It has been suggested, for example, that the introduction of greater marketing skills may be the key to faster economic development (Drucker 1958; Dholakia and Firat 1976). A contrary suggestion, however, is that businesses in less developed countries in fact adjust very well to markets, within their existing institutional arrangements (Simmonds 1994). Once institutional barriers preventing efficiency are broken down, the already adequate marketing skills will operate as effectively as they do in more developed countries.

International firms striving for profits, moreover, may have little incentive to break down such institutional barriers if the outcome would be perfect competition and the elimination of excess profits.

Whatever the country impacts of international firms may be, there is an evident demand for an International Business discipline that can provide understanding as to what they are.

SUMMARY

International Business has its own domain that other subjects in business cannot cover coherently. The domain is important because of its size, its role in allocating wealth and activity, and its impact on country development. The competing players within International Business are countries, firms and individuals, all competing at their own level and with interests that may cause conflict with the other two levels. Individual countries and firms, moreover, are significant enough to have positions and strategies within the complex interaction that can be separately identified. The positions held are also longitudinal rather than cross-sectional in that the effects of actions can be traced over many periods and at any one period average positions mean little. International Business is thus a complex field that requires and is clearly building its own special discipline and rigour.

REFERENCES

Bloom, Allan 1987. *The Closing of the American Mind,* New York: Simon & Schuster.

Dholakia, Nikhilesh and Firat, Fuat A. 1976. The role of marketing in the development of non-market sectors and condition necessary for success. In Izraeli et al., *Marketing Strategies for Developing Countries*, New York: John Wiley and Sons.

Drucker, Peter 1958. Marketing and economic development. *Journal of Marketing*, January: 252–259.

Newman, John Henry 1852. *Idea of a University.* Oxford (various republications).

Simmonds, Kenneth 1994. Transition marketing. *Society and Economy: Journal of the Budapest University of Economic Sciences,* XVI(3): 9–22.

Wilkins, Mira 1970. *The Emergence of Multinational Enterprise: American Business Abroad from the Colonial Era to 1914*, Cambridge, Mass: Harvard University Press.

2. Internationalising the Business Curriculum: Obstacles and Strategies

Stefan Robock

'Changing the curriculum is like trying to move a graveyard.' This observation, attributed to Woodrow Wilson when he served as president of Princeton University, is an apt characterisation of the United States experience in trying to internationalise the curriculum of its business schools. More than three decades were needed to make significant progress toward this goal and the process is still far from complete.

Management training in the United States expanded rapidly during the decade following the end of World War II, but the business school curriculum in virtually all American universities focused almost exclusively on preparing managers for domestic business operations. Aside from foreign trade and export marketing courses offered in a few schools, all courses were taught as if the United States was the world. Accounting rarely touched on the subject of foreign exchange. Labor management dealt only with United States patterns of labor unions and labor legislation. Business law courses were limited to United States laws. And the management courses implicitly assumed that the principles of management, derived almost exclusively from studies in the United States, were universal and applied equally to all national environments.

During this same post-World War II period, many United States firms were internationalising rapidly through foreign direct investments and facing new management challenges that were not being recognised by the business schools. Awareness of this deficiency, however, slowly began to emerge in the mid-1950s and early 1960s. A few pioneering business school professors began to develop courses on international marketing, as replacements for export marketing, and on managing international operations. And a more significant 'breakthrough' occurred in 1956 when Courtney Brown, who had worked for a major international petroleum company, became Dean of the Columbia University Business School and added a specific international business (IB) program to the curriculum. Shortly thereafter, IB programs were added to the curriculum at several other business schools including Indiana

University in 1959, Harvard University in 1961 and New York University in 1963. A parallel and related event was the formation by a small group of a professional association, the Association for Education in International Business (AEIB), later renamed the Academy of International Business (AIB), that came into being at the end of 1959 (Fayerweather 1986).

Spurred on by these initiatives, the long and challenging process began of creating a new field of study and inserting it into an established academic framework. The long process included (1) defining the field of international business studies; (2) developing concepts, information and teaching materials; (3) designing courses; and above all (4) internationalising the professors.

DEFINING THE FIELD

During the 1960s, defining the field of international business became a popular parlour game — always enjoyable, usually spirited, frequently controversial, and eventually productive. And it was the leading topic at several conferences, beginning with the first conference on education for international business held in the United States in December 1963 at Indiana University and attended by deans or their representatives from more than 80 business schools (Robock and Nehrt 1964). Some academics questioned whether there actually was such a distinctive new field. Some argued that IB was nothing more than applied economics. Others argued that nothing more was required than adding an international dimension to existing functional disciplines. Others took the position that the main focus of IB training should be on doing business within specific foreign countries or on international corporate business studies that identified similarities and differences among countries and business systems. The issues of whether IB discipline and whether a concept of IB existed that differentiated it from other academic fields were also debated.

Out of these discussions, a consensus gradually emerged that the instructional and research focus of IB should be on those unique issues that arose when business activities crossed national boundaries. Recognising the emergence of multinational business firms, this meant that future managers should be trained to operate in a number of different business environments. Studies limited to a specific country and comparative business studies were considered valuable sub-areas for the international business field, but the main thrust of the field was to be the management of the cross-border flows of goods, services, capital, personnel, transfers of technology, etc. Within this concept, the international environment, including such issues as treaties, institutions for facilitating the transfer of money across national boundaries, and regional groupings such as the European Common Market (now the European Community, EC) became an important component of IB studies, as well as the national environments of different countries.

This consensus shoved aside the academic debates about whether IB was a discipline (an issue that continues to be discussed), and whether IB consisted of completely new and unique content. The rationale for IB as a field of study for business schools recognised that many concepts and much knowledge that could be drawn upon for IB courses already existed in the fields of political science, anthropology, law and economics. At the same time, new concepts and new information would be needed. The practical question became whether business schools were giving future managers the necessary training for operating in the globalising world economy. The task of defining the field of international business therefore shifted to that of identifying the special issues that arose when business transactions crossed national boundaries and that were not presently covered in the business school curriculum.

The unique variables and considerations that have fostered the field of international business as a separate area in business school training have been identified as international risk elements, the potential for multinational conflicts, the multiplicity of environments and the role of international business as a major change element in the economic and social development of a nation. The field also includes problems of decision-making by public officials who must understand the effects of government policies and actions on international business activities and take such effects into account in the formation and implementation of public policies.

The special risk elements confronted in international business activity include financial, political, regulatory and tax risks. They arise because of the existence of different currencies, monetary standards and national goals, but these risks are all measurable through their effect on profitability or ownership. The multinational conflict elements arise because of different national identities of owners, employees, customers and suppliers and because national interests and the business goals of multinational corporations diverge in many respects. The multiplicity of environments with different cultures and diverse institutional settings is perhaps the most pervasive distinction between multinational and domestic business operations. The role of international firms as change agents requires an understanding of what can and cannot be achieved by a change agent as well as an appreciation of the potential contributions that international business can make to the process of economic and social development.

To reach a consensus on defining the field represented great progress in the evolution of international business studies. When I joined Indiana University in 1960 to head a new international business program, I asked the dean ''What do we teach?' His answer was 'That is what you have to decide'. The same problem was encountered by other early professors in the field. The functional interests and disciplines of the early United States pioneers in international business were remarkably diverse and included business school areas such as accounting, labour relations and marketing as well as the traditional disciplines of economics, political science, law and anthropology. And all of these functional areas and disciplines made contributions toward defining the field of international business.

DEVELOPING CONCEPTS, INFORMATION AND TEACHING MATERIALS

A definition of the field was a beginning. The next challenge was to develop or find concepts, information and teaching materials needed for internationalising the business curriculum. A few schools like Harvard and IMEDE in Switzerland, had prepared a number of cases with some international business content. But, as Professor Vernon explained in describing the evolution of the IB program at Harvard, 'I could find no packaged curriculum, no textbook, that would offer a spoor of the trail others had beat before me. There were texts in international economics, histories of foreign direct investment, treatises on international antitrust problems, stories of Standard Oil, Unilever, and General Motors; but a text for an international business course, according to my lights, was not to be had' (Vernon 1994).

An early contribution to the field was a bibliography: *Cases, and Other Materials for the Teaching of Multinational Business* published by Harvard in 1964 (Bishop and Lindfers 1964). One of the first textbook efforts for the international business field came from Professor John Fayerweather. As he recounts, in the late 1950s a growing number of cases were becoming available but more was needed. 'Out of this situation came my first textbook, *Management of International Operations*', (Fayerweather 1960). Cases were the heart of the book. But as he explained, 'The book was ahead of its time commercially. The market was thin and the book did not get beyond its first printing' (Fayerweather 1994). Several other authors followed Fayerweather's effort with international business textbooks that, likewise, didn't go beyond a first printing. The problem in my view, aside from the thin market, was that the development of concepts and information on international business had not yet progressed sufficiently to provide enough substantive material. In fact, it was not until the late 1960s and early 1970s that IB textbooks began to be reprinted.

The contribution of private foundations and the United States government, towards financing international business research by faculty and graduate students greatly expanded the materials available for business school training. This contribution deserves special mention. The Ford Foundation in particular made substantial grants to Harvard and Indiana Universities in the early 1960s to support the IB programs at those schools. These grants financed a number of international business monographs by professors and doctoral theses based largely on empirical research and field studies. The United States government, through the *National Defense Education Act,* provided a large number of generous doctoral fellowships for new business school programs, which included the field of international business.

Along with the development of general specific IB textbooks, specific IB textbooks for courses in the functional fields began to appear in the late 1960s. These included textbooks in international and multinational marketing, business finance, accounting and management. These functional textbooks generally had earlier success than the broader IB survey textbooks because many schools were responding to the need to internationalise their curriculum by first offering international courses in the traditional functional areas.

The accepted definition of international business studies implied that the content of the field must include disciplines other than economics and the traditional functional business areas. Consequently, part of the task of developing teaching materials was to identify work in other disciplines related to IB issues. At the early stages of developing IB materials, the available contributions from these other disciplines were mixed and generally limited. In the field of anthropology, there were a few 'gems' like *The Silent Language* by Edward T. Hall (1959) on problems of cross-cultural communications. In contrast, the field of political science had little to contribute on the important subject of international business political risk. Political scientists were interested in the subject of political stability as related to revolution. But this approach was not appropriate for international business operations because many political changes short of revolutions can have a major impact on international business operations. The field of international economics made significant contributions to international business in the area of the international economic environment, but the overlap with international business, as Professor Robert Aliber has noted, is partial. International economics, he noted, were concerned with a large number of welfare propositions that international business ignored, but gave scant attention to the relationships that the international manager needs to understand between similar economic and business variables located in different countries (Aliber 1968).

Another important aspect of the evolution of IB instructional materials was the early shortage of professional journals in which IB research could be published. The *Harvard Business Review* published some articles directed to business managers that were useful for IB instruction, but it was not a refereed journal and not particularly interested in so-called scholarly papers. The *Columbia Journal of World Business,* established in the mid-1960s and directed also toward a business audience, was more receptive to scholarly pieces but did not have the desired cachet of being a refereed journal. The problem of professional journals was greatly alleviated by the establishment in 1970 of the *Journal of International Business* (JIBS) by the Academy of International Business. And as the IB field developed, other professional journals began to emerge in the functional fields such as marketing and finance.

ORGANISING THE CURRICULUM

International business training in United States business schools advanced most at the postgraduate level and in programs leading to the Master of Business Administration (MBA) degree. Some steps were also taken to include the international dimension of business in undergraduate business programs and in executive development programs. In addition, some business schools had 'semester abroad' programs which permitted the student to complete part of his or her course work in a foreign university. Living in a foreign country can 'internationalise' the student, yet foreign study per se does not necessarily include training in the substantive aspects of international business.

At the MBA level, the design of the IB program had to take into account the characteristics of the students and the different types of careers they expected to pursue. Some students wanted to study international business as a field of concentration, intending to follow a career working in foreign countries or in the headquarters of a multinational firm that uses mainly local nationals in its foreign subsidiaries. Others would study IB as a supplement to their functional concentration in accounting, marketing, finance and so on. Some students were interested in IB as preparation for working in government positions responsible for the development of policies for assisting and controlling foreign direct investment. Still others intended to work for domestic firms, but needed some IB background because their firms faced competition from foreign firms in their home markets. For all of these kinds of clientele, a minimum preparation needed for dealing effectively with the international dimension of business included two goals: to develop familiarity with the body of knowledge on international business and to develop personal traits of special sensitivities, attitudes, flexibility and tolerance.

The need for personal and emotional training to deal with international business matters deserves particular emphasis because such training requires more than academic reading and lectures. Ethnocentrism can be diluted in several ways, some of which can be part of the academic program. Recruitment from various countries exposes the IB student to other cultures and values through class discussion and through working on projects with students of different nationalities. Also, student exchange programs that arrange short internships with business firms in foreign countries, such as AIESEC (Association Internationale des Etudiants en Sciences Economiques et Commerciales), founded in Europe in 1948 can accomplish some of the necessary personal reconditioning through giving students experience of living and working in a foreign environment.

Given these goals, a number of different strategies have been tried by various United States business schools since the early 1960s for internationalising the business curriculum, with varying degrees of success. In all situations, the internationalisation movement meant changing both the organisational structure of the business school and the content of instruction. It also meant looking at other divisions of the university for courses that might be valuable for IB students. But, as academic institutions rank among the most difficult institutions to accept change, the pace and degree of success in implementing a strategy invariably depended upon the role of the dean. In internationalising the curriculum, the administration cannot play a neutral role.

The ideal situation would be to revise the functional courses to include an international dimension where appropriate, and an early effort was made in this respect by a committee of eight business scholars in four functional fields: accounting, business policy, finance and marketing (Otteson 1968). This strategy, of course, was limited by the reality that professors teach what they know. Consequently, most professors had first to become internationalised for their courses to be internationalised. But even where internationalisation was accepted, it was generally recognised that many concepts and significant information about international business did not fit into the traditional functional courses and required that new courses be added to the curriculum.

From the organisational standpoint, the issue arose as to how the international business responsibility should be handled. Should there be a separate IB department or division? When I joined Indiana University in 1960 to teach IB, I asked the dean, 'What department will I be in? And even though I was a staff of one person, the dean replied, 'You should not be in any of the traditional departments. If we make IB everyone's business it becomes no one's business.' A number of other schools followed the same pattern and created a separate nucleus and advocacy group for IB. At the same time, an inter-departmental committee was often established to assist in the infiltration of international content into the functional courses. In some cases, the resistance to internationalising functional courses was so strong that the IB group had to design and offer the international marketing, international finance and international management courses. Where professors in the functional departments established advanced international courses, they usually became members of the inter-departmental committee as well as of their departments.

As Professor Lee Nehrt commented in 1968 on the issue of a separate IB group:

> Most people are in agreement that the most desirable method is through an internationalisation of existing courses. The problem seems to be in the implementation of such a scheme and the probability that this will happen quickly is very low. I do feel, however, that an International Business department or area must be established initially and that it must then work diligently and continually to diminish its role. If a dean feels that he can achieve the internationalisation of the various functional courses without establishing some central organism from which the spirit of internationalisation emanates, he is either fooling himself or he has established for himself another full-time job. (Nehrt 1968)

It is interesting to note that, in the late 1960s, after a decade of having a separate IB group, the Dean of the Harvard Business School proposed the abolition of the international business area. As Professor Vernon recounts:

> It seemed to me a reasonable and logical step. Thenceforth, according to the proposed plan, the various functional areas would internationalize their respective curricula. And to ensure that the shift occurred, the handful of faculty members associated with the international business area would be distributed strategically among the various functional areas. With hindsight, it seems evident to me that the shift came too early by a decade or two, and the hope that erstwhile faculty members from the liquated international business area could exert much influence over the curricula of their new colleagues appears to have been grossly inflated. (Vernon 1994)

The response of MBA students to international business studies during the 1960s and 1970s was strong and many of them chose IB as their area of concentration. From the job placement standpoint, however, IB majors generally encountered difficulties. Although many chief executives of companies doing recruitment were making statesmanlike speeches about the internationalisation of their firms, the lower level recruitment personnel of these companies were continuing their traditional pattern of looking for functional expertise. To meet this problem, many schools urged their students to take dual concentrations, one of which was in the functional areas.

The various sorts of early faculty resistance to the development of an IB program have been characterised by Professor Franklin Root of the Wharton School. First, there is the resistance of professors who have taught the traditional courses in foreign trade for many years and are emotionally and intellectually committed to a foreign trade concept of international business. Second, there is the resistance of professors in the traditional business fields who regard IB programs as a transgression on their own disciplines, in large part because IB appears to ignore the lines that separate the functional disciplines. A third group denies that IB is a new and unique field of study but rather a mix of the functional disciplines with an international ingredient. 'Finally,' he says, 'Note should be taken of simple inertia. There are always professors who distrust any proposal to institute a new program of study simply because it is new. These persons always favour a postponement of curriculum decisions' (Root 1968).

The resistance of business school deans to internationalising their curricula should also be noted. It was not until 1973 that the American Assembly of Collegiate Schools of Business (AACSB) added the simple phrase 'domestic and worldwide' to its standards for accrediting business schools. And it was not until 1980 that the AACSB interpreted 'worldwide' to require that every student should be exposed to the international dimension through one or more elements of the curriculum — still not much guidance.

INTERNATIONALISING THE PROFESSORS

In the final analysis, the successful implementation of a strategy to internationalise the business curriculum depends on internationalising the professors. As mentioned previously, professors teach what they know. And although the experience of having being in several national cultures may not be sufficient preparation for becoming a professor of international business, overseas working experience can be a beginning. Many academics who pioneered in the IB field had various types of international and multicultural experiences early in their careers.

Some were internationalised by World War II military service, including foreign language training and participating in military government. A surprising number of the American academics attracted to the IB field were of the Mormon faith, and had fulfilled their religious commitment of spending several years abroad as missionaries. Others had their foreign exposure through the Peace Corps and still others were immigrants to the United States who became multicultural by doing graduate training there..

The United States government helped to internationalise professors through its Fulbright Scholars program and its foreign aid programs, especially through getting American schools involved in the establishment of foreign business schools. And the United Nations provided other opportunities for international working experience through its technical assistance program, as was the case for this author. Also important were the summer international business workshops for professors first initiated by New York University in 1964-66 and later continued by the Academy of International Business. But the process of internationalising present and future professors was slow and these various efforts only began to have an impact of the curriculum of business schools in the late 1970s and 1980s.

CONCLUSION

On several occasions, I recommended to deans that the process of internationalising the business curriculum could be accelerated: (1) by establishing as a criterion for recruitment that candidates must be, or become, familiar with the international dimension of their field; (2) by making resources and time off available when needed for the new professor to fulfil this requirement; and finally, (3) by making proficiency in the international dimension of the professor's field one of the requirements for the granting of tenure. But I never encountered a dean who felt that he or she had the 'muscle' to implement my recommendations. To be sure, moving graveyards is difficult, but they can be moved — given enough time.

REFERENCES

Aliber, Robert Z. 1968. Research needs in international business. In Stephen A. Zeff (ed.), *Business Schools and the Challenge of International Business,* New Orleans: Tulane University.

Bishop, Harvey P. and Lindfers, Grace V. 1964. *Bibliography: Cases and other Materials for the Teaching of Multinational Business*, Boston: Harvard Graduate School of Business Administration.

Fayerweather, John 1960. *Management of International Operations*, New York: McGraw-Hill.

Fayerweather, John 1986. A history of the Academy of International Business. *South Carolina Essays in International Business*, 6 November.

Fayerweather, John 1994. A personal odyssey through the early evolution of international business pedagogy, research and professional organisation. *Journal of International Business Studies*, 25(21), First Quarter: 8.

Nehrt, Lee. C. 1968. The imperative of international business for the
    international business student. In Zeff, *Business Schools and the Challenge of
    International Business*, pp.81–82.

Otteson, Schuyler (ed.) 1968. *Internationalising the Traditional Business
    Curriculum*, Bloomington: Bureau of Business Research, Indiana University.

Robock, Stefan H. and Nehrt, Lee C. (eds) 1964. *Education in International
    Business*, Bloomington, IN: Graduate School of Business.

Root, Franklin 1968. International business as a field of study. In Zeff, *Business
    School and the Challenge of International Business*, p.101.

Vernon, Raymond 1994. Contributing to an international business curriculum: An
    approach from the Hank. *Journal of International Business Studies*, 25(2),
    Second Quarter: 217.

PART TWO

IB as an Interdisciplinary Field of Inquiry

3. The Conceptual Frontiers of International Business

Brian Toyne

THE CHALLENGE OF DEFINING INTERNATIONAL BUSINESS INQUIRY

For a coherent discussion about the conceptual frontiers of international business (IB), it is desirable to have some consensus regarding the definition of international business and its domain. For example, there needs be some agreement concerning what kinds of phenomena and relationships are to be termed IB phenomena. There also needs to be some agreement as to how international business activities are to be differentiated from national1 business activities, and how the international business process is to be distinguished from other social processes.

Unfortunately, defining the domain of IB inquiry is not easy, since there is little agreement among IB scholars regarding the scope and nature of international business, and the levels of abstraction and analysis to be use when describing it in conceptual terms. Unlike their parochial, functionally specialised counterparts who periodically discuss what knowledge they seek, for what purpose and for whose benefit, IB scholars have not been inclined to question the boundaries and content of their investigative domain. In fact, the issue of domain has not been central to most IB scholarship. This, of course, is, at least in part, the consequence of the paradigms they have unquestioningly adopted to describe international business. Moreover, this willingness to leave domain discussions to others has reinforced a predilection among IB scholars to accept the received wisdom of their respective business disciplines. As a consequence, and unlike other fields of inquiry, IB inquiry lacks coherence, a single defining paradigm and a central theory.

Nonetheless, there are several streams of literature that can be tapped to gain an appreciation for the general scope and nature of international business, and to identify the assumptions that have been made in order to study it. To ensure reasonable representation of those interested in international business, these streams of literature could include such topics as international production (Dunning 1958, 1981, 1988a), state–enterprise relations (Bergsten et al. 1978), government policies (Doz 1986b), international trade policy (Aggarwal 1985), parent–subsidiary relations (Beechler and Yang 1994), and such topics as marketing program standardisation decisions (Jain 1989). At the same time, however, it needs to be noted that this body of knowledge lacks coherence and internal consistency. Except, perhaps, for international microeconomics, it is also somewhat difficult in many cases to link this body of knowledge in a direct, theoretical way to other bodies of knowledge dealing with human experience and expression (e.g. the social sciences and the humanities).

The field of IB, to use Whitley's (1984) typology of the intellectual and social organisation of the sciences, is a fragmented adhocracy. The failure to agree upon an overarching paradigm has resulted in a body of research that is personal, idiosyncratic and only weakly linked to research undertaken by the traditional business disciplines and social sciences (see Whitley 1984). The field of IB also fails to be a discipline since its many scholars have not been able to agree on the tools, procedures, exempla, concepts and theories that account coherently for a set of objects or subjects. That is, many IB leaders have objected to the adoption of an overarching conceptualisation of international business, such as that advocated by Toyne (1989).

The purpose of this chapter is twofold: to present various representations of international business that underpin the diverse streams of knowledge that IB inquiry has generated, and to examine the impact that these conceptualisations may have on the questions yet to be addressed by IB scholars. To achieve these goals, first the major paradigms that have guided IB inquiry for the last 40 years are identified and briefly described. Next, a more inclusive paradigm is presented that is based on recent developments in the physical and social sciences. To complete this examination, and to lay the foundation for understanding the scope and nature of IB inquiry to date, the various forms of inquiry that have been used by IB scholars are then briefly reviewed. Finally, the chapter concludes with a brief examination of the evolving frontier of IB inquiry that includes a discussion of the likely directions that will be taken by IB scholars in their generation of IB knowledge.

ALTERNATIVE DEFINITIONS OF INTERNATIONAL BUSINESS

What is international business? This question has perplexed and dogged many IB writers. Ultimately, the problem stems from the failure of business scholars to develop a satisfactory definition of business, and from the persistent, even tenacious, epistemological belief held by most business scholars trained in the United States that the whole can be understood as a consequence of studying its parts. In the United States, for example, business has been artificially defined as the functional activities undertaken by enterprise to achieve its economic objectives and goals (e.g. finance, marketing, production, and so on).[2] Moreover, this piece-meal, task-focused approach to the study of business is predicated on the Anglo-American ideals espoused by liberal economists (i.e. economic and socio-political separation).

Naturally, the same reductionist approach to the study of business is evident in what is viewed by many as constituting IB inquiry. At the popular end of the scale, international business has been defined as, or implicitly assumed to be, firm-level activities that cross national borders or are conducted at locations other than the firm's home country primarily, if not exclusively, for economic motives (Behrman and Grosse 1990; Fayerweather 1960; Nehrt, Truitt and Wright 1970; Wilkins 1996; Vernon 1964). At the other, less examined and even less understood end of this scale, international business is seen as a multi-level, economic exchange process (Toyne 1989), and as a socially embedded interactive process (Toyne and Nigh 1996).

More specifically, Wilkins (1996), like many others, takes the position that international business is the consequence of economic-driven firm-level activity. Thus, in her words, IB inquiry must be linked to a viable and rich theory of the firm. She offers the work of such IB scholars as Buckley (1990) and Pitelis and Sugden (1991) as evidence in support of this firm-level definition of the field of IB. Boddewyn (1996), while agreeing with the economic *raison dêtre* of international business and the centrality of the firm, recognises a need to explicitly include environmental influences, such as government. At the same time, he limits the range of these influences by asserting that not all environmental influences are germane to an understanding of international business.

Toyne (1989), in attempting to make IB inquiry more inclusive and more open to other forms of inquiry, such as those that address both international economic exchange issues and international policy issues at more macro levels, has argued that the international firm is merely one mechanism used by societies to satisfy their domestic needs. He also argues against the emphasis placed on liberal economic assumptions by Anglo-American scholars, and their proclivity for cross-sectional examination of phenomena. Instead, he recommends approaches that appear to more accurately reflect reality,[3] that emphasise process and thus longitudinal examination, believing these to be more attractive to the other social sciences, and thus more conducive to multi-disciplinary dialogue.

Toyne and Nigh (1996) advance the argument by suggesting that business (and thus international business) needs to be seen as a hierarchical, relational process that is an inextricable part and expression of the societies in which it emerged and in which it subsequently evolves as a consequence of culture-bound and history-bound learning (see also Granovetter 1985; Mattsson 1996; Wartick 1996). This evolving social process view of business is in sharp contrast to the dominant economic view that assumes economic and social separation (Gilpin 1987), an assumption that has at its core the desocialisation of human constructions (e.g. human activity and creativity succumbing to the pricing mechanism). It is also in sharp contrast to the reductionistic, cross-sectional approaches developed and used by business scholars to understand the evolving human phenomena they examine.

There are, of course, other definitions of international business. For example, for some IB scholars probably those most interested in examining exporters and exporting international trade could be viewed as international business. For others, the comparison of business practices could be viewed as international business. For a third group, such as political science scholars, international business could be viewed merely as an uninteresting consequence of international policy.[4] Ultimately, the choice of definition is dependent on the paradigm that an international scholar adopts in order to model the reality he or she is interested in examining.

The implications of these different perspectives for the study of international business are quite apparent. For example, the national competitiveness topics covered by Jackson (1993), Thurow (1992), Reich (1991), and Ohmae (1995) are viewed by some as central to an understanding (explanation) of international business (i.e. the public policy process and its outcomes/initiatives viewed as endogenous). For others, these topics are merely of passing interest. They may give colour to the fabric of understanding, but not necessarily structure (i.e. public policy initiatives viewed as exogenous). The result, of course, is confusion and considerable arbitrariness among IB scholars concerning what should be examined, what is important, what is significant and what is excellent scholarship (Toyne and Nigh 1996). It also leaves underdeveloped the theoretical linkage between changes in upper levels of society and those of the firm.[5]

PARADIGMIC APPROACHES TO IB INQUIRY

Like the social sciences and the business disciplines, IB inquiry is experiencing paradigmic conflict. Toyne and Nigh (1996), for example, note that the dominant paradigms that have guided and influenced the social sciences in their quest for knowledge are facing increasingly strong contenders. They point out that Berger (1992) finds sociology afflicted with parochialism, triviality, rationalism and ideology. In economics, Mirowski (1988) leads a pragmatist institutionalist challenge to a neoclassical economics he decries as 'imitation 19th century physics'. In anthropology, Fox (1992) accuses other anthropologists of abandoning science by extending the traditional cultural relativism of anthropology to embrace cognitive relativism as well. There is also debate across traditional disciplinary boundaries. For example, in sociology, Granovetter (1985) argues that economic actions are embedded in concrete, ongoing systems of social relations and that economic institutions are social constructions. The preceding examples highlight the serious debates that are taking place today within and across the social sciences concerning appropriate domains and methods of inquiry.

Challenges to the paradigmic underpinnings of the business disciplines are also evident in the business literature. For example, Hunt (1991) reviews the crisis literature that challenges his philosophical foundation of marketing, and rejects the relativistic/constructionist science of Anderson (1983) and Peter and Olson (1983). In sharp contrast, Mintzberg (1994) argues that process rather than outcomes should be the focus of management inquiry since such a perspective provides a richer and more accurate understanding of human activities and advancements.

IB inquiry is an eclectic field that draws from the business disciplines, and from the various humanities and social sciences and their sub-branches for guidance, inspiration and paradigmic structure and focus. Thus it is not too surprising to find that the dominant paradigms that have guided IB inquiry since the late 1950s are also being questioned. As a consequence of the debate within the various business disciplines and within the field of IB inquiry itself, the conceptual frontiers of international business are in the process of being reshaped.

To better understand these fluid frontiers of IB inquiry, it is necessary to examine, if only briefly, its paradigmic roots. Essentially, two paradigms (or orientations) have guided much of IB inquiry for the past four decades. They are the extension and cross-border management paradigms (Vernon 1964).

THE EXTENSION PARADIGM

The extension paradigm has strongly influenced IB inquiry since its inception in the early 1950s.[6] Reflecting both the outward investment pattern of United States firms and the activity-based definition of business adopted by United States business scholars at that time, it holds that international business is the extension of a firm's activities across national borders, and that IB inquiry is the study of the adjustment and adaptation to these activities because of the environmental differences found to exist between the firm's home and host countries. That is, the firm is the unit of analysis, and the paradigm-inspired questions guiding the research activity are those asked of nation-bound firms by the various business disciplines of finance, marketing and so on. To paraphrase Kuhn (1970: 10), extension paradigm-inspired IB inquiry is based on the past achievements acknowledged by the various business disciplines as supplying the foundation for their further practice. Thus this form of IB research is traditional and parochial in the sense that the questions asked, and the knowledge and methodologies employed to answer these questions, are guided by the paradigms, theories, metaphors and methodologies accepted and used by business researchers to study nation-bound firm behaviour. Pick up any academic journal and it will include various examples of the extension paradigm form of IB research (Bird and Beechler 1995; Samiee 1994; Wright and Ricks 1994).

THE CROSS-BORDER MANAGEMENT PARADIGM

The second conceptualisation of international business that has strongly influenced IB inquiry since the late 1950s deals with the problems that arise from the movement of goods and capital across national boundaries and the monitoring, coordinating and integrating from headquarters of operations existing in more than one country. Unlike the extension paradigm, however, this conceptualisation presents international business as distinct from nation-bound business since it necessitates the development of an effective method for managing environmental diversity (e.g. governmental entry barriers, foreign exchange risk management, international taxation, international logistics, and industrial relations regulations and policies) (Vernon 1964: 9–10). Examples of contemporary IB research based on this paradigm include Bartlett and Ghoshal (1991) and Kobrin (1994).

Although the questions raise by this paradigm are distinctive, they are not unique since the paradigm suffers from the same conceptual constraints as the extension paradigm. It is a firm-level paradigm that focuses attention on the outward movement of firms and their activities. It also assumes that business is business no matter where it is practised,[7] and consists of the United States-defined tasks of marketing, manufacturing, personnel management, finance, accounting and so on. Furthermore, it views both the firm's market and industry as acted upon by the firm (see Mattsson 1996). That is, the cross-

Table 3.1: The extension and cross-border management paradigm criteria for international business research

---

- International business research is concerned with firm-level business activity that crosses national boundaries or is conducted in a location other than the firm's home country. (This activity may be the movement of goods, capital, people and knowledge, or it may be manufacturing, extraction, construction, banking, shipping, advertising and the like.)
- International business research is concerned with the interrelationships between the operations of the business firm and international or foreign environments in which the firm operates.
- International business research does not include studies devoted to economic development, development planning, foreign trade and the international monetary system, which belong to development and international economics. Excluded also are studies of foreign legal, political, economic and social environments. These belong to the fields of law, political science, economics and behavioral science unless the study itself relates the environment directly to the organisational, operational, or decision-making problems of international business firms.
- International business research does not include studies of business activities in given foreign countries. A study of marketing channels in Turkey, whether it is done by a US, French or Turkish professor of marketing, is still a study about domestic business in Turkey. This would not be international business any more than would the study of motivation levels of Portuguese workers or the study of personal income distribution in Japan, though each may be of interest to international business firms.
- As an exception to the last point, however, *comparative* business studies are included within this definition. For example, a study of pharmaceutical marketing channels in Germany, Italy, Brazil and Japan, which makes comparisons and analyses the causes and effects of similarities and differences, would be considered international business research although it is not concerned with the relationship between the marketing channels within each country and international business firms.

Source: Adapted from Nehrt, Troitt and Wright (1970), pp. 1-2.

border management paradigm unquestioningly supports the assumption that there is a single definition of business with variants that are the result of environmental (structural) differences (i.e. it is based on the liberal economic assumption of economic and socio-political separation). All that the firm needs to do is stand back, observe, and then modify the application of its universal tools to the various alien market and industry situations that it is confronted with.

The framework developed by Nehrt, Truitt and Wright (1970) for the preparation of 'an inventory of recent and current research in international business and recommendations for further research' presents an excellent synthesis of the research implications of the extension and cross-border management paradigms. These authors defined IB research as the interdisciplinary study of a phenomenon that satisfies the five criteria presented in Table 3.1. Unfortunately, the call for an interdisciplinary approach to the study of IB was either ignored or overlooked by the already well-entrenched 'functional groups' in the United States. It is only recently that there has again been a call for either a multidisciplinary or an interdisciplinary approach to the study of IB, this time by Dunning (1989)[8] and Toyne (1989), respectively.

THE EVOLVING INTERACTION PARADIGM

As noted earlier, the social sciences and the business disciplines are in the process of reformulating the central questions guiding their respective inquiries. In attempting to do this, they are seeking new paradigms and new ways of conceptualising the world that are based on the relatively new thinking emerging in the physical sciences (i.e. relativity, quantum mechanics, chaos theory). In line with these more complex, holistic representations of reality, Toyne and Nigh (1996) recently advanced a new paradigm that builds on the insights gained as a consequence of the extension and cross-border management paradigms. It presents international business as a multi-level, hierarchical process that evolves over time as a consequence of the interaction of two or more socially embedded, multi-level business processes.[9]

International Business as a Hierarchical Social Process

The reason for adopting an expanded representation of international business is as follows (Toyne and Nigh 1996):

1. The phenomena examined as IB phenomena are identical neither within

nor across national borders. They are the indeterminate outcomes of particular social processes and are subsequently affected by other business processes.

2. A firm's indeterminancy is minimised by exogenating the business process, such as is done when a firm-level conceptualisation of international business is adopted. It is then easier to assume that it is not part of a process, but merely affected by a process. Thus it can then be assumed that IB phenomena are identical, irrespective of their origins (e.g. firm-level contingency theory); only their similarities are recognised and considered of interest and value.

3. However, if business and international business phenomena are acknowledged to be indeterminate yet socio-culturally distinguishable at the national level, an understanding of their interaction with one another and with the business processes of different locales requires including those processes that explain their emergence, continuance and individuality.

4. Missing from current research on IB phenomena is a theory of IB phenomena differences. What is needed to understand IB entities are theories that explain differences, initially at the national level and subsequently at the international level (e.g. what role does culture-bound learning, recognised as both a socialising and an individualising activity, play in the emergence of similarities and differences among organisations.)

5. To make sense of IB phenomena it is not sufficient to study just the phenomena involved in international business, even if this study involves organisations from different socio-cultural contexts and thus the products of uniquely different processes.

For explanation and prediction, IB inquiry must include an examination of the sources of the similarities and differences found in phenomena from different national business processes. This, of course, requires the simultaneous study of the processes that created them and which are transforming them. It is insufficient to include an exogenised immediate context (industry) within which they exist, such as that advocated by Porter (1980) and the Anglo-American industrial organisation theorists from whom he draws so heavily. The sciences of anthropology, political economy and sociology can contribute as much to an understanding of IB phenomena and the national business processes from which they spring as can economics (Dunning 1989; Toyne 1989).

Table 3.2: Characteristics of the emerging international business paradigm

CORE ORIENTATION	BUSINESS is an emerging, recursive, hierarchical social process, the outcomes of which are indeterminate (e.g. firms, industry associations, etc.)
	INTERNATIONAL BUSINESS is an emerging, hierarchical social process that is the result of the interaction of national business processes and their outcomes. The outcomes of this international process are indeterminate.
Implicit/explicit assumptions	A business process evolves over time because of internal review, change (e.g. economic, technological, political, sociological), and its inter-connectedness with other business processes and the IB process (i.e. evolution is the consequence of individual and organisational learning at all levels of the hierarchical process.
	All levels of a society's hierarchical business process impacted by the IB process are central to IB inquiry.
	Phenomena at each level of the business process are expressions of current knowledge, information and experience received from upper and lower levels.
Implications for IB inquiry	Future business activity is dependent on learning that is related to such things as previous experience, self-study, transfer of the response to practices of other business processes, and environmental discontinuities (e.g. scientific breakthrough, etc.)
	IB knowledge (certified and generalised) is gained from the development and testing of theories and concepts that seek to explain and predict the outcome of the interaction of two or more social-embedded business processes.

STRENGTHS OF PARADIGM	Recognises the new 'reality' — increasing complexity and interconnectedness of business processes and their outputs.
	Requires increased understanding of, and knowledge about, the basic social sciences and the contributions they make in explaining and predicting the international business process.
	Brings comparative business studies 'centre stage' by requiring an understanding of the evolving differences of business processes and their outputs.
	Results in 'new' theories and concepts that have value by contributing to a better understanding and explanation of single business processes.
WEAKNESSES OF PARADIGM	Increased sense of 'uncertainty' because of the indeterminacy of outcomes (e.g. government, industry, firm, individual).
	Deficiency of theories and concepts explaining the outcome and directions of interconnected organisations and systems.
	Rigourous research methodology is underdeveloped.

Source: Adapted from Toyne and Nigh (1996), Chapter 1.

The Evolving Interaction Paradigm

Table 3.2 describes an 'emerging' interaction paradigm that is an evolving hierarchical representation of IB. At its core is the idea that the evolution of international business is the consequence of two or more business processes in interaction. Also, the evolution of the international and national business processes is intermittent because of informed hunch, intuition and vision (learning and inductive thinking) that can originate at any level in the processes (i.e. above the focal level, at the focal level, or below the focal level). A national example would be a group of firms (focal level phenomena) vying for market exchanges. The idiosyncratic approaches used by these firms would be initiated by their intrinsic properties (e.g. lower level phenomena such as individuals and groups), yet regulated by industrial and governmental properties and purposes (e.g. upper level phenomena including trade associations, government agencies, supranational organisations and the consequences of their actions — agreements, regulations, laws, etc.).

Choice of Hierarchical Levels

There are various levels of organisation that describe, constrain, stimulate and shape international business. They extend from the individual to the suprasocietal, and should satisfy the following criteria:

1. Phenomena at each level must be capable of being 'seen' or 'sensed' (e.g. product divisions, firms, nation states, EU, WTO, UN).
2. Phenomena at lower levels must constitute intrinsic properties of contiguous upper level phenomena (e.g. individuals are in firms, firms are in industries, and so on).
3. Interactions between phenomena at contiguous levels must establish the initiating or boundary conditions. Initiating conditions are lower level constraints that give rise to focal-level processes and outcomes (e.g. management capabilities, organisational slack). Boundary conditions are higher level constraints regulating focal-level processes and outcomes (e.g. governments and industries contextualising or informing the responses of firms).
4. Phenomena at the different levels must serve different functions (i.e. levels are functionally incommensurable).
5. Level classification must depend on the principle of robustness..[10]

Using these criteria, one possible hierarchy of levels for studying IB, along with examples of their initiating and boundary conditions, is presented in Table 3.3. The phenomena included in each level are observable and functionally incommensurable with phenomena in contiguous levels. Finally, all phenomena above the individual are manifestations of contemporary knowledge, information, and experience.[11]

The dynamic for this IB representation consists of three elements that are common to all levels of a business process: (1) self-interest; (2) the available pool of knowledge, information and experience; and (3) the learning process (which includes awareness, discernment, interpretation and judgment). Each

Table 3.3: Different levels of international business

Hierarchical level	Examples of initiating and boundary conditions
Suprasocietal	The suprasocietal level imposes boundary conditions on the contiguous level of nation-states. Examples of boundary conditions include human rights, environmental concerns, multilateral trade agreements, international monetary system. Examples of suprasocietal organisations include the United National, the World Trade Organisation, the European Union and so on.
Societal (or nation-state level)	Nation-states are embedded in an emerging suprasocietal world and constitute the suprasocietal level's initiating conditions. These arise from the historical, socio-cultural, economic and political distinctiveness of nation-states and their individual and collective (regional/global) political and economic aspirations. They also constitute the boundary conditions of lower levels (e.g. laws, rules and regulations governing business, tax structures, education of the workforce and their enforcement organisations).
Industry	Industries are embedded in national business processes and constitute initiating conditions (e.g. economic efficiency, economic specialisation, satisfaction of indigenous needs/wants). They also provide the boundary conditions of lower levels (e.g. competitive intensity, technology and investment characteristics).
Firm	Firms are embedded in industries and constitute their initiating conditions (e.g. inventiveness, organisational capabilities, resource bases, labor pools, geographic scope). Firms also constitute the boundary conditions for lower levels (e.g. policies and procedures, strategic direction budgets).

Table 3.3 cont'd

Group	Groups are embedded in firms and constitute their initiating conditions (e.g. divisional focus, functional expertise, managerial capabilities and talents). Groups are algo the boundary conditions for individuals (e.g. they contextualise and inform individuals concerning possible behaviours, the scope of their authority).
Individual	Individuals are embedded in groups, and constitute their initiating conditions or intrinsic properties (e.g. the group's potential motivation, talents, capabilities, skills and knowledge/expertise).

Source: Adapted from Toyne and Nigh (1996), Chapter 1

level of the business process and its phenomena change incrementally, sometimes radically, as a result of the interaction of these three elements. These changes, in turn, affect that particular level's initiating and boundary conditions and thus affect both higher and lower levels since the relationship between contiguous levels is changed.

Self-interest, articulated in economic, political, and social terms, is at the core of most explanations dealing with business, regardless of organisational level. It is accepted by most business scholars as the motivator or galvaniser of action. Learning is also common to all levels of organisation. It is central to what individuals and organisations seek to become within an already ongoing world of ideas. Finally, the world of ideas upon which individuals and organisations depend for meaning is the pool of contemporary knowledge, information and experience that is available to them at a particular point in time.

There are two distinguishing features to national business processes (apart from the physical resource base on which they may depend). One is the interpretation given self-interest by individuals and organisations. The other is the available pool of contemporary knowledge, information and experience on which individuals and organisations depend when making decisions and creating their organisations. Collectively, they distinguish between national business processes because they reflect the socio-cultural and historical differences that distinguish nation-states. They also distinguish between the national and international business processes, since the latter is the process that is continuously harmonizing national differences as a consequence of knowledge, information and experience transfers. In fact, the IB process can be viewed as an 'ongoing', continuous reconciliation process, the purpose of which is domain consensus, ideological consensus, positive evaluation and work coordination (Toyne 1989, 1996). For example, the suprasocietal level's organisations can be viewed as the multinational manifestation of this reconciliation process. It appears that the purpose of the process is to bring about agreed-upon interpretations of order to exchange relations among nations partly through transparency requirements and partly through the creation of external impartial monitoring mechanisms that increasingly have the ability to persuade, but not yet enforce (e.g. the WTO).

A Note on Paradigmic Choice

Paradigms either contract or expand scientific inquiry. The difference, of course, is extremely important when setting out to understand some new or ill-defined phenomenon, such as international business. The extension and cross-border paradigms are contractionary in that the contemporary knowledge used to speculate about and to explain the examined phenomena is parochial; as noted earlier, the body of knowledge is the result of separating the examined phenomena from the processes that created them, and then examining them from the researcher's nationalistic (cultural, economic and political) viewpoint. The emerging interaction paradigm, on the other hand, is expansionary, since it speaks directly to the processes that created the phenomena under examination. That is, to understand or explain the phenomena under examination, the researcher is required to have some understanding of the pool of contemporary knowledge, information and experience that is informing these phenomena; this, of course, is an investigative activity that is intrinsically expansionary, not contractionary.

MODES OF IB INQUIRY

It is also necessary to make clear the type of inquiry that is under review when discussing the conceptual frontiers of IB inquiry, since inquiry can be categorised as discovery, integration and application. The inquiry of discovery is defined as a unidisciplinary, multidisciplinary or interdisciplinary commitment to the production of knowledge that involves the discovery of scientific hypotheses, laws and theories (also see Hunt 1991: 21–25).[12] Integrative inquiry is defined as the bringing together of two or more streams of knowledge across the social sciences and business disciplines (i.e. the placing of specialties in a larger context). In contrast to the investigative and synthesising traditions of discovery and integration, respectively, the inquiry of application is defined as the demonstration of how knowledge can be applied to important problems and how important problems can define an agenda for scholarly investigation that is unidisciplinary, multidisciplinary or interdisciplinary.

Since, like business inquiry in general, IB inquiry includes discovery, integration and application, both confusion and disagreement can and do occur when a discussion takes place on the merits and contributions of IB inquiry (see, for example, Behrman 1996). The reason for the existence of either confusion or disagreement is that the three forms of inquiry have essentially different investigative objectives and methodologies, and these objectives and methodologies often take on misplaced values. Depending on whose point of view is being sought, IB inquiry could be classified as irrelevant, too esoteric, too empirical or too descriptive. For example, some researchers say that the purpose of science (discovery and integration) is to seek truth, not usefulness (application). At the same time, others say that only application has merit, since it seeks a utilitarian end. Since the debate over pure and applied is not of much help in understanding the actual growth of IB knowledge, all three forms of inquiry will be addressed in the next section of this chapter. As Kaplan (1964: 398) notes, all problems are really problems in research, and can lead to advancements in knowledge (see, for example, the work done by Doz 1986a).

THE CONCEPTUAL FRONTIERS OF INTERNATIONAL BUSINESS

Table 3.4 summarises the core points discussed so far by contrasting the three paradigms with each mode of IB inquiry in terms of its level (unit) of analysis, disciplinary emphasis and purpose. The shading of the table's cells also provides some clues as to the relative intensity of IB inquiry within the boundaries of each paradigm. The deeper the shading, the more intense the inquiry.

IB's most impressive contributions are the consequence of examining the firm and its activities within and across multiple countries in a uni-disciplinary and multi-disciplinary fashion. The IB literature is replete with examples of this form of scholarship (e.g. Bartlett and Ghoshal 1991; Doz 1986b; Doz and Prahalad 1994; Perlmutter 1969; Stopford and Wells 1972; Vernon 1970). These studies, mostly anecdotal, descriptive, empirical or reflective, have highlighted a wide assortment of interesting problems confronting firms operating in an international context. In addition, while

Table 3.4: IB paradigms, mode of IB inquiry, and the phenomena and relationships studied

Mode of inquiry	Paradigms guiding IB inquiry		
	Extension	Cross-Border	Interaction
Discovery	*Level of analysis:* the firm.	*Level of Analysis:* the firm.	*Level of analysis:* the multi-level societal business process and its outcomes (individual-to-suprasocietal).
	Disciplinary emphasis: uni-disciplinary.	*Disciplinary emphasis:* uni-disciplinary.	*Disciplinary emphasis:* multi-disciplinary and inter-disciplinary.
	Purpose of inquiry: to test the explanatory power of home-country generated business knowledge in foreign settings (i.e., replication of 'normal science').	*Purpose of inquiry:* to explain how firms simultaneously adjust/adapt/respond to environmental diversity and its opportunities.	*Purpose of inquiry:* to explain the outcomes of international interaction for particular societies, across societies, and the suprasocietal business process.

Table 3.4 cont'd: IB paradigms, mode of IB inquiry, and the phenomena and relationships studied

Mode of inquiry	Paradigms guiding IB inquiry		
	Extension	Cross-Border	Interaction
Integration	*Levels of analysis*: the firm.	*Level of analysis*: the firm.	*Level of analysis*: the multi-level societal business process and its outcomes (individual-to-suprasocietal).
	Disciplinary emphasis: multi-disciplinary.	*Disciplinary emphasis*: multi-disciplinary.	*Disciplinary emphasis*: multi-disciplinary and inter-disciplinary
	Purpose of inquiry: to develop a comprehensive, integrated explanation of home-country firm-level responses in foreign settings.	*Purpose of inquiry*: to develop a comprehensive, integrated explanation of firm-level responds to environmental diversity and its opportunities.	*Purpose of inquiry*: to develop a comprehensive, multi-disciplinary (social sciences and the humanities), and integrated understanding of the business process and its outcomes in particular societies, across societies, and of the suprasocietal business process.

Table 3.4 cont'd: IB paradigms, mode of IB inquiry, and the phenomena and relationships studied

Mode of inquiry	Paradigms guiding IB inquiry		
	Extension	Cross-Border	Interaction
Application	*Level of analysis:* the firm.	*Level of analysis:* the firm.	*Level of analysis:* the multi-level societal business process and its outcomes.
	Disciplinary emphasis: multi-disciplinary.	*Disciplinary emphasis:* multi-disciplinary.	*Disciplinary emphasis:* multi-disciplinary and inter-disciplinary.
	Purpose of inquiry: to provide possible solutions to uni-disciplinary, firm-level, and country-specific problems and to generalise these problems/solutions across categories of firms.	*Purpose of inquiry:* to provide possible solutions to uni-disciplinary, firm-level, across-country specific problems and to generalise these problems/solutions across categories of firms.	*Purpose of inquiry:* to provide possible solutions to societal business-related problems and to generalise these problems/solutions across societal categories, and to the suprasocietal context.

these studies were not designed to build theory or test parochial theories (Doz and Prahalad 1994), they do contribute to the theory-building activity that is taking place in the various business disciplines by raising questions that challenge the assumptions underpinning their generalised parochial theories. The reason that IB contributions can successfully challenge the fragmented and increasingly specialised developments in the business disciplines is that IB's research agenda is focused on a major source of business innovation. While the research undertaken by IB scholars is mostly a consequence of the questions raised by the extension and cross-border management paradigms, and utilises the theories, concepts and methodologies of the parochial business disciplines, the phenomena studied are the consequence of the reconciling interaction of two or more socio-culturally distinct business processes that are learning in dissimilar ways. That is, IB inquiry is at the frontier of business process change, and is focused on firm-level activities and practices that are ahead of those being examined by parochial business scholars. Moreover, the reason that IB scholars can recognise the innovations that are a consequence of business process change is that they are not as specialised as their parochial counterparts, and are thus more willing to use a multi-disciplinary approach when examining the firm. While most IB inquiry cannot be classified as either theory building or theory testing, business scholars are involved in theory testing and methodology design activities that can be classified as IB inquiry. There is an abundance of examples of this unidisciplinary form of scholarship (e.g. Green and White 1976; Gregersen and Black 1992; Parkhe 1993; Thomas and Toyne 1995). Essentially, the theory-testing studies replicate and elaborate on single-country, uni-disciplinary theory-testing activities. Their major contribution to the theory-building activity is the extension and clarification of the boundaries of theories that have been developed by parochial business scholars using single-country observations. Unfortunately, this particular fraternity of IB scholars has not placed much emphasis on theory development.

The need for multi-disciplinary and interdisciplinary research is most strongly felt in the international business arena. While firms recognise the merits of specialisation, they also recognise the compelling need for integration (Lawrence and Lorsch 1967). This dual requirement for differentiation and integration has been recognised by some IB scholars, primarily those who have emphasised a holistic and complex understanding of business activity, not rigorous, fractionated theory-building. As Table 3.4 suggests, most IB scholarship that can be classified as integration has involved the study of firm-level activity that crosses borders. This, of course, is to be expected since this form of management is the most advanced and most complex, and demands a holistic appreciation of a firm's totality as an organisation.

CONCLUSION

IB inquiry has advanced along several fronts. Conceptually, the contributions made by IB scholars are challenging the tendency of single-country business scholars, particularly United States business scholars, to claim universal understanding based on their narrowly-defined, parochial studies. IB scholars are also contributing to a much deeper, yet broader, understanding of the growing complexities of the business world as it becomes increasingly globalised in terms of competition, markets, information flows and experience. Also, in a unique fashion, they have identified and started to explore the issues and challenging confronting firms that operate in a number of countries requiring different strategic initiatives, and have raised serious questions concerning the symbiotic relationship of firms and the environments that spawned them. As such, IB scholars are beginning to make significant contributions to a richer understanding of the dynamics of socio-cultural and economic and political interactions.

Advancement in IB inquiry is also occurring as a consequence of the globalisation of the research activity itself. As noted by Wright and Ricks (1994) and Toyne and Nigh (1996), the influx of IB scholars from divergent socio-cultural, economic and political background are challenging the universality of United States theories. Increasingly, cutting-edge contributions are made by Asian and European-based and foreign-trained IB scholars.

At the same time, however, Table 3.4 suggests that there are still fundamental gaps in our understanding if some credence is given to the possibility that firm-level evolution is at least in part a consequence of the cross-national interaction of evolving, hierarchical business processes. That is, firm-level evolution is not exhaustively the consequence of firm-level competitive interaction.

The core problem, and I don't believe it is a serious one, is that there are no clearly defined frontiers to IB inquiry; the frontiers are emergent. That is, they are the consequences of international organisations, governments, firms and individuals learning how to accommodate their persistently changing cultural, social and political differences through an ongoing interactive process of reconciliation. This problem of indeterminacy is only a serious one to those IB scholars who wish to be mere extensions of their home country counterparts.

NOTES

1   For illustrative purposes only, the words 'nation', 'cultural group,' and society are used interchangeably throughout this chapter. I recognise, of course, that when these words are used to describe a particular geographic area or group of people, their boundaries may not coincide.

2   One possible explanation for this task-oriented perspective is the vocational training roots of business inquiry. Another possible explanation is the Anglo-American penchant to emphasing task.

3   This, of course, tends to make outcomes somewhat uncertain, and thus creates unease among reductionists because of their particular perspective and assumptions.

4   Uninteresting in the sense of being outside the scope of their study.

5   Lower levels, such as groups and individuals and their intrinsic attributes, are viewed as endogenous to the firm, so are of interest to IB scholars. However, the primary focus is on questions of interest to management (e.g. how can we get the most out of our employees, how can we get them to behave in ways that will benefit the firm).

6   The study of international phenomena, such as the multinational firm and exporting, was undertaken much earlier than the 1950s. However, these studies were not viewed as part of a separate, distinct field of inquiry. That is, they were not viewed as distinct from business history, economics and the business disciplines. I believe that the field of IB can be traced to the establishment of the Association for Education in International Business (now the Academy of International Business) in 1958.

7   Such an assumption might be true in the long run (i.e. when the world has become one homogeneous group of acultural, ahistorical yet economically driven humans).

8   Although Dunning uses the word interdisciplinary in the title to his speech, he subsequently speaks of complementary assets and perspectives. This suggests that what he is calling for is a multidisciplinary study of IB phenomena, not an interdisciplinary study, since the former retains clear separation of the disciplines, and the latter results in the merging of disciplines and their eventual replacement with a new field of inquiry.

9   See Root (1969) for an earlier discussion of a static interaction model.

10 For example, if we detect the same things in two different ways, we increase our confidence of their reality — they are robust to perceptual confidence.

11 Knowledge is used here in both its tacit sense and in its most rigorous sense (certified and generalised). Information refers to non-generalised knowledge collected and used by focal-level phenomena (e.g. individuals, groups, firms, government agencies) when making decisions. Experience is idiosyncratic to a particular focal-level phenomenon.

12 Unidisciplinary research is defined here as the study of business phenomena from a single functional perspective (i.e., accounting, finance, information systems, management, marketing and so on). Multidisciplinary research is the simultaneous study of a particular business phenomenon from two or more functional perspectives. Interdisciplinary research is the study of business phenomena from a functionally integrated perspective.

REFERENCES

Aggarwal, V.K. 1985. *Liberal Protectionism: The International Politics of Organized Trade*, Berkeley and Los Angeles: University of California Press.

Anderson, Paul F. 1983. Marketing, scientific progress, and scientific method, *Journal of Marketing*, 47(4): 18–31.

Bartlett, Christopher A. and Ghoshal, Sumantra 1991. *Managing Across Borders*. Boston, MA: Harvard Business School Press.

Beechler, Schon and Yang, John Zhuang 1994. The transfer of Japanese-style management to American subsidiaries: Contingencies, constraints, and competencies. *Journal of International Business Studies*, 25(3): 467–91.

Behrman, Jack N. 1996. Discussion of conceptual domain of IB. In Brian Toyne and Douglas Nigh (eds), *International Business: An 'Emerging' Vision*, Columbia, SC: The University of South Carolina Press.

Behrman, Jack N. and Grosse, Robert E. 1990. *International Business and Government*, Columbia: University of South Carolina Press.

Berger, Peter L. 1992. Sociology: A disinvitation? *Society*, 30(1): 12–18.

Bergsten, C. Fred, Horst, Thomas and Moran, Theodore H. 1978. *American Multinationals and American Interest*, Washington: Brookings Institute.

Bird, Allan and Beechler, Schon 1995. Links between business strategy and human resource management strategy in United States-based Japanese subsidiaries: An empirical investigation. *Journal of International Business Studies*, 26(1): 23–46.

Buckley, Peter J. 1990. Problems and developments in the core theory of international business. *Journal of International Business Studies*, 21(4).

Doz, Yves L. 1986a. *Strategic Management in Multinational Companies*, New York: Pergamon Press.

Doz, Yves L. 1986b. Government policies and global industries. In Michael E. Porter (ed.), *Competition in Global Industries*, Boston: Harvard Business School Press.

Doz, Yves L. and Prahalad, C.K. 1994. Managing DMNCs: A search for a new paradigm. In Richard P. Rumelt, Dan E. Schendel and David J. Teece (eds), *Fundamental Issues in Strategy: A Research Agenda*, Boston, MA: Harvard Business School Press.

Dunning, John H. 1958. *American Investment in British Manufacturing Industry*, London: Allen and Unwin.

Dunning, John H. 1981. *International Production and the Multinational Enterprise*, London: Allen & Unwin.

Dunning, John H. 1988. The eclectic paradigm on international production: A restatement and some possible extensions. *Journal of International Business Studies*, 19(1): 1–31.

Dunning, John H. 1989. The study of international business: A plea for a more interdisciplinary approach. *Journal of International Business Studies*, 20(3): 411–36.

Fayerweather, John 1960. *Management of International Operations, Text and Cases*, New York: McGraw-Hill.

Fox, Robin 1992. Anthropology and the 'teddy bear' picnic. *Society*, 30(1): 47–55.

Gilpin, Robert 1987. *The Political Economy of International Relations*, Princeton, NJ: Princeton University Press.

Granovetter, Mark 1985. Economic action and social structure: The problem of embeddedness. *American Journal of Sociology*, 91(3): 481–510.

Green, Robert T. and White, Phillip D. 1976. Methodological considerations in cross-national consumer research. *Journal of International Business Studies*, 7(2): 81–88.

Gregersen, Hal B. and Black, J. Stewart 1992. Antecedents to commitment to a parent company and a foreign operation. *The Academy of Management Journal*, 35(1): 65–90.

Hunt, Shelby D. 1991. *Modern Marketing Theory: Critical Issues in the Philosophy of Marketing Science,* Cincinnati: South-Western Publishing Company.

Jackson, Tim 1993. *The Next Battleground: Japan, America, and the New European Market,* New York: Houghton Mifflin Company.

Jain, S.C. 1989. Standardization of international marketing strategy: Some research hypotheses. *Journal of Marketing,* 53(January): 70–79.

Kaplan, Abraham 1964. *The Conduct of Inquiry: Methodology for Behavioral Science,* New York: Harper & Row, Publishers.

Kobrin, Stephen J. 1994. Is there a relationship between a geocentric mind-set and multinational strategy? *Journal of International Business Studies,* 25(3): 493–511.

Kuhn, Thomas S. 1970. *The Structure of Scientific Revolutions,* Rev. 2nd edn, Chicago, IL: University of Chicago Press.

Lawrence, P.R. and Lorsch, J.W. 1967. *Organization and Environment: Managing Differentiation and Integration,* Boston, MA: Division of Research, Harvard Business School.

Mattsson, Lars-Gunnar 1996. Exchange approaches and marketing's contributions to international business research. In Brian Toyne and Douglas Nigh (eds), *International Business: An 'Emerging' Vision,* Columbia, SC: University of South Carolina Press.

Mintzberg, Henry 1994. *The Rise and Fall of Strategic Planning,* New York: The Free Press.

Mirowski, Philip 1988. *Against Mechanism: Protecting Economics from Science,* Ottowa: NJ: Rowman & Littlefield.

Nehrt, Lee, Truitt, Frederick and Wright, Richard 1970. *International Business Research: Past, Present, and Future,* Bloomington, IN: Bureau of Business Research, Indiana University.

Ohmae, Kenichi 1995. *The End of the Nation State: The Rise of Regional Economies,* New York, The Free Press.

Parkhe, Arvind 1993. Strategic alliance structuring: A game theoretic and transaction cost examination of interfirm cooperation. *The Academy of Management Journal,* 36(4): 794–829.

Perlmutter, Howard 1969. The tortuous evolution of the multinational corporation. *Columbia Journal of World Business,* January–February: 9–18.

Peter, J. Paul and Olson, Jerry C. 1983. Is science marketing? *Journal of Marketing,* 47(4): 111–125.

Pitelis, Christos N. and Sugden, Roger 1991. On the Theory of the Transnational Firm. In Christos N. Pitelis and Roger Sugden (eds), *The Nature of the Transnational Firm,* London: Routledge.

Porter, M.E. 1980. *Competitive Strategy: Techniques for Analyzing Industries and Companies,* New York: Free Press.

Reich, Robert B. 1991. *The Works of Nations: Preparing Ourselves for 21st-Century Capitalism,* New York: Alfred A. Knopf.

Root, Franklin R. 1969. A conceptual approach to international business. *Journal of Business Administration,* 1(1): 18–28.

Samiee, Saeed 1994. Customer evaluation of products in a global market. *Journal of International Business Studies,* 25(3): 579–604.

Schumpeter, J. 1979 (1926). *The Theory of Economic Development,* 2nd edn, New Brunswick: Transaction Press.

Stopford, John M. and Wells, Louis T. Jr. 1972. *Managing the Multinational Enterprise: Organization and Ownership of the Subsidiaries*, New York: Basic Books, Inc.

Thurow, Lester 1992. *Head to Head: The Coming Economic Battle Among Japan, Europe, and America*, New York: William Morrow and Company, Inc.

Thomas, David C. and Toyne, Brian 1995. Subordinates' responses to cultural adaptation by Japanese expatriate managers. *Journal of Business Research*, 32(January): 1–10.

Toyne, Brian 1989. International exchange: A foundation for theory building in international business. *Journal of International Business*, 20(1): 1–17.

Toyne, Brian 1996. International business inquiry: Does it warrant a separate domain? In Brian Toyne and Douglas Nigh (eds), *International Business: An 'Emerging' Vision*, Columbia, SC: The University of South Carolina Press.

Toyne, Brian, and Nigh, Douglas 1996. *International Business: An Emerging Vision*, Columbia, SC: University of South Carolina Press.

Vernon, Raymond 1964. Comments. In Stefan H. Robock and Lee C. Nehrt (eds). *Education in International Business*, Bloomington, IN: Graduate School of Business, Indiana University.

Vernon, Raymond 1970. *Sovereignty at Bay: The Multinational Spread of United States Enterprise*, New York, NY: Basic Books, Inc.

Wartick, Steven L. 1996. From 'business in society' to 'business in societies': Comments on the papers by Hogner, Freeman, and Wood and Pasquero. In Brian Toyne and Douglas Nigh (eds), *International Business: An 'Emerging' Vision*, Columbia, SC: The University of South Carolina Press.

Whitley, Richard 1984. *The Intellectual and Social Organization of the Sciences*, Oxford: Clarendon Press.

Wilkins, Mira 1996. The conceptual domain of international business. In Brian Toyne and Douglas Nigh (eds), *International Business: An 'Emerging' Vision*, Columbia, SC: The University of South Carolina Press.

Wright, Richard W. and Ricks, David A. 1994. Trends in international business research: Twenty-five years later. *Journal of International Business Studies*, 25(4): 687–701.

4. The Economic Theory of the Firm as the Basis for a 'Core' Theory of International Production

John Dunning

INTRODUCTION

Over the past three decades, economists have taken two broad approaches to explaining the presence and growth of foreign owned and controlled value-added activities. The first is to treat such activities as the geographic extension of the domestic firm and to explain why firms choose to engage in foreign direct investment (fdi), rather than to seek other avenues of acquiring resources and capabilities or of penetrating markets (e.g. exports, licensing, subcontracting, etc.). The second is to treat international production, that is, production financed by fdi and undertaken by multinational enterprises (MNEs) as a form of international business activity, similar in many respects to international trade, but distinctive from it.

While the first approach has legitimately used the theory of the firm as its starting point for a 'core' paradigm of international business, the latter has taken a more macroeconomic stance and it has attempted to explain the totality of foreign value-added activity by MNEs, rather than by explaining why firms engage in fdi per se.

Not all explanations by economists of the remarkable growth in international business activity since the Second World War fit neatly into one or another of these categories.1 But, in general, the early partial theories of international production and the MNE2 put forward by Stephen Hymer, Richard Caves, Raymond Vernon and R.Z. Aliber in the 1960s and early 1970s fall into the second category;3 while writings on the theory of the MNE (qua MNE) by such scholars as J.C. McManus, Mark Casson and Peter Buckley, Alan Rugman, Birgitta Swedenborg and Jean Francois Hennart date back only to the mid-1970s and early 1980s.4 However, unlike their predecessors, this latter group of economists, who are best associated with the internalisation theory or paradigm of the MNE, attempted to put forward a general or core theory of international business which, in the mid-1990s, remains a rich and powerful framework for analysis.

Our own approach to explaining international business activity draws upon both strands of thinking but, in terms of what it is seeking to explain, draws upon a much wider (and richer) vein of economic analysis than the internalisation paradigm. It, too, seeks to offer a general, rather than a partial, analytical framework for understanding the growth and pattern of international production. However, unlike the internalisation paradigm, it is not only concerned with why firms supplant cross-border intermediate product markets by administrative fiat and why, indeed, they choose to locate these value-added activities in a foreign, rather than a domestic, location. It also seeks to identify and evaluate the advantages or assets which enable the investing firms to out-compete their foreign rivals in the first place. We choose to call our paradigm the 'eclectic' paradigm of international production because we believe that, to fully understand the extent and pattern of foreign owned value-added activities, economists need to draw upon several separate, but interrelated, strands of received theory.[5] In more recent years, we have also attempted to extend the original version of the eclectic paradigm to incorporate strategic and dynamic elements of business behaviour,[6] but such attempts will not be the focus of this chapter.

LOCATION AND OWNERSHIP OF PRODUCTION

Any 'core' theory of international business must seek to explain both the location of value-added activities and the ownership and organisation of these activities. As such, it needs to draw upon and integrate three branches of economic theory. The first is the theory of international resource allocation, which is based upon the spatial distribution of natural and created assets[7] and of markets. This theory chiefly addresses questions relating to the spatial distribution of economic activity by firms. The second is the theory of economic organisation, which is essentially concerned with the ownership of that production and the situations in which firms, rather than markets, choose to coordinate the transactions relating to it (including those which impinge upon its location). This theory draws heavily on the subtheory of market failure. The third is the theory of industrial organisation, which attempts to explain why the competitive advantages or ownership-specific assets of firms are not evenly spread, but tend to be concentrated in some, rather than other, firms. It is the inclusion of this element of economic theory which the eclectic paradigm, but not the internalisation paradigm, embraces — at least not in its static form. Inter alia, it helps to explain the changing geographical or sectoral composition of fdi and MNE activity over the past 30 years, although the reasons why, for example, Japanese or United States firms choose to exploit their competitive or ownership as opposed to specific advantages by foreign production, rather than by licensing or other non-equity arrangements, can still largely be explained by the internalisation paradigm.

Perhaps the main unique contribution of economists to our understanding of international business activity in recent years has been to resurrect and extend the Coasian idea that firms exist because they can coordinate economic activity more effectively than markets (Coase 1937). Until the 1950s, for example, neoclassical models of international economics located the firm as a 'black box', and completely neglected questions relating to economic organisation. This was because the market was considered to be the perfect mechanism for the exchange of goods and services and involved zero transaction costs. Furthermore, resources were presumed to be immobile across national boundaries, but mobile within national boundaries. Similarly, for much of the last century, microeconomic analysts have considered the firm primarily as a production, rather than as a transaction, unit — that is, as a transformer of valued inputs into more valued outputs, rather than as a coordinator of interrelated activities and exchanges. Even in the 1970s, most economics textbooks confined their attention to single-activity firms, and assumed that managerial strategy was solely concerned with identifying the optimum level of output and minimising the costs of producing that output. The transaction and coordinating costs and benefits of a firm's activities were largely ignored.

Much of the inability of traditional economics to explain international business activity, then, arises because of its limited perception of the functions of the firm, and the belief that where markets failed they did so because of structurally distorting conduct on the part of sellers or buyers, rather than because of any intrinsic or endemic characteristics of the market. However, in conditions of demand or supply instability and/or uncertainty, in the presence of economies of scale where elasticity for demand for the product being supplied is less than infinity, where there is an increasing public goods component of many products, where the reality of market situations involves only a few buyers and sellers, and in an innovation-driven economy, the ideal of a perfect market is neither practical, nor necessarily desirable. And it is precisely these endemic market failures which have increased as national economies have become more sophisticated and more closely linked with each other.

Economists generally accept that, without a degree of market imperfection in the exchange of intermediate products (e.g. technology, management skills, semi-finished goods) across national boundaries, there would be no impetus for firms to engage in fdi — that is, there would be no MNEs. Hence any theory of international business would be confined to explaining why firms engage in international trade — whether it be in intermediate or in final products. The fact that the major form of cross-border commerce now takes the form of international production (UNCTAD 1994), rather than trade, however, suggests that market failure issues must form an important component of any core theory of international business.[8] So must the related issue of innovation, which until the 1980s was given little attention by the mainstream theories of international business.[9]

In hindsight, it is clear that the early work of the internalisation economists was as much directed to explaining the growth of national firms as to the *raison d'être* of the MNE per se. It was, indeed, the beginning of a reconsideration of the very nature and functions of the firm. It is true that the MNE is, in essence, a diversified firm, but most of the elements of market failure identified and analysed by internalisation scholars have not been uniquely applicable to cross-border markets. However, by implication, such elements (notably uncertainties of one kind or another) are assumed to be more pronounced once a firm sells or buys its intermediate products from or to other firms in foreign countries.

Over the past 30 years, there has been a good deal of empirical testing of both general and specific explanations for international business activity. This is described in Dunning (1993a). The explanations are seen to vary a great deal according, for example, to the issues being addressed, and industry- and country-specific circumstances. Certainly, the fact that MNEs tend to concentrate in certain types of value-added activity, and that the propensity of countries to be outward or inward direct investors, can be explained by the location and organisational variables identified by the internalisation and eclectic paradigms. Research also suggests that the technological and political developments of the last decade or so are causing economists to reappraise some of their reasoning about the core determinants of international business activity. The following section deals with this issue in more detail.

NEW CHALLENGES FOR THE CORE THEORY OF INTERNATIONAL BUSINESS

Perhaps the two outstanding developments of the world economy over the last decade have been the renaissance of the free market system and the more gradual regionalisation and/or globalisation of business activity. Both reflect the dynamic interaction between political and technological events, and especially the increasing ease with which people, knowledge, finance and ideas are now moving across national boundaries. Together with the impressive and speedy industrialisation of many developing countries, the opportunities and challenges for crossborder business are much more extensive than they were when the dominant explanatory paradigms were first put forward.

Increasingly, to become or remain competitive, firms are being forced to engage in fdi or cross-border alliances. The number of MNEs has trebled since the early 1980s and it now stands around 37 000 (UNCTAD 1994), while the significance of the outward fdi stock of developed countries as a proportion of their gross domestic product (GDP) increased from an average of 6.2 per cent in 1980 to 10.2 per cent in 1992 (Dunning 1995b). The propensity of firms to conclude cross-border alliances or to participate in networks with suppliers, customers or competitors, particularly in high-technology sectors, has increased even more dramatically, with the average annual number being more than 50 per cent higher in 1992–93 than in 1981–85.

Yet, in spite of the growth of first-time foreign investors, 80 per cent of the growth by international production since 1980 has been by MNEs already established in that date. And much of the sequential investment has occurred through mergers and acquisitions (M&As). Indeed, between 1985 and 1993, between 60 per cent and 65 per cent of all fdi by US firms in Europe and by European firms in the United States took this form (UNCTAD 1994). Often, the rationale for the investment was not so much to exploit the existing competitive advantages of firms by foreign production (cf. exports or licensing), but to gain access to new resources, capabilities and markets perceived necessary to protect or advance the global competitive position of the investing firms. Similarly, firms are now increasingly engaging in cross-border strategic alliances with a view to acquiring complementary assets or accelerating the rate at which new assets are created and marketed.

There is little in the core theories of international business to explain the remarkable growth of strategic asset acquiring (or sharing) activity by MNEs, although, to the extent that M&As are undertaken by firms to internalise the transaction costs and benefits of using cross-border markets, the predictions of the internalisation paradigm are upheld. But we believe that it is only by embracing the concept of alliance capitalism and the realisation that the competitiveness of firms is becoming increasingly dependent on their ability to harness the competitive advantages of other firms and also the location specific created assets of other countries that the economic paradigms of the 1970s and 1980s can retain their explanatory power in the 1990s.[10] The implications of global economic events, of course, go well beyond the international business research. It is, for example, giving new credence to the resource-based theory of the firm, which dates back to the writings of Edith

Penrose in the 1950s. Perhaps even more significantly, it is fashioning a new trajectory of research on innovatory or evolutionary microeconomics, especially that of scholars such as John Cantwell (1992, 1993), and Bob Pearce and Satwinder Singh (1992), who are seeking to unravel the interaction between the technology of firms and the extent, modality and location of their innovating activities. In both areas of research, the simplistic transaction cost models, used to explain the *raison d'être* for first time market seeking or resource based fdi, fail to capture the critical determinants of sequential investment — and particularly so where this is intended to strengthen the core competencies or strategic positioning of the investing firms.

Some interesting research on the dynamics of MNE activity, using the concept of the investment development path, first put forward by the author in 1971,[11] is offering some glimpses of the way in which the core theories of international business may be modified to embrace contemporary theories of innovatory development. From a series of country case studies (Dunning and Narula 1995) and a study by Ragnit Narula (1995), it is clear that countries, like firms, proceed through various stages of internationalisation; and that, according to the particular stage at which they happen to be, the mobile competitive advantages of domestic- and foreign-based MNEs interact differently with their location-bound assets. At early stages of a firm's or country's development, its prosperity is likely to rest primarily on its capacity to adapt imported assets to enhance their indigenous capabilities. However, when firms grow and become more competitive and develop their own core competencies, they are increasingly likely to engage in foreign trade and investment, and/or form alliances with foreign firms in order to enhance the value of their own assets. In their more advanced stage of growth and development, firms and countries — especially those whose prosperity rests on their ability to innovate new products and upgrade human skills — tend to be both exporters and importers of capital and technology, and to both exploit and acquire their competitive strengths through fdi and strategic alliances.

The dynamic interplay between inward fdi and the performance of indigenous firms, as well as that between outward fdi and the competitiveness of domestic MNEs, has recently been explored by UNCTAD (1995). This study reveals that, depending on the efficacy of the macroeconomic and organisational policies of home and host governments, MNEs can play a critical role as arbitragers in competitive enhancing strategies via leveraging the resources and capabilities of the firms with which they have dealings, and the location-bound assets of the countries, or regions within a country, in which they operate. It is those MNEs which are successful in recognising that competitive success requires the integration of multiple firm-specific competencies both across and between functional areas to coordinate these assets in the context of an innovatory driven competitive environment which are likely to be the global winners of the future.

In a recent contribution, (Dunning 1995a) the author has attempted to 'add on' to the variables which were initially considered by the eclectic paradigm of international production, those which arise specifically as a result of collaboration between firms of different ownership.

CONCLUSION

The internalisation and eclectic paradigms continue to offer a rich framework for analysing the economic determinants of the cross-border business activities of both firms and countries. Within these frameworks a whole variety of partial economic and strategically oriented theories can be accommodated.

However, the emphasis of the competitive (or ownership) advantages of firms and those of countries, and the ways in which firms organise the use of the two kinds of assets, is changing as the socio-institutional structure of capitalism is shifting from that primarily based on hierarchies and markets to that based on a more pluralistic combination of hierarchies, inter-firm alliances, networks and markets, not to mention the role of governments. Increasingly, any 'core' theory of international business needs to incorporate the consequences which cross-border inter-firm cooperation has on the resources and capabilities of MNEs (or potential MNEs), and the ways in which MNEs choose to organise these assets. Increasingly, too, in their examination of location-specific characteristics of countries, economists need to give more attention to the external economies of the clustering or agglomeration of similar activities in a particular geographical area. While organisational scholars have long recognised the benefits of spatial networking, economists have been slow to resuscitate and update Alfred Marshall's analysis of agglomerative economies (Marshall 1920)

It is, perhaps, the challenges of one of the emerging paradoxes of an innovation driven globalising economy — how to reconcile the advantages of inter-firm cooperation with those of effective inter-firm competition — that will most tax the intellect of economists seeking to develop a core theory of international business and international business activity in the early twenty-first century. It is a challenge which not only requires the input from various strands of economic thought, but also that of several related business disciplines. For, at the end of the day, a complete explanation of the ownership, location and organisation of international business, and the propensity of industries and countries to engage in inbound and outbound

MNE activity, rests as much on the political, cultural and strategic goals and aspirations of firms and governments as it does on purely economic considerations. Such issues are the subject of later chapters in this volume.

NOTES

[1]   As, for example, is reviewed by Dunning (1993a), and more recently updated by UNCTAD (1994, 1995).

[2]   So called because they sought to explain specific kinds of international business activity, or used very distinctive analytical tools in so doing. For a review of these partial theories, see Dunning (1992).

[3]   The key contributions of these scholars are contained in Dunning (1992).

[4]   Also fully described in Dunning (1992).

[5]   This is not the place to give a full discussion of the eclectic paradigm; this is set out in Chapter 4 of Dunning (1993a). However this chapter, we do outline some modifications of the original paradigm recently suggested by the author (Dunning 1995a).

[6]   See Chapters 3 and 4 of Dunning (1993b).

[7]   Natural assets may be defined as land and the stock of untrained labour. All other assets are created from natural assets. They may be tangible (e.g. the stock of physical and financial assets) or intangible (e.g. technological know-how, trademarks. goodwill and the culture and organisational structure of institutions).

[8]   Business and organisational scholars would (rightly) argue that the presence of an imperfect market widens the strategic options of firms to respond to any particular portfolio of endogenous and exogenous variables affecting fdi related decisions. We accept that, as and when endemic market failure becomes more pronounced, the way in which firms react to these failures — bearing in mind that, *ex ante,* it may not be possible to identify an optimum reaction (Dunning, 1995a); and that an understanding of the determinants of a firm's strategy becomes an important component of any core theory of international business.

[9]   With the exception of Vernon's product cycle theory (Vernon 1966, 1979).

[10]   The concept of alliance capitalism was first introduced by Michael Gerlach (1992) to describe the social organisation of Japanese business. Our interpretation of the terms 'relational', new' and collective' — which other scholars (e.g. Best 1990, Lazonick 1992) associate with capitalism — is much broader. Indeed, we regard alliance capitalism as much a socio-cultural phenomenon as a technolo-organisational one. The former suggests a change in the ethos and perspective towards the organisation of capitalism, and, in particular, towards the relationships between the participating institutions and individuals. The latter embraces the formal structure of the organisation of economic activity, including the management of resource allocation and growth. Alliance capitalism is an eclectic (sic) concept. It suggests both cooperation and competition between institutions (including public institutions) and between interested parties within institutions. De facto, it is also leading to a flattening out of the organisational structure of decision-taking of business enterprises, with a pyramidal chain of command being increasingly replaced by a more heterarchical interplay between the main participants in decision-taking. Finally, we would emphasise that we are not suggesting that alliance capitalism means the demise of hierarchies, but rather that the rationale and functions of hierarchies requires a reappraisal in the socio-economic climate of the global marketplace now emerging.

[11]   See Dunning (1993a) for a full explanation.

REFERENCES

Best, M. 1990. *The New Competition: Institutions of Restructuring*, Cambridge, MA: Harvard University Press.

Cantwell, J. 1992. The theory of technological competence and its application to international production. In D.G. McFetridge (ed.), *Foreign Investment. Technology and Economic Growth*, Calgary: University of Calgary Press.

Cantwell, J. 1993. *Transnational Corporations and Innovatory Activities*, United Nations Library on Transnational Corporations, 17. London and New York: Routledge.

Coase, R.H. 1937. The nature of the firm, *Economica*, 4: 386–405.

Dunning, J.H. (ed.) 1992. *The Theory of Transnational Corporations*, United Nations Library on Transnational Corporations, 1. London: Routledge.

Dunning, J.H. 1993a. *Multinational Enterprises and the Global Economy*, Wokingham, England and Reading, Mass.: Addison Wesley.

Dunning, J.H. 1993b. *Globalization of Business: The Challenge of the 1990s*, London and New York: Routledge.

Dunning, J.H. 1995a. Reappraising the Eclectic Paradigm in the Age of Alliance Capitalism. *Journal of International Business Studies*, 26(3).

Dunning, J.H. 1995b. The role of foreign direct investment in a globalizing economy. *Banca Nazionale del Lavoro Quarterly Review*, 193 (June): 12544.

Dunning, J.H. and Narula, R. (eds) 1995. *Foreign Direct Investment and Governments*, London and New York: Routledge.

Gerlach, M.J. 1992. *Alliance Capitalism: The Social Organization of Japanese Business*, Oxford: Oxford University Press.

Lazonick, W. 1992. Business organization and competitive advantage: capitalist transformation in the twentieth century. In G. Dosi, R. Giannelti and P.A. Toninelli (eds), *Technology and Enterprise in a Historical Perspective*, Oxford: Clarendon Press, pp. 119–163.

Marshall, A. 1920. *Principles of Economics*, 8th edn, London: Macmillan.

Narula, R. 1995, *Multinational Investment and Economic Structure*, London and Boston: Routledge.

Pearce, R. and Singh, S.A. 1992. *Globalizing Research and Development*, London: Macmillan.

UNCTAD 1994. *World Investment Report 1994: Transnational Corporations. Employment and the Workplace*, New York and Geneva: United Nations.

UNCTAD 1995. *World Development Report 1995: Transnational Corporations and Competitiveness*, New York: United Nations.

Vernon, R. 1966. International investment and international trade in the product cycle,' *Quarterly Journal of Economics*, 80: 190–207.

Vernon, R. 1979. The product cycle hypothesis in the new international environment. *Oxford Bulletin of Economics and Statistics*, 41: 255–67.

5. International Political Economy and MNEs' Strategies: New Directions for Interdisciplinary Research

Thomas Brewer

PURPOSE AND SCOPE

This chapter addresses the following question about the literature of international business (IB) and the literature of international political economy (IPE): how can each enrich the other for the intellectual advancement of both? The answer developed here is that there are two promising directions for such an effort: one is to combine the IB literature on fdi theory and strategy with the political science literature on political economy to advance our understanding of MNEs' fdi strategies and interactions with governments. A second is to focus on international regime change, which is a particularly promising direction for research because of the changes in both the strategies of firms and the policies of governments concerning fdi during recent years. The IPE literature has not yet reflected the changes in the former, and the IB literature has not yet reflected changes in the latter.[1]

The most pertinent IPE literature can be divided into two groups — one that is principally concerned with the interests and power of MNEs and national governments and their interactions, and another that is principally concerned with the evolution of international regimes. A critical differentiating criterion between these two groups of studies is the level of analysis: whereas the former focuses on the nation-state and thus the national as well as international levels of analysis, the latter focuses on international organisations and thus the international and supranational levels of analysis. Another critical difference concerns types of international business transactions: whereas the former has been very much concerned with the fdi of MNEs, the latter has generally ignored fdi and focused almost exclusively on trade instead.[2] The concern with the power of MNEs and their relations with national governments is the focus of the next section, and the concern with international regimes is the focus of the subsequent section.

POLITICAL ECONOMY, MNES' STRATEGIES AND NATIONAL GOVERNMENTS

The power of MNEs, their relations with home and host governments and their role more generally in political economies can be analysed through the prism of diverse notions of politics, economics and political economy.

Concepts of Politics, Economics and Political Economy

Political economy, as an interdisciplinary domain of analysis, can be defined in a straightforward manner as the study of the interactions of politics and economics.[3] One notion of politics is that it is the exercise of power in the sense of one actor inducing another to do something it would not otherwise do; the inducement is based on threatened or actual deprivations, and/or promised or actual indulgences. In this notion of politics, there is the conception of politics as a decision calculus utilised by actors in strategic situations involving a high degree of interdependent behaviour. Although there is a strong emphasis on conflicts of interest and behaviour in this definition of politics, there are also many opportunities for cooperation as actors pursue common interests. Much of the international relations scholarship on international security affairs explicitly or implicitly adopts this notion of power. A second notion of politics defines it as collective goal-seeking, or as a social problem-solving process. This view of politics treats it as a goal seeking activity and emphasises common interests and cooperative relationships among political actors; politics is, accordingly, an on-going, iterative process that is embedded in social contexts. A third notion of politics defines it as an authoritative value-allocation process in which values (i.e. human preferences) are shaped and shared. A central feature of politics, therefore, is that it entails a struggle over the distribution of values in society. This view of politics is particularly evident in studies of domestic political processes that emphasise the interests and political activities of groups.

Economics can also be defined in three ways, and these three definitions of economics parallel the three definitions of politics. First, economics can be defined as a decision calculus that focuses on the relationship between means and ends, including especially the selection of means that are efficient in the achievement of given ends. This notion of economics thus treats behaviour as rational in the sense that maximising alternatives are preferred over less efficient alternatives. A second notion of economics treats it as a goal-oriented provisioning activity — as a process that produces goods and services for the satisfaction of wants and needs. A third notion of economics treats it as an institutionalised process in which exchanges take place among participants in markets or otherwise-organised social structures.

Although this definitional exercise is necessarily proscrustean, it is a useful way to think about politics and economics because it highlights key underlying similarities as well as differences in them. In particular, the first definition of each is based on the notion of a *decision calculus,* in which actors can pursue their ends rationally. There is thus not only economic rationality, in the sense of linking means to ends in maximising ways, but there is also political rationality, in the sense of maximising power. In fact, game theory and deterrence studies reflect the intersection of these definitions of politics and economics, with their underlying emphasis on rational calculations in the choice of strategic alternatives as actors pursue their ends. Both are concerned with the effectiveness of strategies in the pursuit of interests. There is a key difference between politics and economics, though: whereas politics is concerned with power, conflict and cooperation as means to achieve goals when actors calculate in strategic situations, economics is concerned with the efficiency of the means.

The second definitions above reflect social-functional views of politics and economics inasmuch as both focus on *collective goal-seeking* activities that produce outcomes of utility to society. In economics the products are the goods and services that satisfy people's wants and needs, while in politics the products are authoritative decisions and rules. The key difference between politics and economics in this view, lies in the nature and function of the end product — whether goods and services for consumption or investment, as produced by the economic system, or decisions and rules for the maintenance of order and for other social functions, as produced by the political system.

The underlying theme in the third notion of politics and economics above is that both are *institutionalised allocation processes.* In market economies, allocative processes are based on price mechanisms that rely on the forces of supply and demand; in command economies, allocative processes are based on centralised material input–output matrices and administered prices. In democratic political systems, allocation processes are based on elections, representative institutions and other mechanisms that facilitate the expression of popular preferences; in authoritarian political systems, allocation processes are based on the preferences of dictators or oligarchies. A key difference between politics and economics lies in the scope of what is being allocated.

In the economic system, wealth is allocated; in the political system, a broad range of diverse 'values', including power, status and a variety of other intangible and tangible values, as well as wealth, are allocated.[4]

Thus, each of these paired definitions identifies both similarities and differences between politics and economics. These three paired definitions also make it possible to identify nine potential foci of the analysis of political economy, based on the combinations of the three definitions of politics and three definitions of economics. These nine notions of political economy have much potential for enriching the literature of IB strategy, including the development of new paradigms of international business strategy. Within the broad range of IB topics, I restrict the chapter to the application of selected notions of political economy to fdi in particular, and I leave to others the opportunity to apply these notions of political economy to additional current issues of international business.

The Power and Strategies of MNEs

In the columns of Table 5.1, several of the abovementioned notions can be used as a basis for identifying the multiple ways in which multinational firms are political actors — that is, as power seekers in interactions with other political actors, as participants in collective goal-seeking processes, and as allocators of values in societies. Table 5.1 also depicts — in the rows — key questions in the fdi theoretical literature.

The underlying analytic issue of the table is how these notions of political economy can improve upon common questions and answers about fdi strategy. MNEs' behavior as power-seeking political actors (in the first column) can be easily and directly related to MNEs' strategic decisions and fdi theory, and more generally to MNE–government interactions (Boddewyn 1988; Boddewyn and Brewer 1994; Brewer 1992). For instance, uncertainty about the enforcement of international licensing agreements is one of the reasons fdi is often preferred as a strategic alternative to arms-length licensing agreements with unrelated firms in foreign countries. Thus the lack of power of a given multinational firm to induce a government to enforce a licensing agreement is at issue. Similarly the lack of power of a firm to induce a government to lower its trade barriers often makes fdi the preferred strategic alternative to trade. In both instances, in other words, it is the MNE's power over its own internalised transactions through fdi, compared with the lack of power over government policy obstacles to licensing and trade, that makes fdi a relatively attractive strategic alternative. On the other hand, in those instances when an individual MNE's power (or several MNEs' power collectively) is sufficient to reduce uncertainty about licensing agreement enforcement, or is sufficient to obtain reductions in trade barriers, then those strategic alternatives become more attractive.

An MNE's power, furthermore, may be country-specific; that is, a firm may have political resources that enable it to exercise more power in one country than in others. Thus the locational advantage of one prospective host country over others depends not only on the features of the country, but the variability across countries in the political power of particular MNEs. Political power is therefore a partial answer to the question in the second row: Why does a firm undertake fdi in a given host country rather than another?

Table 5.1: Fdi strategic issues in a political economy context

Fdi strategic issues	MNE as actor in political economies		
	Power seeker	Participant in collective goal-seeking	Value allocator
Why Fdi, not trade or licensing?			
Why Fdi in one country instead of other countries?			
Why can firm compete despite being foreign?			

The power-seeking behavior of MNEs, moreover, offers a partial answer to the question in the third row of Table 5.1: why is the firm able to compete in a foreign country despite the disadvantages of being foreign and operating at a cultural and geographic distance, compared with its domestic competition? The political power answer is that firms sometimes are able to exercise power to gain favoured treatment from the host government that increases its revenues and/or reduces its costs. Sometimes, for instance, multinational firms are able to obtain tax advantages and other government subsidies while local firms are not.

It is also possible to relate the types of political behavior of MNEs represented by the second and third columns of Table 5.1 to questions about their strategies. For instance, in the second column an MNE's ability to contribute to a country's goal-seeking concerning international technology inflows may enable it to gain preferred treatment over local firms, which do not have the same capacity to bring in new technology to the local economy. An example in the third column is that the potential impact of an fdi project on the allocation of values in some countries makes the project unacceptable to some countries but not others. For instance, firms that are known to have strong policies against discrimination based on gender and race may be perceived as unacceptably threatening to the current distribution of status in a prospective host society.

PUBLIC POLICY REGIMES FOR FDI AND THE STRATEGIES OF MNES

Another logical topic for interdisciplinary IB–IPE research is international regimes, and this section of the paper therefore briefly reviews changes in public policy regimes for fdi since the early 1980s, presents key concepts of international regime analysis in the IPE literature, and discusses the interactions of public regimes and MNEs' strategies.[5]

Changes in Fdi Regimes

There have been significant changes in fdi public policy regimes at the national, bilateral, regional and multilateral levels since the early 1980s. A United Nations study (1992) analysed the fdi policies of 46 host countries over the 1977–87 period for evidence of change in either a more liberal or more restrictive direction; these included 20 developed market economy countries, five newly industrial countries, and 21 developing countries, which altogether received more than 90 per cent of world fdi inflows. Of the 321 policy changes observed, 70 per cent were of a liberalising nature: this preponderance of liberalising changes over restrictive changes occurred within each of the three groups of countries. Studies for the World Bank by Becsky, Ordu and Lee (1991) and by Brewer (1991) of the twelve major fdi recipient countries in Asia, Africa and Latin America also found significant liberalisation tendencies during the 1980s.[6] In addition, an overview of fdi policies in selected industrial and developing countries by Behrman and Grosse (1990: 112) revealed strong tendencies towards fdi policy liberalisation: of the seven industrial countries included, two adopted more open fdi policies during the 1980s, none adopted more restrictive policies, and five remained the same; of the nine developing countries, four adopted more liberal fdi policies, and the remainder maintained the same general level of restrictiveness/openness.[7] The trend towards more liberalised policies has continued and gathered momentum in the 1990s. For instance, surveys by UNCTAD (1993, 1994) for the years 1991 and 1992 found, respectively, 30 and 36 non-OECD countries in those years that had undertaken unilateral fdi

Table 5.2: Unilateral Fdi policy changes by non-OECD countries

	1991 More/less liberal	1992 More/less liberal
Number of countries	30/0	36/0
Number of policy changes	88/0	67/0
Foreign ownership/sectoral restrictions	15/0	24/0
Approval procedures	13/0	17/0
Operational conditions[a]	12/0	19/0
Guarantees	16/0	13/0
Controls[a]	12/0	12/0
Incentives	More/less attractive 13/0	More/less attractive 23/0

Note: a The distinction between operational conditions and controls is not evident in the source.

Sources: UN, *World Investment Report*, 1992, Table m.3, pp. 80–81, Annex Table 11, pp. 337–345, for 1991; *UN, World Investment Report*, 1993, Table I.13, pp. 32–33, and Annex Table 6, pp. 267–28, for 1992.

policy reforms. In every instance, the changes were in the direction of liberalisation — or otherwise more favourable policies to investors, in the case of incentives (see Table 5.2).

At the bilateral level, there has been a big increase in the number of bilateral investment treaties (BITs). Table 5.3 indicates the number of such treaties entering into force or signed in the early 1990s. By May 1994, there were 569 treaties between OECD countries and non-OECD countries.[8]

Table 5.3: Bilateral investment treaties between OECD countries and non-OECD countries[a] (number of treaties entering into force or signed)

Region of OECD non-members	1950–1989	1990–1993	Cumulative EOY 1993
Africa[b]	149	22	171
Asia[c]	76	31	107
Central and East Europe	53	110	163
Latin America	42	57	99
Total	320	220	540[d]

Notes: a. Period prior to Mexico's membership . b. Includes Middle East., c. Includes West Asia. d. There were an additional 29 treaties signed between January and may 1994, when Mexico became an OECD member. The total as of the end of May 1994, therefore, was 569.

Sources: Computed by the author from UN, *World Investment Report*, 1992, Table II.2, p. 77; UN, *World Investment Report*, 1993, Table I.12, p. 28, and Annex Table 5, pp. 256–66; UN, *World Investment Report*, 1994, Table VII.2, p. 279, and Annex Table 6, pp. 427–40.

At the regional level, there have been two significant tangible developments in recent years — the North American Free Trade Area (NAFTA) and the Asia Pacific Economic Cooperation forum (APEC). NAFTA contains extensive provisions concerning fdi, including for instance dispute settlement procedures for disputes between governments and disputes between investors and governments (Brewer 1995a; Gestrin and Rugman 1994; Graham and Wilkie 1994). Although the future of APEC in institutional and rulemaking terms remains highly uncertain, its governments have adopted a set of non-binding international investment principles (Green and Brewer 1995).

At the multilateral level, the General Agreement on Trade in Services (GATS), the agreement on Trade Related Investment Measures (TRIMs), the agreement on Trade Related Intellectual Property Rights (TRIPs), and the Dispute Settlement Understanding (DSU) from the Uruguay Round have established a new multilateral fdi regime centred on the World Trade Organisation (WTO). The explicit inclusion of fdi-related rules within the WTO institutional framework marks an historic change from the GATT (Brewer 1995b; OECD 1994, chs. 19–24; Sauvé 1994, 1995; UNCTAD Uruguay 1994). In addition to these changes reflected in the transformation of the GATT into the WTO, the Organisation for Economic Cooperation and Development (OECD) has initiated negotiations on a new Multilateral Agreement on Investment (Brewer and Young 1995a, 1995b; Graham 1995; Rugman and Gestrin 1995; Smith 1995).[9]

In their totality, these changes in fdi regimes at the multilateral, regional, bilateral and national levels create a new era in the public policy environment of MNEs. The IPE literature on international regimes offers an array of concepts and theoretical approaches that could be incorporated in interdisciplinary studies of the interaction of public policy regime change and MNEs' strategies.

IPE Literature on International Regimes

The focus of the IPE literature on regimes has been on multilateral agreements. Although this is a limitation of its applicability to fdi regime change in light of the important changes at the national, bilateral and regional levels noted above, this IPE literature is directly relevant for understanding changes at the multilateral level. Furthermore, although the focus in that literature has been on *trade* — to the neglect of investment in general and fdi in particular — many of the central concepts and theoretical approaches are nevertheless applicable to fdi regime change.[10]

In a review of the IPE literature on regimes, Haggard and Simmons (1987) identify four theoretical approaches: structural, functional, cognitive and game-theoretic. *Structural* analyses of regimes have been embodied specifically in hegemonic stability explanations of regime creation, maintenance and demise; the fate of regimes, in such analyses, thus depends on the existence of dominant national governments in the international system and their ability and willingness to support international regimes. The outlines of the theory were first developed by Keohane and Nye (1977); although it assumed the status of the prevailing paradigm in regime studies, particularly as an explanation of the development of the GATT centred international trade regime, its applicability in the current more pluralistic world political economy is problematic.[11]

Functional theoretical analysis focuses on the actual and expected effects of regimes as causal factors that explain the maintenance of regimes, the modification of regimes, and the strength of regimes. Regimes may persist or be modified or retain their strength, 'even when the structural conditions that initially gave rise to them' no longer pertain, simply because governments find them useful (Haggard and Simmons 1987: 506). For instance, regimes can reduce information and transaction costs or uncertainties — much like the internalisation of economic transactions within firms in lieu of market-based transactions. Functional analyses tend to focus on common interests and cooperation in regimes, and to neglect the roles of conflict, power and inequalities in regimes'.[12]

Cognitive theories of regimes suggest that:

> cooperation cannot be completely explained without reference to ideology, the values of actors, the beliefs they hold about the interdependence of issues, and

the knowledge available to them about how they can realise specific goals. Cooperation is affected by perception and misperception, the capacity to process information, and learning. While structural and functional theories assume that cooperation operates within an issue-area which is relatively unambiguous, cognitivists point out that issue-areas are never simply given. Cognitive approaches are therefore particularly important in explaining the substantive context of regime rules and why they evolve. By elevating the importance of actor learning, cognitive theories have a dynamic other approaches lack. (Haggard and Simmons 1987: 510)

Table 5.4: Analytic foci of international regime change in IPE literature

| Theoretical | Dimensions of change | | | |
approaches	Strength	Form	Scope	Allocation Mode
Structural				
Functional				
Cognitive				
Game Theory				

Source: Derived by the author from Haggard and Simmons (1987: 491–517).

Though *game theory* has not been applied extensively to the topic of international regimes, it 'can readily explain the conditions under which regimes might arise as an instance of cooperative behavior, and it can also suggest the conditions conducive to stable compliance' (Haggard and Simmons 1987: 504).[13]

These four theoretical approaches could be applied to multilateral regime changes, with a focus on the four key dimensions of change evident in that literature: strength, form, scope and mode of allocation (see Table 5.4).

IB Strategies and Fdi Regimes

There are important overlaps between the topic of fdi regime change and the earlier concern of the chapter with the political economy and strategies of MNEs. For instance, understanding the role and power of MNEs in the development of a new multilateral regime of rules and institutional arrangements for fdi has become more timely as both the OECD and WTO assume additional fdi rule-making responsibilities. Also, as multilateral rules and institutional arrangements become more elaborate and as enforcement mechanisms become more effective, the need to understand the constraints and opportunities that they create for both MNEs' strategies and national governments' policies has similarly become more current.

The combination of the proliferation of international investment agreements among governments and the proliferation of international strategic alliances among MNEs (Dunning 1995; US Office of Technology Assessment 1993) marks a new era of international business-government relations. Neither the IB literature nor the IPE literature by itself will provide an adequate understanding of the interactions of firms and governments in the new era. More interdisciplinary IB–IPE research will be needed.

CONCLUSION

This chapter has focused on two key topical concerns in the intersection of international business strategy and international political economy. One is a traditional concern in both the IB and IPE literature, namely the power of MNEs, particularly in relation to national governments. The other is a new but increasingly important concern, namely the interaction of international public policy regime change and MNEs' strategies. The theme of the chapter is that the analysis of the former can be enriched by the application of core notions of political economy to the analysis of MNEs' strategies and that analysis of the latter can be enriched by the integration of the IPE literature on international regime change with the IB literature on MNEs' strategies. These two suggested directions for research, of course, only begin to explore interesting possibilities for IB–IPE interdisciplinary studies. However, they are 'current issues' of special significance.

NOTES

[1]   A collection of 37 articles on IPE and FDI from 1966–91 has been collected by Gomes-Casseres and Yoffie (1993).

[2]   The literature of IB on business–government relations is of course massive, and it overlaps in many ways with the IPE literature on the interactions of national governments and MNEs. Indeed, many of the individual items in that literature could be treated as both IB and IPE literature and could have been published in journals in either field. However, the empirical emphasis of the IPE literature is on the development of theory focused on the interests and power of actors in political processes and ultimately the explanation of the political outcomes of those processes and their implications for governments, while the parallel emphasis in the IB literature of business–government relations is on the political behaviour of firms and on the consequences of the behavior of governments for firms. Similarly, to the extent that there are normative concerns — either explicitly stated or implicitly reflected — in the bodies of literature, there is also an important difference of

emphasis: whereas the IPE literature emphasises the implications for public policy, the IB literature emphasises the implications for business management.

3 This is not intended to be an exhaustive presentation of definitions of politics, or economics or political economy; rather, it suggests some notions that would be useful to expand and focus interdisciplinary IB–IPE research. The discussion draws extensively on Brewer (1995a, 1995b) and Caporaso and Levine (1992: 8–21), which is an excellent introduction to theories of political economy. The definitions of politics presented here are drawn from Dahl (1991), Deutsch (1966), Easton (1970), Lasswell (1936) and Lasswell and Kaplan (1950). Three related, but somewhat differently explicated, concepts of power in the international politics literature are identified by Hart (1976). The literature of political science has recently eschewed generalised definitions of politics in favour of more specific notions of types of polities, political institutions and political economies; see, for instance, Putnam (1993). Although we can define politics and economics as analytically separable, the political and economic phenomena that we study are of course highly interdependent and intertwined in the 'real world'.

4 Lasswell and Kaplan (1950) present a carefully structured and encompassing list of values that are allocated in political systems: power, enlightenment, wealth, well-being, skills, affection, righteousness, and deference. One could add the aesthetic value of beauty.

5 Portions of this section of the chapter have been adapted from Brewer (1993) and from Brewer and Young (1995a, l995b, 1995c, 1995d). Also see Preston (1992), Preston and Windsor (1992), Carnegie Bosch Institute (1995), Rugman and Gestrin (1995), Graham (1995) and Dunning (1993, ch. 23) on international institutional arrangements affecting FDI.

6 The countries were Argentina, Brazil, Columbia, Mexico, India, Indonesia, Korea, Malaysia, Thailand, Kenya and Nigeria.

7 The industrial countries were Canada, France, Germany, Italy, Japan, United Kingdom and United States; the developing countries were Argentina, Brazil, China, India, Indonesia, Korea, Mexico, Singapore, Taiwan. These findings are reinforced by data generated from the annual *Report on Exchange Restrictions and Exchange Arrangements of the International Monetary Fund* by Quinn and Inclan (1992) in a study of 21 industrial countries. Evidence of liberalising tendencies during the 1980s in both restrictions on capital account transactions and restrictions on current account transactions was found for all four subgroups of countries in the study. In addition, a study by the World Bank (1991) found a clear shift away from import-substitution to export-oriented economic growth strategies by developing countries.

8 Although much of the interest in creating additional BITs is focused on the industrial countries' need to expand their networks of BITs to the countries of Central and Eastern Europe and the former Soviet Union, there has also been increased activity involving Mexico and West European governments. See United Nations Center on Transnational Corporations and International Chamber of Commerce (1992) and UNCTAN–DTCI World Investment Report (1994, Annex Table 6 427-40).

9 The Multilateral Agreement on Investment (MAD at the OECD was initially referred to as a Wider Investment Instrument (WII), in comparison with the OECD Codes on the Liberalization of Capital Movements and Current Invisible Operations, and then subsequently as the Multilateral Investment Agreement (MIA).

10 Three definitions of international regimes have been identified by Haggard and Simmons (1987: 493–96). One conceives regimes to be 'multilateral agreements among states which aim to regulate national actions within an issue-area' (also see Young 1993). According to the second, regimes are 'implicit or explicit principles, norms, rules and decision-making procedures around which actors' expectations converge in a given area of international relations' (Krasner 1983: 1–21). Third, regimes can be defined even more generally as 'patterned behaviour' (Puchala and Hopkins 1983: 61–91). As Haggard and Simmons (1987: 495–6) note, the first definition 'allows a sharper distinction between the concept of regime and several [cognate concepts]' — in particular 'cooperation', and 'order' or 'stability', as well as 'normative consensus'. In each instance, regimes may be causally

connected to those other phenomena, as either cause or consequence, but regimes are not synonymous with them; indeed, the potential causal connections between regimes and those other phenomena constitute a set of important theoretical and empirical issues in the analysis of regimes. Nor does a focus on multilateral agreements as the essence of regimes exclude analysis of their relationship to the variables that are included in the more encompassing definitions — for instance, norms, principles and other forms of patterned behaviour, whether explicit or implicit. Again, however, those are matters for empirical analysis rather than definitional semantics.. Second, ... we search for the authoritative statements of powerful actors in the issue area ... [which] can be found in UN resolutions on the topic, the annual reports of the international organization concerned, the speeches of policy makers at fora or at national legislative bodies, and the like.'

[11] Haggard and Simmons (1987: 504) note that 'hegemonic interpretations may have missed this century's most important "structural" cause of cooperation among the advanced industrial states' — namely, the polarisation of international security relations in the Cold War bi-polar system.

[12] Studies by Keohane (1985) are prominent items in this literature. The former has observed, for instance (103–6), 'that the marginal cost of dealing with an additional issue will be lower with a regime, an insight that casts light on the important question of why regimes often expand in scope' (Haggard and Simmons 1987: 507–8).

[13] Game theory is also deficient in its neglect of the domestic national politics in regime analysis, but this is a potentially correctable deficiency through the use of two-level game analysis. Haggard and Simmons (1987: 506) conclude as follows about the utility of this approach. 'Game theoretic approaches are strongest when they reveal the conditions which enable cooperation and stability; they say far less about whether regimes will actually arise, how they will be institutionalized, and, above all, the rules and norms which will comprise them.'

REFERENCES

Becsky, G., Ordu, A. and Lee, 1991. *Foreign Direct Investment in Selected Developing Countries in the Last Two Decades*, Washington, DC: The World Bank.

Behrman, Jack N. and Grosse, Robert E. 1990. *International Business and Governments: Issues and Institutions,* Columbia, S.C.: University of South Carolina Press.

Boddewyn, Jean J. 1988. Political aspects of MNC theory. *Journal of International Business Studies,* 19: 341–63.

Boddewyn Jean and Brewer, Thomas L. 1994. International business political behavior: New theoretical directions. *Academy of Management Review,* 19(1) January 1994: 119–43.

Brewer, Thomas L. 1991. *Foreign Direct Investment in Developing Countries: Patterns Policies and Prospects,* Washington, DC: The World Bank.

Brewer, Thomas L. 1992. An issue–area approach to the analysis of mnc–government relations. *Journal of International Business Studies,* 23(2): 295–309.

Brewer, Thomas L. 1993. Government policies, market imperfections, and foreign direct investment. *Journal of International Business Studies,* 24(1): 101–20.

Brewer, Thomas L. 1995a. International investment dispute settlement procedures: The evolving regime for foreign direct investment. *Law and Policy in International Business,* 26(3): 633–73.

Brewer, Thomas L. 1995b. Investment issues in the WTO and the implications for APEC's agenda. In Carl J. Green and Thomas L. Brewer (eds), *Investment Issues in the Asia Pacific Region: The Role of APEC*, Dobbs Ferry, NY: Oceana.

Brewer, Thomas L. and Young, Stephen 1995a. Towards a new multilateral framework for FDI: Issues and scenarios. *Transnational Corporations*, 4(1) (April): 69–83.

Brewer, Thomas L. and Young, Stephen 1995b. The multilateral agenda for foreign direct investment: Problems, principles and priorities for negotiations at the OECD and WTO. *World Competition,* 18(4): 67–83.

Brewer, Thomas L. and Young, Stephen 1995c. European union policies and the problems of multinational enterprises. *Journal of World Trade*, 29(1): 33–52.

Brewer, Thomas L. and Young, Stephen 1995d. FDI policies in regional and multilateral agreements. Paper prepared for the annual meeting of the European International Business Academy, Urbino, Italy.

Caporaso, James A. and Levine, David P. 1992. *Theories of Political Economy*, Cambridge: Cambridge University Press.

Carnegie Bosch Institute 1995. Conference on Governments, Globalization and International Business. Washington, DC.

Dahl, Robert A. 1991. *Modern Political Analysis*, 5th edn. Englewood Cliffs, NJ, Prentice-Hall.

Deutsch, Karl W. (1966), *The Nerves of Government*, 2nd edition. New York: Free Press.

Dunning, John H. 1993. *Multinational Enterprises and the Global Economy,* Wokingham, England: Addison-Wesley.

Dunning, John H. 1995. Reappraising the eclectic paradigm in an age of alliance capitalism. *Journal of International Business Studies*, 26(3), third quarter.

Easton, David 1970. *The Political System*, New York: Knopf.

Gestrin, Michael, and Rugman Alan M. 1994. The North American Free Trade Agreement and foreign direct investment. *Transnational Corporations*, 3 (February): 77–95.

Gomes-Casseres, B. and Yoffie, David B. 1993. *The International Political Economy of Foreign Direct Investment*, Edward Elgar.

Graham, Edward M. 1995. Direct investment in the new multilateral trade context. Paper presented at a meeting of the OECD Trade Committee, Paris, 22 February, 1995, and at a meeting of the Council on Foreign Relations, Washington, DC, 15 March, 1995; revised version presented at a meeting of the C.D. Howe Institute, Montreal, 3 June, 1995.

Graham, Edward M. and Wilkie Christopher 1994. Multinationals and the investment provisions of the NAFTA. *The International Trade Journal*, 8 (Spring): 9–38.

Green, Carl J. and Brewer, Thomas L. (eds) 1995. *Investment Issues in the Asia Pacific Region: the Role of APEC*, Dobbs Ferry, NY: Oceana.

Haggard, Stephan and Simmons, Beth A. 1987. Theories of international regimes. *International Organization*, 41: 491–517.

Hart, Jeffrey 1976. Three approaches to the measurement of power in international relations. *International Organization*, 30: 289–305.

Keohane, Robert 1985. *After Hegemony: Cooperation and Discord in the World Political Economy*, Princeton: Princeton University Press.

Keohane, Robert and Nye, Joseph 1977. *Power and Interdependence*, Boston: Little, Brown.

Krasner, Stephen D. 1983. *International Regimes*, Ithaca: Cornell University Press.

Lasswell, Harold D. 1936. *Politics: Who Gets What, When and How*, New York: New American Library.

Lasswell, Harold D. and Kaplan, Abraham 1950. *Power and Society*, New Haven, Yale University Press.

Organization for Economic Cooperation and Development 1994. *OECD Documents: The New World Trading System, Readings*, Paris: OECD.

Preston, Lee E. 1992. *The Rules of the Game in the Global Economy: Policy Regimes for International Business*, Occasional Paper 7, Center for International Business Education and Research, University of Maryland at College Park.

Preston, Lee E. and Windsor, Duane 1992. *The Rules of the Game in the Global Economy: Policy Regimes for International Business*, Boston: Kluwer.

Puchala, Donald J. and Hopkins, Raymond F. 1983. International regimes: lessons from inductive analysis. In Stephen D. Krasner (ed.), *International Regimes*, Ithaca, NY: Cornell University Press.

Putnam, Robert D. 1993. *Making Democracy Work: Civic Traditions in Modern Italy*, Princeton: Princeton University Press.

Quinn, Dennis and Inclan, Carla 1992. International capital flows: A twenty one country study of financial liberalization, 1950–1988. Paper prepared for presentation at the Annual Meeting of the American Political Science Association.

Rugman, Alan M. and Gestrin, Michael 1995. A conceptual framework for a multilateral agreement on investment: Using NAFTA as a prototype. Paper prepared for the annual meetings of the Canadian Economics Association, Montreal, 3 June, 1995; to be published in a book by C.D. Howe and OECD.

Sauvé, Pierre 1994. A first look at investment in the final act of the Uruguay round. *Journal of World Trade*, 28(5) (October): 5–16.

Sauvé, Pierre 1995. Assessing the general agreement on trade in services: Half full or half empty? *Journal of World Trade*, 29(4) (August), forthcoming.

Smith, Alister 1995. The development of a multilateral investment agreement at the OECD: A preview. In Carl J. Green and Thomas L. Brewer (eds), *International Investment Issues in the Asia Pacific Region and the Role of APEC*, New York: Oceana, Chapter 6.

United Nations Centre on Transnational Corporations and International Chamber of Commerce 1992. *Bilateral Investment Treaties, 1959–1991*, New York: United Nations.

UNCTAD 1994. *The Outcome of the Uruguay Round: An Initial Assessment*, Supporting Papers to the Trade and Development Report, 1994. New York: United Nations.

UNCTAD, Division on Transnational Corporations and Investment 1994. *World Investment Report, 1993*, New York and Geneva: United Nations.

UNCTAD, Division on Transnational Corporations and Investment 1994. *World Investment Report, 1994*. New York and Geneva: United Nations.

United States Office of Technology Assessment 1993. *Multinationals and the National Interest: Playing by Different Rules,* Washington, DC: GPO.

World Bank 1991. *World Development Report 1991*, Washington, DC: World Bank.

PART THREE

Current Issues and Controversies

6. A 'Borderless' World: Issues and Evidence

George Yip

Kenichi Ohmae (1990) has proclaimed a 'borderless world'. The extent to which this condition holds has severe implications for governments, individuals and companies. Of most interest to the field of international business are the implications for the strategies of multinational companies. In a truly borderless world, multinational companies (MNCs) should adopt global strategies that have maximal integration across countries and minimal differentiation between them. Thus, global strategy can be defined as a globally coordinated or integrated approach to operating multinationally, particularly in contrast to multidomestic (Porter 1986) or multilocal (Yip 1992) strategies. In terms of Prahalad's (1975) integration–responsiveness grid, MNCs should tilt heavily towards integration. This chapter addresses whether they do or should.

Many forces affect whether or not the world is borderless. At the societal level these forces are very broad indeed. Even at the business level, they include many aspects, such as culture and language, that are clearly not globally homogeneous. Yip's framework presents a set of four drivers. Similarly, industries vary in the extent to which they are globalised, such that some think global strategies are not possible (Douglas and Wind 1987). The interesting question, however, is not whether industries are fully globalised, but what companies should do to exploit the globalisation potential that exists (Johansson and Yip 1994). So the key issues that need to be addressed are as follows:

- Should companies have a global strategy?
- Do companies have a global strategy?
- What are the determinants of global strategy?
- Does company nationality affect global strategy?
- Does global strategy bring about better performance?

This chapter addresses arguments and evidence on the above issues, and frames this discussion in the context of a general model of globalisation. Despite the importance of the subject, there exists only limited evidence on the use of global strategy and its performance effects. Most research has been normative rather than empirical, and most of the empirical work has covered small samples of companies or industries rather than large samples. Conversely, the large sample studies that have been conducted all cover relatively narrow issues, a significant problem in a field concerned with many inter-related constructs. This chapter reviews most of these empirical studies.

NORMATIVE ARGUMENTS FOR AND AGAINST GLOBAL STRATEGY

The case for global strategy can be viewed as having been started by Levitt's (1983) article in *Harvard Business Review*, proclaiming, *inter alia* that the 'global corporation ... sells the same things in the same way everywhere'. Such an unequivocal stand prompted strong reactions, including articles arguing against global strategy, such as Douglas and Wind (1987). But the period of 'black-and-white' arguments was soon dispelled by the introduction of a contingency approach to global strategy. Porter (1986) applied an industrial organisation approach arguing that the case of a global strategy depends very much on industry conditions. Yip (1989 and 1992) further developed this contingency approach to a fully fledged framework for systematically analysing how 'industry globalisation drivers' set the level of globalisation potential for different industries. Most of the conceptual literature since the mid-1980s has focused on examining ways in which companies might use global strategy. Quite rightly, researchers have implicitly or explicitly understood that, in dealing with a new type of strategy, progress is made more by focusing on possible reasons for using it and ways to make it work than focusing on reasons not to use it and why it does not work. Increasingly, this has become the attitude of managers also, with some companies' practice and consultants' advice at times leading academic research.

The essence of global strategy lies in global rather than local optimisation — that is, the performance outcome of global optimisation is superior to the combined results from local optimisation. This is the theoretical basis of the arguments for the use of global strategy. The potential benefits can be summarised as follows:

- cost reductions (via economies of scale, lower factor costs, flexibility and enhanced bargaining power [Kogut 1985a]);

- improved quality (by focusing resources and efforts on a smaller number of products and programs [Yip 1989]);
- enhanced customer preference (through global availability, global serviceability and global recognition [Levitt 1983]);
- increased competitive leverage (by providing more points to attack and counter-attack against competitors [Hout, Porter and Rudden 1982; Hamel and Prahalad 1985]).

NATURE AND USE OF GLOBAL STRATEGY

Prior literature and empirical studies have clearly established that forms of global strategy are multi-dimensional. These dimensions include:

- *global market participation,* such as building major share in strategic as opposed to profitable countries (Ohmae 1985; Porter 1990; Rugman and D'Cruz 1993);
- *global product standardisation* rather than local product adaptation (Levitt 1983; Kogut 1985a; Walters 1986; Samiee and Roth 1992);
- *global activity location* such as building a global value chain rather than self-sufficient local value chains (Hout, Porter and Rudden 1982; Kogut 1985b; Bartlett and Ghoshal 1989), exemplified by the Japanese approach in many industries (Yip 1995) and increasingly by the MNCs of other countries, Eastman Kodak's operation of its various manufacturing facilities as a single worldwide plant or 'global factory' (Murphy 1985); in global production-sharing (Kim 1986); or at the very least, using offshore production, as in the semiconductor industry (Saghafi and Davidson 1989). A global location strategy also includes global sourcing (Murray, Kotabe and Wildt 1995);
- *globally uniform marketing* such as global brand names or advertising rather than more locally responsive approaches (Quelch and Hoff 1986; Takeuchi and Porter 1986; Douglas and Craig 1989; Jain 1989). Huszagh, Fox and Day (1986) empirically examined the feasibility of global marketing in terms primarily of similarity across countries in product acceptance rates. Kashani (1989) studied nine successful and eight failed efforts at global marketing by American and European MNCs, focusing on implementation management as the key differentiator. Sandler and Shani (1992) found in a study of brand managers in Canada that global standardisation is practised more for brands than for advertising, with the most common combination being standardised brand names and non-standardised advertising. Rosen, Boddewyn and Louis

(1989) found that only a few United States brands had wide distribution in foreign markets. But Syzmanski, Bharadwaj and Varadarajan (1993), using the PIMS database, found that performance relationships to marketing resource allocations were similar for businesses operating in the United States, Canada or Western Europe, suggesting that it is possible to use a standardised approach in serving multiple national markets. Yavas, Verhage and Green (1992), in a survey of consumers in the United States, Mexico, the Netherlands, Turkey, Thailand and Saudi Arabia, found consumer segments that transcended national boundaries, concluding that companies can adopt a modified global marketing approach;

- *globally integrated competitive moves* such as cross-subsidised competitive moves or sequenced moves, rather than only local moves (Hamel and Prahalad 1985; Porter 1986; Jatusripitak, Fahey and Kotler 1985).

Yip (1989, 1992) tied these different dimensions into a common framework, and Johansson and Yip (1994) have provided validation on a sample of 36 American and Japanese worldwide businesses. Some studies have tried to identify clusters of strategies, at least one of which is a global strategy of some sort. Morrison and Roth (1992) identified, in a study of 115 business units, a 'quasi-global, combination strategy', as distinct from a domestic, product–specialisation strategy, an exporting, high quality offerings strategy, and an international, product-innovation strategy. Roth (1992) found that selective globalisation (in which the firm defines its global strategy around a narrow subset of the value chain) may lead to the most effective outcomes.

A number of case-study type articles have described the global strategies of individual companies with conflicting emphases. Some stress how these companies succeed via localisation in global strategy: Honda (Sugiura 1990); BHP (Lewis, Clark and Moss 1988); and Vicks/Procter and Gamble (Das 1993). Some stress a balanced global and local approach: GFT, an Italian company that is the world's largest manufacturer of designer apparel (Howard 1991), and Asea Brown Boveri (Taylor 1991). Lastly, some studies stress how some companies primarily use globally integrated strategy: Caterpillar, Ericsson and Honda Motor (Hout, Porter and Rudden 1982), Volkswagen (Avishai 1991), Thomson SA (McCormick and Stone 1990), and Whirlpool (Maruca 1994). Bartlett and Ghoshal (1989) have also provided in-depth descriptions of the global or 'transnational' strategies of nine MNCs: Unilever, Kao, Procter and Gamble, Philips, Matsushita, General Electric, ITT, NEC and Ericsson. The differences reported among companies, and between different articles on the same company (e.g. Honda Motors), suggest inevitably that successful global strategies have both local and global elements.

DETERMINANTS OF GLOBAL STRATEGY

What explains the use of global strategy? An industrial organisation perspective would argue that industry conditions constitute the primary determinant. Porter (1986) and Yip (1989), took such an approach, developing a contingency framework linking industry conditions to when global strategy would be appropriate. In a 'perfect' world, that of traditional economic theory, industry factors or industry globalisation drivers would be the sole determinants of strategy. But in a world of company heterogeneity and human actors, this linkage from industry to strategy needs to be moderated by other factors, including organisation structure, management processes, human resources, corporate culture, and corporate characteristics. In particular, these other factors can delay or change the global strategy that should be adopted given industry drivers. Thus, there may well be a lag or gap between the optimal global strategy indicated by industry globalisation drivers and the actual global strategy achievable by an MNC. Lastly, globalisation forces and the use of global strategy should affect business performance.

Industry Globalisation Drivers

In the industry structure approach, industries vary in globalisation potential because of underlying industry structure or conditions (Porter 1986; Yip, Loewe and Yoshino 1988; Morrison 1990). These industry globalisation conditions can be summarised as market, cost, government and competitive drivers. Each set of drivers has its proponents, with market drivers (e.g. globally common customer needs) being particularly associated with Levitt (1983), cost drivers (e.g. global scale economies) with Porter (1986), government drivers (e.g. absence of trade restrictions) with Doz (1979) and competitive drivers (e.g. cross-country subsidisation) with Hamel and Prahalad (1985). Yip (1994) analysed the strength of globalisation drivers for 18 different industries, finding wide variations both in total and in categories of drivers.

In terms of cross-industry empirical studies, Kobrin (1991) examined 56 manufacturing industries containing United States-based firms and found technological intensity and advertising intensity to be key industry drivers of global integration by firms, while manufacturing scale economies was not a significant driver. Johansson and Yip (1994) examined industries involving

36 American and Japanese MNCs and found market and cost drivers to be the most significant for globalisation, while government and competitive drivers were not significant.

In terms of single-industry empirical studies, Yip and Coundouriotis (1991) found in the chocolate confectionery business that market and competitive drivers provided the strongest spurs to globalisation, while government drivers did not pose significant barriers, nor were cost drivers crucial. Baden–Fuller and Stopford (1991) challenge the common view that mature industries are always ripe for global strategies. Based on 1975–87 data from the European domestic appliance industry, they found that changing economic conditions can diminish the value of global strategies. Critical in these shifts were simultaneous rises in demand for variety (that eroded the benefits of scale and continental market share) and decreases in manufacturing scale (that permitted new supply options), which reduced the extent of the strategic market to national dimensions. In contrast, Whirlpool, a leading participant in this worldwide industry, is now aggressively pursuing global strategy both worldwide and in Europe (Maruca 1994).

Organisation Factors

Organisation factors such as structure, management processes, people and culture clearly affect how well a desired global strategy can be implemented, probably more so than for most other types of strategy (Prahalad and Doz 1987; Ghoshal 1987; Bartlett and Ghoshal 1989). Roth, Schweiger and Morrison (1991) found that for 82 business units competing in global industries, business unit effectiveness was a function of the fit between the international strategy and the organisational design. In another empirical study, Johansson and Yip (1994) found, for 36 American and Japanese MNCs, that organisation and management factors played a major intervening or moderating role between industry globalisation drivers and the implementation of global strategy. There has, of course, been extensive work on the subject of MNC control and coordination mechanisms (reviewed by Martinez, Jarillo and Carlos 1989), but this mostly predates the current debate on global strategy.

Organisation structure
Much early research on MNC management has confirmed the critical role of formal organisation structure in influencing both parent and subsidiary strategy. More recently, and focusing on global strategy *per se*, Bartlett and Ghoshal (1987, 1989) have argued for a network structure that facilitates global learning. Ghoshal (1987) argues that the tendency of global strategy

toward a centralised global authority, and the potential corresponding erosion of global learning benefits, is one of the 'strategic tradeoffs' associated with pursuing a global strategy. A special aspect of global authority is whether control of a worldwide business is split between separate domestic and international divisions. Yip, Loewe and Yoshino (1988) argue that American MNCs are more likely than European and Japanese MNCs to have such a split, and that this split reduces the ability to implement global strategy; this argument was empirically validated by Johansson and Yip (1994). Malnight (1995) examined the globalisation process of Eli Lilly and found the process to be an evolutionary one that occurred at the level of the function rather than of the firm. Global authority or 'mandates' may also be delegated to subsidiaries from headquarters. Roth and Morrison (1992) examined 578 foreign subsidiaries in six country locations to find the subsidiary characteristics that are associated with these mandates.

Management processes
Prahalad and Doz (1987, Ch. 8) down-played the role of organisation structure in global strategy, emphasising instead integrative management processes such as global information systems, global business teams, coordination committees, task forces and other cross-country coordination devices. Similarly, much of the more recent research (e.g. Hedlund 1980; Edström and L'orange 1984) has found evidence of more informal and subtler mechanisms as MNC control processes. Bartlett and Ghoshal (1989) also stress the importance of management processes that allow a balance between headquarters and subsidiary. Chakravarthy and Perlmutter (1985), Shanks (1985) and Prahalad and Doz (1987) have all argued that a global strategic planning process, as opposed to multiple national ones, aids the use of global strategy. Prahalad and Doz (1987) and Dyment (1987) argued that global organisations need to create performance review and compensation systems based on achieving strategic objectives that cross national borders. Hence, the use of cross-country coordination mechanisms should facilitate the implementation of global strategy. Roth, Schweiger and Morrison (1991) found in a study of 147 business units, that increased coordination was associated with implementation of global strategy. Johansson and Yip (1994) found, global budgeting and global group meetings to be the two most important global management processes in fostering the implementation of global strategy. Kim and Mauborgne (1995) have developed a model that stresses the role of procedural justice in enabling the implementation of global strategy, and validated this model on a sample of 63 subsidiaries of 25 MNCs.

People
Extensive literature exists with respect to human resource practices in MNCs, most of it related in some way to international coordination or the dissemination of best practice. For example, Edström and Galbraith (1977) found that international transfer of career employees greatly helped the flow of information (see also the literature on the use of expatriates, for example, Tung 1984). More direct implications for the implementation of global strategy are fewer. Franko (1978) found the use of home-country nationals overseas to be a highly effective means of central control. Prahalad and Doz (1987) recommended the use of foreign nationals in key positions and multi-country careers as ways of enhancing an MNC's global capability. Thus, the use of multi-country careers should enhance the implementation of global strategy.

Culture
Various aspects of corporate culture can affect an MNC's ability to develop and implement global strategy. Beginning with Perlmutter (1969), the degree of international or global orientation in corporate culture has been viewed as an important influence on MNC strategy and performance — with Perlmutter distinguishing among ethnocentric, polycentric and geocentric cultures. Another relevant aspect of corporate culture is the degree to which the culture of the home country company is transmitted to international subsidiaries. But dominance by the home-country culture probably does not foster the neutral viewpoint needed in global strategy. Thus, Ohmae (1985) argues that managers and units should be treated as if they were 'equidistant from the corporate center'. So a culture of a global rather than a national identity should help the implementation of global strategy.

EFFECT OF NATIONALITY ON GLOBAL STRATEGY

Previous research has tended to address only in passing the issue of nationality and its possible effect on global strategy. In one sense, the essence of global strategy lies in overcoming the effects of national differences. Ohmae (1990) has gone so far as to argue that multinational companies (MNCs) should consider themselves stateless (see also Stopford and Strange 1991). In contrast, Porter (1990) argues strongly for the importance of the role of the home country.

Parent nationality can affect global strategy in a number of ways. First, national history has affected the general order of entry into international markets: Western Europeans first, Americans second, Japanese third, and other

Asian countries and some Latin American ones going international most recently. Early entry clearly leads to greater global dominance. The timing of entry should also affect global strategy. In particular, the standardisation and specialisation in global strategy requires conditions of low trade barriers and few differences in national customer tastes. More recent international entrants, like the post-war Japanese companies, have faced increasingly lower trade and taste barriers.

Some overall characterisations of possible national differences in globalisation can be made, particularly in regard to the most studied nationalities — American, European and Japanese. In their response to globalisation forces, MNCs from these countries are likely to be affected by their history of internationalisation, to some extent following Stopford and Wells' (1972) stages of international development.

European MNCs

Following their colonial flags, or imitating neighbours in the case of countries without colonies, European MNCS were often the first to internationalise, many beginning in the nineteenth century. In this early period of poor transportation and communications, and high trade barriers, European MNCs typically built up overseas subsidiaries that enjoyed a large degree of autonomy. Many European MNCs are now finding that this local autonomy greatly inhibits the ability to formulate and implement globally integrated strategies. For example, Philips N.V.'s problems with its overly independent subsidiaries have been well documented (Aguilar and Yoshino 1988; Jeelof 1989). Both perceptions and the reality of their many historical, cultural and political differences may spur Europeans to favor local rather than global solutions. A study over the time period, 1972–1987, found that national or local businesses performed better than continental ones in Europe, while the reverse held in North America (Yip 1991). A study of the European food industry in the 1980s found that European companies mostly marketed national brands while it was left to American companies to succeed with pan-European ones (Bennigson 1992). On the other hand, because of the small size of their home markets, European companies tend to have a very high percentage of revenues being international, and also have a long history of moving managers around the world. The overall globalisation challenge for the typical European MNC seems to be to move from the direction of local autonomy towards global integration.

American MNCs

Perhaps the key distinguishing feature of American MNCs is their huge home market. This large domestic base has frequently resulted in the building of separate United States and international divisions, with a large wall between them. Another consequence has been a tendency to under-adapt for local markets, utilising American products and programs rather than tailoring for international markets. This orientation towards the home market also makes it difficult to achieve a global strategy that best exploits opportunities around the world and leverages worldwide capabilities.

Japanese MNCs

Later than Europeans and Americans to internationalise, most Japanese MNCs have until recently pursued an export-based model, with its concomitant centralisation. Some aspects of this centralisation favour global strategy, particularly in terms of integration. Other aspects hurt global strategy, as in the lack of a globally dispersed network, like that advocated by Bartlett and Ghoshal (1989). As cost pressures and trade frictions spur Japanese MNCs to relocate manufacturing activities, they face the challenge of preserving the advantages of their unique system.

These historical differences are likely to affect all aspects of globalisation, from perceptions of industry globalisation drivers to the actual use of global strategy. Various studies have found differences in organisation structure and management processes among American, European and Japanese companies (e.g. Franko 1971; Jaeger 1983; Egelhoff 1984; Abegglen and Stalk 1985; Tsurumi 1986), although mostly without relating these differences to global strategy. Bartlett and Ghoshal (1989) argue that American MNCs stress formalisation of structure and processes to achieve global integration, European MNCs stress socialisation, and Japanese MNCs centralisation. In one of the few empirical studies directly examining the role of nationality on global strategy, Johansson and Yip (1994) found that Japanese firms have more globalised strategies than do American firms.

EFFECT OF GLOBAL STRATEGY ON PERFORMANCE

The existence of industry globalisation potential implies that companies can derive globalisation-related benefits from the use of globally integrated strategy, and hence improve performance. Conversely, a strategy that is more global than warranted by industry globalisation potential will yield drawbacks that result in worse performance.

Studies have provided limited evidence, all in favour of — or at least neutral toward — global strategy. Roth and Morrison (1990) found no significant difference in profit performance among businesses facing: (1) global integration pressures; (2) local responsiveness pressures; and (3) both pressures. A narrower study, by Kotabe and Omura (1989), found that the market share and profit performance of 71 European and Japanese firms serving the United States market was negatively related to the extent to which products were adapted for the United States market, so that businesses with globally standardised products performed better. More broadly, Johansson and Yip (1994) found a strong positive relationship between the use of global strategy and superior performance in terms of relative market share and relative profitability. Morrison (1990) found that, in his sample of global industries, companies with a 'global, combination' strategy had the best performance on measures of return on assets and those with an 'international, product innovation' strategy had the best performance on return on investment, while the companies with the worst fit — 'domestic, product specialisation' strategy — had the poorest performance. In conclusion, very few empirical studies, indeed, have examined the performance consequences of global strategy.

MODELS OF GLOBAL STRATEGY

The above analysis has identified the following constructs:

- global strategy and its various dimensions
- industry globalisation drivers
- organisation factors (including organisation structure, management processes, people and culture)
- nationality
- performance.

How do these constructs relate? Most of the literature has concentrated on relationships among subsets of these constructs. Both Prahalad and Doz (1987) and Bartlett and Ghoshal (1989) stressed the interplay between strategy and organisation, particularly in terms of the latter acting as a moderating effect on the implementation of global strategy. Porter (1986) pioneered the link from industry conditions to global strategy choices. Various studies, cited above, have examined the empirical links between some of these constructs.

Johansson and Yip (1994) proposed and tested a series of models that related the constructs in increasing levels of complexity (Figure 6.1). Their simplest model (Specification 1) had all constructs directly affecting performance. Their most complex models had industry globalisation drivers affecting organisation structure and management processes, which in turn affect global strategy, and in turn again affect performance (Specification 4), and an alternate model with global strategy coming before organisation structure and management processes (Specification 5). They also allowed nationality to directly affect each of the constructs. Using causal modelling, they found that the more complex models had much stronger explanatory power than the simpler models, confirming that the various constructs do relate to each other in a systemic mode. Furthermore, they found a gap between what executives perceived to be the optimal level of global strategy and the actual level their companies had achieved.

Figure 6.1: Alternative models of globalisation

Specification 1 (one level) — Direct effects on performance

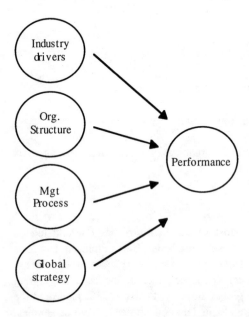

Other researchers are now increasingly using complex, causal models to explain global strategy, although this work is still at the stage of conference papers rather than published articles. Future research on global strategy should use models of the general nature shown in Figure 6.2. In this general model of global strategy, industry globalisation drivers and company characteristics

Specification 2 (two levels) — Only global strategy affects performance

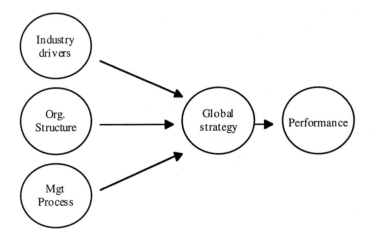

Specification 3 (two levels) — All factors affect performance

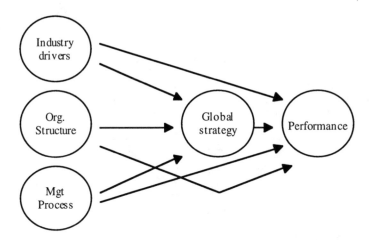

Specification 4 (three levels) — Strategy follows structure

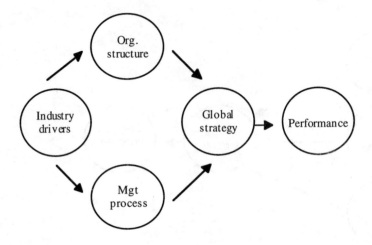

Specification 5 (three levels) — Structure follows strategy

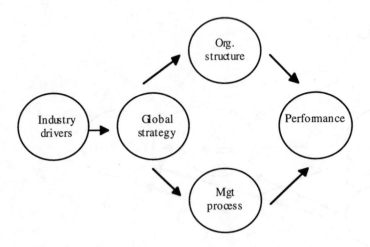

Source: Johansson and Yip (1994).

(including size, history and extent of internationalisation, and competitive position) combine to yield an optimal global strategy (specified in terms of

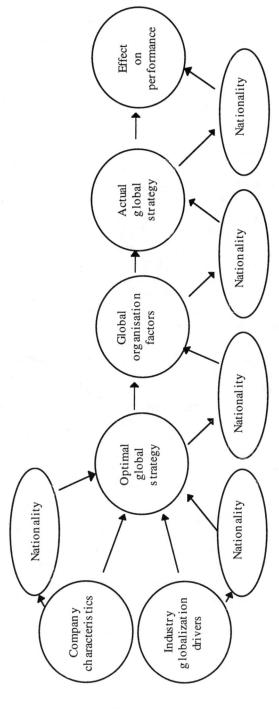

Figure 6.2: A general model of global strategy

multiple dimensions). Organisation factors (including structure, processes, people and culture) then moderate the extent to which the optimal global strategy is implemented as an actual global strategy. This actual strategy then has an effect on performance. Lastly, nationality can moderate the effect of each path in the model.

CONCLUSION

This chapter has addressed the question of whether the world is borderless as far as business strategy is concerned. Specifically, it has examined the viability of global strategy as a response to the globalisation drivers that contribute to a borderless condition. While ten years ago, the viability of globally standardised strategies was seriously questioned, a review of published research suggests that the debate has moved on. Although still limited, the empirical evidence mostly supports a view that companies are finding ways to use global strategy effectively. In particular, this effective use of global strategy involves a flexible approach that globally integrates or standardises some activities or functions while localising others. It has also become clear that successful implementation continues to be difficult and depends greatly on effective change of organisational factors. Corporate nationality continues to play an important role. The use and consequences of global strategy are determined by multiple causal and moderating factors. Research needs to use more complex models than has been the case in many instances. Lastly, some evidence is emerging that use of global strategy is associated with performance not just when matched to the appropriate industry conditions, but under any conditions. There are at least three possibilities:

1. Most companies are so far below their globalisation potential that studies have not observed examples of companies that are over-globalised ('asymmetric populations');
2. Better performing companies have the resources and strategic degrees of freedom to implement global strategy ('cause and effect');
3. The organisational capabilities (e.g. coordination and cooperation) that make it possible to implement global strategy are the same ones that allow for excellent management in general ('global excellence').

Investigating this last set of possibilities poses the next frontier in global strategy research.

REFERENCES

Abegglen, James C. and Stalk, George Jr 1985. *The Japanese Corporation*, New York: Basic Books Inc.

Aguilar, Francis J. and Yoshino, Michael Y. 1988. The Philips Group: 1987. Case no. 9, 388–050. Harvard Business School, Boston, MA.

Avishai, Bernard 1991. A European platform for global competition: An interview with VW's Carl Hahn. *Harvard Business Review*, 69(4), July/August.

Baden–Fuller, Charles W.F. and Stopford, John M. 1991. Globalization frustrated: The case of white goods. *Strategic Management Journal*, 12(7), October.

Bartlett, Christopher A. and Ghoshal, Sumantra 1987. Managing across borders: New organizational responses. *Sloan Management Review*, Fall: 43–53.

Bartlett, Christopher A. and Ghoshal, Sumantra 1989. *Managing Across Borders: The Transnational Solution*, Boston, MA: Harvard Business School Press.

Bennigson, Lawrence A. 1992. The food industry jousts for Europe. In Liam Fahey (ed.), *Winning in the New Europe: Taking Advantage of the Single Market*, Englewood Cliffs, N.J.: Prentice-Hall, pp. 154–65.

Chakravarthy, Balaji S. and Perlmutter, Howard V. 1985. Strategic planning for a global business. *Columbia Journal of World Business*, Summer: 3–10.

Das, Gurcharan 1993. Local memoirs of a global manager. *Harvard Business Review*, 71(2), March–April.

Douglas, Susan P. and Craig, C. Samuel 1989. Evolution of global marketing strategy: Scale, scope and synergy. *Columbia Journal of World Business*, (24)3, Fall.

Douglas, Susan P. and Wind, Yoram 1987. The myth of globalization. *Columbia Journal of World Business*, 22(4), Winter: 19–29.

Doz, Yves 1979. *Government Control and Multinational Management*, New York: Praeger.

Dyment, J.J. 1987. Strategies and management controls for global corporations. *Journal of Business Strategy*, Spring: 20–26.

Edström, A. and Galbraith, J.R. 1977. Transfer of managers as a coordination and control strategy in multinational organizations. *Administrative Science Quarterly*, 22: 246–63.

Edström, A. and L'orange, P. 1984. Matching strategy and human resources in multinational corporations. *Journal of International Business Studies*, Fall: 125–37.

Egelhoff, William G. 1984. Patterns of control in U.S., U.K. and European multinational corporations. *Journal of International Business Studies*, Fall: 73–83.

Franko, Lawrence G. 1971. *European Business Strategies in the United States*, Geneva: Business International.

Franko, Larry G. 1978. Organizational structures and multinational strategies of continental European enterprises. In M. Ghertman and J. Leontiades (eds), *European Research in International Business*, Amsterdam: North Holland.

Ghoshal, Sumantra 1987. Global strategy: An organizing framework. *Strategic Management Journal*, 8(5), September–October: 425–40.

Hamel, Gary and Prahalad, C.K. 1985. Do you really have a global strategy? *Harvard Business Review*, 63(4), July–August: 139–48.

Hedlund, Gunnar 1980. The role of foreign subsidiaries in strategic decision-making in Swedish multinational corporations. *Strategic Management Journal*, 1: 23–26.

Hout, Thomas, Porter, Michael E. and Rudden, Eileen 1982. How global companies win out. *Harvard Business Review*, 60(5), September/October.

Howard, Robert 1991. The designer organization: Italy's GFT goes global. *Harvard Business Review*, 69(5), September/October.

Huszagh, Sandra M., Fox, Richard J. and Day, Ellen 1986. Global marketing: An empirical investigation. *Columbia Journal of World Business*, 20(4), Commemorative Issue.

Jaeger, A.M. 1983. The transfer of organizational culture overseas: An approach to control in the multinational corporation. *Journal of International Business Studies*, Fall: 91–114.

Jain, Subhash C. 1989. Standardization of international marketing strategy: Some research hypotheses. *Journal of Marketing*, 53, January: 70–79.

Jatusripitak, Somkid, Fahey, Liam and Kotler, Philip 1985. Strategic global marketing: Lessons from the Japanese. *Columbia Journal of World Business*, 20(1), Spring.

Jeelof, Gerrit 1989. Global strategies of Philips. *European Management Journal*, 7(1): 84–91.

Johansson, Johny K. and Yip, George S. 1994. Exploiting globalization potential: U.S. and Japanese strategies. *Strategic Management Journal*, 15(8), October.

Kashani, Kamran 1989. Beware the pitfalls of global marketing. *Harvard Business Review*, 67(5), September/October.

Kim, W. Chan 1986. Global production sharing: An empirical investigation of the Pacific electronics industry, *Management International Review*, 26(2), Second Quarter: 62–70.

Kim, W. Chan and Mauborgne, René 1995. A procedural justice model of strategic decision making. *Organization Science*, 6(1), January–February: 44–61.

Kobrin, Stephen J. 1991. An empirical analysis of the determinants of global integration. *Strategic Management Journal*, 12, Summer.

Kogut, Bruce 1985a. Designing global strategies: Comparative and competitive value-added chains. *Sloan Management Review*, Summer: 27–38.

Kogut, Bruce 1985b. Designing global strategies: Profiting from operational flexibility. *Sloan Management Review*, Fall: 27–38.

Kotabe, Masaaki and Omura, Glenn S. 1989. Sourcing strategies of European and Japanese multinationals: A comparison. *Journal of International Business Studies*, 20(1), Spring: 113–30.

Levitt, Theodore 1983. The globalization of markets. *Harvard Business Review*, May–June: 92–102.

Lewis, Geoffrey, Clark, John and Moss, Bill 1988. BHP reorganizes for global competition. *Long Range Planning*, 21(3), June.

Malnight, Thomas W. 1995. Globalization of an ethnocentric firm: An evolutionary perspective. *Strategic Management Journal*, 16(2), February.

Martinez, Jon, Jarillo, I. and Carlos, J. 1989. The evolution of research on coordination mechanisms in multinational corporations. *Journal of International Business Studies*, 20(3): 489–514.

Maruca, Regina Fazio 1994. The right way to go global: An interview with Whirlpool CEO David Whitwam. *Harvard Business Review*, March–April: 134–49.

McCormick, Janice and Stone, Nan 1990. From national champion to global competitor: An interview with Thomson's Alain Gomez. *Harvard Business Review,* 68(3), May/June.

Morrison, Allen J. 1990. *Strategies in Global Industries: How U.S. Businesses Compete*, Westport, Connecticut: Quorum Books.

Morrison, Allen J. and Roth, Kendall 1992. A taxonomy of business-level strategies in global industries. *Strategic Management Journal*, 13(6), September.

Murphy, Cornelius J. 1985. Kodak's 'global factory'. *Planning Review*, 13(3), May.

Murray, Janet Y., Kotabe, Masaaki and Wildt, Albert R. 1995. Strategic and financial performance implications of global sourcing strategy: A contingency analysis. *Journal of International Business Studies*, 26(1), First Quarter.

Ohmae, Kenichi 1985. *Triad Power: The Coming Shape of Global Competition*, New York: Free Press.

Ohmae, Kenichi 1990. *The Borderless World: Power and Strategy in the Interlinked Economy*, New York: Harper Business.

Perlmutter, Howard V. 1969. The tortuous evolution of the multinational corporation. *Columbia Journal of World Business*, January–February: 9–18.

Porter, Michael E. 1986. Changing patterns of international competition. *California Management Review*, 28(2), Winter: 9–40.

Porter, Michael E. 1990. *The Competitive Advantage of Nations*, New York: The Free Press.

Prahalad, C.K. and Doz, Yves L. 1987. *The Multinational Mission: Balancing Local Demands and Global Vision*, New York: Free Press.

Quelch, John A. and Hoff, Edward J. 1986. Customizing global marketing. *Harvard Business Review,* May–June: 59–68.

Rosen, Barry Nathan, Boddewyn, Jean J. and Louis, Ernst A. 1989. U.S. brands abroad: An empirical study of global branding. *International Marketing Review,* 6(1): 7–19.

Roth, Kendall 1992. International configuration and coordination archetypes for medium-sized firms in global industries. *Journal of International Business Studies*, 23(3), Third Quarter.

Roth, Kendall and Morrison, Allen J 1990. An empirical analysis of the integration-responsiveness framework in global industries. *Journal of International Business Studies*, 21(4), Fourth Quarter.

Roth, Kendall and Morrison, Allen J. 1992. Implementing global strategy: Characteristics of global subsidiary mandates. *Journal of International Business Studies*, 23(4), Fourth Quarter.

Roth, Kendall, Schweiger, David M. and Morrison, Allen J. 1991. Global strategy Iimplementation at the business unit level: Operational capabilities and administrative mechanisms. *Journal of International Business Studies*, 22(3), Third Quarter.

Rugman, Alan M. and D'Cruz, Joseph 1993. How to operationalize Porter's diamond of international competitiveness. *The International Executive*, 35(4), July/August: 283–99.

Saghafi, Massoud M. and Davidson, Chin-Shu 1989. The new age of global competition in the semiconductor industry: Enter the dragon. *Columbia Journal of World Business*, (24)4, Winter.

Samiee, Saeed and Roth, Kendall 1992. The influence of global marketing standardization on performance. *Journal of Marketing*, 56(2), April: 1–17.

Sandler, Dennis, M. and Shani, David 1992. Brand globally but advertise locally? An empirical investigation. *International Marketing Review*, 9(4): 18–31.

Shanks, David C. 1985, Strategic Planning for Global Competition, *Journal of Business Strategy,* Winter: 80–89.

Stopford, John M. and Wells, Louis T. Jr 1972. *Managing the Multinational Enterprise*, New York: Basic Books.

Stopford, John M. and Strange, Susan 1991. *Rival States, Rival Firms*, Cambridge: Cambridge University Press.

Sugiura, Hideo 1990. How Honda localizes its global strategy. *Sloan Management Review*, 32(1), Fall.

Szymanski, David M., Bharadwaj, Sundar G. and Varadarajan, P. Rajan 1993. Standardization versus adaptation of international marketing strategy: An empirical investigation. *Journal of Marketing*, 57, October: 1–17.

Takeuchi, Hirotaka and Porter, Michael E. 1986. Three roles of international marketing in global strategy. In Michael E. Porter (ed.), *Competition in Global Industries*, Boston, MA: Harvard Business School Press, pp. 111–46.

Taylor, William 1991. The logic of global business: An interview with ABB's Percy Barnevik. *Harvard Business Review*, 69(2), March/April.

Tsurumi, Yoshi 1986. Japanese and European multinationals in America: A case of flexible corporate systems. In Klaus Macharzina and Wolfgang H. Staehle (eds), *European Approaches to International Management*, Berlin: Walter de Gruyter, pp. 23–38.

Tung, Rosalie L. 1984. Human resource planning in Japanese multinationals: A model for U.S. Firms? *Journal of International Business Studies*, 2(15), Fall: 139–49.

Walters, Peter G.P. 1986. International marketing policy: A discussion of the standardization construct and its relevance for corporate policy. *Journal of International Business Studies*, Summer: 55–69.

Yavas, Ugur; Verhage, Bornislaw J. and Green, Robert T. 1992. Global consumer segmentation versus local market orientation: Empirical findings. *Management International Review*, 32(3), Third Quarter: 265–72.

Yip, George S. 1989. Global strategy ... In a world of nations? *Sloan Management Review*, 31(1), Fall: 29–41.

Yip, George S. 1991. A performance comparison of continental and national businesses in Europe. *International Marketing Review*, 8(2): 31–39.

Yip, George S. 1992. *Total Global Strategy: Managing for Worldwide Competitive Advantage*, Englewood Cliffs, N.J.: Prentice Hall.

Yip, George S. 1994. Industry drivers of global strategy and organization. *The International Executive*, September/October: 529–56.

Yip, George S. 1995. Global strategy as a factor in Japanese success. *The International Executive, Special Issue on Japan*, 38(1), January–February: 145–67.

Yip, George S. and Coundouriotis, George A. 1991. Diagnosing global strategy potential: The world chocolate confectionery industry. *Planning Review*, January/February.

Yip, George S., Loewe, Pierre M. and Yoshino, Michael Y. 1988. How to take your company to the global market. *Columbia Journal of World Business*, Winter: 37–48.

7. The Evolution of the Transnational

Christopher Bartlett and Sumantra Ghoshal

The world's largest MNCs have experienced a great deal of turmoil and turbulence over the last decade. Highly publicised problems in companies like IBM, Kodak and Westinghouse have led many to question the fundamental viability of companies as large, as diversified and as geographically dispersed as these corporate behemoths. And it is not just in the United States that such problems have been emerging. In Europe, once-revered names like Volkswagen, Olivetti and Philips have been making headlines more as problem cases than as role models. Even much-admired Japanese companies such as Mazda, Yamaha, Toshiba and the Industrial Bank of Japan have lost their lustre as deteriorating performance has led them to contemplate the once-unthinkable steps of layoffs and top-management changes.

Some critics have interpreted such turmoil in some of the largest and most visible MNCs as a sign that the era of the large worldwide company may be over. Though many still survive and even dominate various geographic and business areas, these critics would have us believe that these are the last generation of dinosaurs still roaming the earth completely unaware of their inevitable and impending fate. The meteor impact of simultaneous market and technological revolutions of the 1990s, they believe, will lead to the extinction of the entire population, to be replaced by more agile small companies or by a completely new genetically engineered species of 'virtual corporations'.

Based on our own ongoing work in a number of companies, we believe that this news of the MNC's death is exaggerated. Indeed, our own research has indicated that it is precisely because of their experience in the international operating environment that such companies develop the best chance of surviving. Most obviously, this is due to their access to a wider

Reprinted with permission from Irwin Publishers

scope of markets and resources and their ability to secure competitive positions and competencies unobtainable by purely domestic companies. But even more important, it is because the management in such companies gains invaluable experience from routinely dealing with the fast-changing, multi-dimensional demands and opportunities that are part of the global business environment. Through this experience, they develop an organisational capability that is increasingly valuable in today's complex and dynamic operating context.

In many ways, therefore, the transnational organisational and management issues we have described represent perhaps one of the most advanced forms of the modern corporation. The core management challenge in all companies is to embrace rather than to deny or minimise the environmental complexity and uncertainty and the demanding context of the transnational organisation provides the ideal laboratory in which to develop such skills. In short, the challenge of managing across borders is the ideal way to develop the skills required for managing across boundaries of all kinds in the modern corporation.

In this chapter, we describe the emerging management model, which is one possible answer to the 'what's new' question. In this process, we also suggest a new way of thinking about large companies. Instead of defining a large company in terms of a formal structure, which divided the overall company into a series of business or geographic functional units, we describe it in terms of three core processes that characterise this new management approach. The *entrepreneurial process* drives the opportunity-seeking, externally focused ability of the organisation to open markets and create new businesses. The *integration process* allows it to link-leverage its dispersed worldwide resources and capabilities to build a successful company. The *renewal process* maintains its ability to challenge its beliefs and practices and to continuously revitalise itself so as to develop an enduring institution. Effective management of these three processes also calls for some very different roles and tasks of front-line, middle and top-level managers. We illustrate these organisational processes and management roles based on the experiences of different American, European and Japanese companies.

THE ENTREPRENEURIAL PROCESS: SUPPORTING AND ALIGNING INITIATIVES

The traditional worldwide organisation was built in a highly structured manner that allowed those at the top to coordinate and control the multifunctional, multibusiness, multinational operations. But this increasingly complex structure looks very different from the top than from the bottom (see Figure 7.1). From the top, the CEO sees order, symmetry and uniformity — a neat instrument for step-by-step decomposition of the company's tasks and priorities. From the bottom, hapless front-line managers see a cloud of faceless controllers — a formless sponge that soaks up all their energy and time. The result, as described so colourfully by GE's Jack Welch, is an organisation that has its face towards the CEO and its backside towards the customer. The key assumption in these companies is that the entrepreneurial tasks will be carried out by the top management, while front-line managers will be primarily responsible for the operational implementation of top-down strategies. Such a management approach had not been a major constraint in the benevolent, high-growth environment that most companies enjoyed in the decades following World War II. Throughout that period of rapid international market expansion, the opportunities for growth were enormous and the key management challenge was to allocate a company's financial resources among competing opportunities.

But in recent years, not only has market growth slowed, but massive investments have led to severe overcapacity in many industries. Simultaneously, the motivation for companies expanding abroad has increasingly shifted from one focused primarily on securing new markets or low-cost productive inputs, to a worldwide search for vital intelligence or scarce competencies not readily obtainable in the home market. As knowledge and specialised skills have gradually replaced capital as the scarcest and most important source of competitive advantage, managers have become increasingly aware that, unlike money, expertise cannot be accumulated at and allocated from the top. The critical task now is to use the knowledge of widely dispersed front-line managers to identify and exploit fast-moving opportunities. In short, the entrepreneurial function must now be focused not at the top of the hierarchy but at the bottom.

The challenge of rebuilding the initiative, creativity and drive of those on the front lines of worldwide operations does not, however, mean that a company must now become a society of geographically spread, independent entrepreneurs held together by a top management acting as a combination of a bank and a venture fund. Instead, companies will be required to build an organisation in which a well-linked entrepreneurial process will drive the company's opportunity-seeking, externally focused ability to create and exploit avenues for profitable growth wherever they may arise. It is this integrated entrepreneurial process that will bring the worldwide company advantages to the local front-line entrepreneurs and save the entrepreneurial transnational corporation from the myths of internal venturing and 'intrapreneurship' that have already proven so flawed in practice. The entrepreneurial transnational corporation will not be an hierarchical organisation with fewer layers of management and a few scattered skunk works or genius awards: it will be a company built around a core entrepreneurial process that will drive everybody and everything the company does.

Figure 7.1: Top-down versus bottom-up view of the organisation

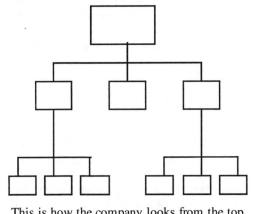

This is how the company looks from the top

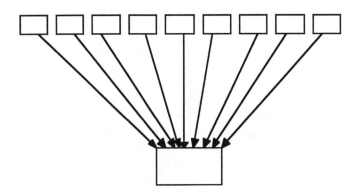

This is how the company looks from the bottom

The entrepreneurial process will require a close interplay among three key management roles. The front-line *entrepreneurs* will be the spearheads of the company and their responsibility will be to create and pursue new growth opportunities. The *coaches* in senior-management positions will play a pivotal role in reviewing, developing and supporting the front-line initiatives. Corporate *leaders* at the top of the organisation will establish the overall strategic mission of the company that will define the boundary within which the entrepreneurial initiatives must be contained; they will also set the highly demanding performance standards that these initiatives must meet (see Figure 7.2). Just as the structural units of corporate, divisional and operating-unit management groups were the fundamental building blocks of the hierarchical, divisionalised company, the three management roles of entrepreneurs, coaches and leaders and their interrelationships will be the core building blocks of the new entrepreneurial transnational corporation. The recent reorganisation of a large American computer company provides an example of how such a management process can be structured.

Confronted with the challenge of rapidly changing customer demands and the constraints of a traditional matrix organisation that impeded the company's ability to marshall its own formidable technological resources to help its customers solve ever-more-complex problems, the company decided to restructure itself to create 'a network of entrepreneurs in a global corporation'. As described by top management, the objective was to create a management approach 'which starts with *opportunity* and capitalises upon the *innovation, creativity* and *excellence* of people to secure the future of the company'. This objective was enshrined in the vision statement: to build 'a global IT service company based on people who are enthusiastic about coming to work every day knowing that they are highly valued, encouraged to grow and increase their knowledge and are individually motivated to make a positive difference'.

To achieve this vision, the company restructured itself into a large number of relatively small units, each unit being headed by a person formally designated as an entrepreneur. There were different kinds of entrepreneurial units, corresponding to different tasks such as product creation, field sales and support, or industry marketing. All shared a common mandate, however: 'to think and act as heads of companies in a networked holding'. Pursuit of opportunities was defined as their key challenge. Each entrepreneur was assured significant support and the top management collectively declared that 'everyone in the company works for the entrepreneurs'. At the same time, it was emphasised that no one could afford to own or control all the expertise, resources or services necessary for achieving his or her objectives; independent judgment and action had to reflect this pervasive interdependence so as to effectively leverage the network of resources available in a global corporation.

Figure 7.2: The entrepreneurial process: management roles and tasks

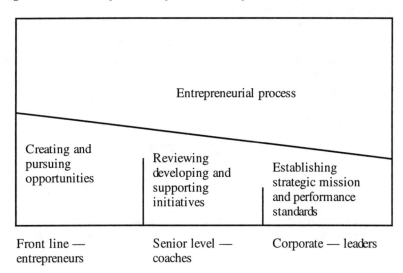

Entrepreneurial process

Creating and pursuing opportunities

Reviewing developing and supporting initiatives

Establishing strategic mission and performance standards

Front line — entrepreneurs

Senior level — coaches

Corporate — leaders

Pursuant to the reorganisation, senior regional, divisional and functional managers were relieved of their normal consolidation and control tasks and were instead regrouped as a pool of coaches. The label of *coach* highlighted that they should not play in the actual game. Yet the metaphor was that of a football coach who bore overall responsibility for the team's success, had the expertise to improve the players' skills, possessed the experience to guide the team's strategy and had the authority to change players when the need arose.

In operational terms, each entrepreneur has an allotted coach to support him or her, but also a separate 'board' that has formal responsibility to 'review and question the validity of the entrepreneur's strategy and plan, provide feedback, monitor performance, encourage, stimulate, support and, via the chairperson, propose rewards or change of the entrepreneur' (see Figure 7.3).

In his or her individual capacity, the coach's main task is to help the entrepreneur succeed both through personal guidance and support on strategic plans and also by acting as a link between the entrepreneur and all others in the company whose resources the entrepreneur might need to succeed. An active role in the entrepreneur's personal development including planning of training inputs and new assignments is defined as an essential part of the coach's role.

The board, of which the assigned coach is often the chairperson, acts in a manner not dissimilar from regular corporate boards. While the chairperson is nominated by the top management, other members are selected by the entrepreneur, in consultation with the chairperson, from the company's pool of coaches. In selecting his or her board members, the entrepreneur looks for specific technological, industry or administrative expertise and, if the desired skills are not available within the company, she can appoint outsiders such as customer representatives, professors in technical or management schools, or even one of the employees within her unit.

Figure 7.3: The operational structure

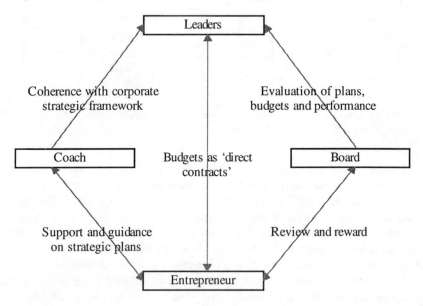

While the coach, in his or her personal capacity, is responsible for developing and supporting the entrepreneurial initiatives, the board is the company's key instrument for maintaining rigorous and disciplined financial control. The board's key tasks are to challenge the entrepreneur's plans, reviews his or her budget proposals, monitor performance against budgets and to continuously advise top management on resource allocation decisions. Budgets are seen as sacrosanct both ways: once the budget is proposed and approved, the entrepreneur must achieve it and must take personal responsibility for initiating any changes in plans that might become necessary because of unforeseen developments. Similarly, no one in the company can tamper with an approved budget except in response to the entrepreneur's demonstrated inability in living up to the contract.

Achievement of budgets is the trigger for release of the next set of resources and managing this multi-stage resource allocation process is a key responsibility of the boards. The separation of the development and support responsibilities, which rests with the coach and the review and reward responsibility, which rests with the board, is designed to prevent both the entrepreneur and the coach from lapsing back into the familiar boss-subordinate role structure and is, therefore, key to protecting the integrity of the system.

While the uniform financial control system provides rigour and discipline to the exercise of bottom-up opportunism, top management of the company also recognised the need for a clear statement of strategic mission to provide direction and coherence to the entrepreneurial process. In contrast to the company's historical focus on proprietary products, the mission statement unambiguously described the need for refocussing on customer service and on providing and integrating multi-vendor products and services. Further elaboration of the mission highlighted particular industry sectors and specific services for priority attention. The simple yet unambiguous statement was explained and debated throughout the company over a six-month period to ensure not only intellectual understanding but also emotional commitment on the part of all employees.

Just the statement and its elaboration were, however, not enough. The process of discussion and debate revealed the need for establishing some clear performance standards and norms to link the mission with specific projects and plans. In response, top management articulated five key performance parameters — each clearly linked to the mission statement — and set specific overall goals against each parameter. For example, 'increase market share faster than competition' or 'profit above local competitors' was translated into tangible but differentiated objectives for the different entrepreneurial units and approval of plans was linked to these objectives.

While this is only one example of how a company can build the entrepreneurial process, it illustrates four key attributes that appear to be common to companies that are able to capture the creative energy of their people to develop new business opportunities.

First, they build their organisations around relatively small units. Matsushita has proliferated the world with its National, Panasonic, Quasar, Technic and other branded consumer electronic products on the strength of its 'one product–one division' concept: as soon as an existing division comes out with a successful new product, it is split up as a separate division. ABB, similarly, is not a $30 billion behemoth: it is a network of 1300 separate companies, each a legal entity with its own balance sheet and profit and loss statement, with an average of 200 employees per company. One can observe the same practice in companies as diverse as Johnson and Johnson, 3M and Bertelsmann: to maintain the entrepreneurial spirit, each unit must be restricted in size so that every member of the unit can personally know all the others.

To build such small units, these companies have abandoned the notion of functionally complete 'strategic business units,' which own all key resources so as to be in full control over their performance. Instead, they have structured incomplete 'performance units' that are interdependent and must use each other's resources to achieve their own goals. The product divisions in Matsushita or Canon do not control the sales units, which are structured as separate companies, as the technology units often are as well. And, in contrast to the arbitrary and conflict-generating distinctions between cost centres, revenue centres and profit centres, the performance centres are not differentiated based on their activities. Whether they sell to customers, or produce for internal customers, or work to build new technologies, all performance centres are treated similarly in the planning, budgeting and control systems.

Second, they create a multi-stage resource allocation process instead of up-front commitment to a clearly articulated long-term plan. Any employee can propose to start a new business at 3M and 'a single coherent sentence can often suffice as starting plan'. But, at each stage of developing his or her proposal, from the initial idea to product development, prototyping, technical and market testing and commercialisation, the entrepreneur must propose a specific budget and clearly quantified mileposts and all approvals are subject to satisfactory performance against the earlier commitments. As 3M managers grudgingly admit, 'We spend all our time preparing budgets, but it seems to help'.

Third, they tend to adopt a highly structured and rigorously implemented financial control system. At 3M, for example, such financial discipline is maintained through a standardised management reporting system that is applied uniformly to all operating units, who are forbidden by a central directive from creating their own systems. At the level of product families, 3900 monthly P&L statements are generated centrally and these are made available on-line to all the units within 10 days of every financial closing. Similarly, at Matsushita, a new division receives start-up capital from the corporate headquarters and loans, when justified under normal commercial conditions; it pays interest on the loans to the corporate 'bank' at regular market rates, together with 60 per cent of pretax profits as dividend. Performance expectations are uniform across all divisions, regardless of the maturity of the market or the company's competitive position. If a division's operating profits fall below 4 per cent of sales for two successive years, the divisional manager is replaced.

An essential corollary of such rigorous financial control is the sanctity of the budget of each entrepreneurial unit. In traditional divisionalised companies, budgets are cascaded down across each layer of the hierarchy and managers at each level are expected to achieve the aggregate budget at their level. Such an aggregation process essentially translates into sudden changes of approved budgets for certain units in response to unanticipated problems faced by other units within the administrative control of a common manager. In contrast, in companies with a firm commitment to bottom-up initiative, the budgets of the small entrepreneurial units are not changed except in response to variances in the unit's own performance. There is neither a cascading down of budget approvals nor an aggregation up of budget achievements: the budget of each unit is approved separately and its performance is monitored individually right up to the very top of corporate management.

And finally, all these companies have a clearly articulated and widely understood and shared definition of the 'opportunity horizon' that provides a lightning rod to direct organisational aspirations and energy into cohesive corporate development. The boundaries of the opportunity horizon tend to be precise enough to clearly rule out activities that do not support the company's strategic mission and yet broad enough to prevent undue constraints on the creativity and opportunism of front-line managers. Without such a clearly defined strategic mission, front-line managers have no basis for selecting among the diverse opportunities they might confront and bottom-up entrepreneurship soon degenerates into a frustrating guessing game. The actual definition of the boundaries may be stated in very different terms — a strong technology focus in Canon or 3M or specific customer groups in SAS or Cartier, for example — but it provides a basis for strategic choice among different initiatives and serves as a guideline for the entrepreneurs themselves to focus their own creative energy.

THE INTEGRATION PROCESS: LINKING AND LEVERAGING COMPETENCIES

In this world of converging technologies, category management and global competition, the entrepreneurial process alone is not sufficient. Tomorrow's successful companies will also have a strong integration process to link their diverse assets and resources into corporate competencies and to leverage these competencies in their pursuit of new opportunities. In the absence of such an integration process, decentralised entrepreneurship may lead to some temporary performance improvement as existing slack is harnessed, but long-term development of new capabilities or businesses will be seriously impeded. Many highly decentralised companies, including Matsushita, have recently experienced this problem. In describing the transnational organisation, we have suggested how worldwide integration can coexist with entrepreneurship at the national level, but the challenge of managing the symbiosis between entrepreneurship and integration extends beyond managing across geographic boundaries to those between the different businesses and functions of a company. The following example will illustrate how such a broader integration process can be built and managed.

Nikkei Business recently ranked Kao as the third in its list of Japan's most creative companies — well ahead of other local superstars including NEC, Toyota, Seibu and Canon. The company had earned this distinction because of its outstanding record of introducing innovative, high-quality products to beat back not only domestic rivals such as Lion but also its giant global competitors such as Procter & Gamble (P&G) and Unilever. Technological and design innovations in Merries, Kao's brand of disposable diapers, reduced P&G's market share in Japan from nearly 90 per cent to less than 10 per cent. Similarly, Attack, Kao's condensed laundry detergent, has seen the company's domestic market share surge from 33 to 48 per cent, while that of Lion declined from 31 to 23 per cent. In the 1980s, this innovative capability allowed this traditional soap company to expand successfully into personal care products where it established Sofina as the largest selling cosmetics brand in Japan and into floppy disks in which it has already risen to be the second largest player in North America.

A powerful entrepreneurial process lies at the heart of Kao's innovative ability. It practises all the elements of the entrepreneurial process we have described: small, functionally incomplete units driven by aggressive targets, rigorous financial discipline, a structured new product creation process supported by a flexible and multi-stage resource allocation system and a clear definition of its strategic mission in terms of utilising its technological strengths to develop products with superior functionality. However, the wellspring behind this entrepreneurial process has been what Dr Yoshio Maruta, the chairman of Kao, describes as 'biological self-control'. As the body reacts to pain by sending help from all quarters, 'if anything goes wrong in one part of the company, all other parts should know automatically and help without having to be asked'. A company-wide integration process has allowed Kao to link and leverage its core competencies in research, manufacturing and marketing not only to solve problems but also to create and exploit new opportunities. And this integration process in Kao, like the entrepreneurial process we have described, is built on some well-defined roles, tasks and value-added on the part of the front-line entrepreneurs, the senior-level coaches and the corporate leaders (see Figure 7.4).

Figure 7.4: The integration process: management roles and tasks

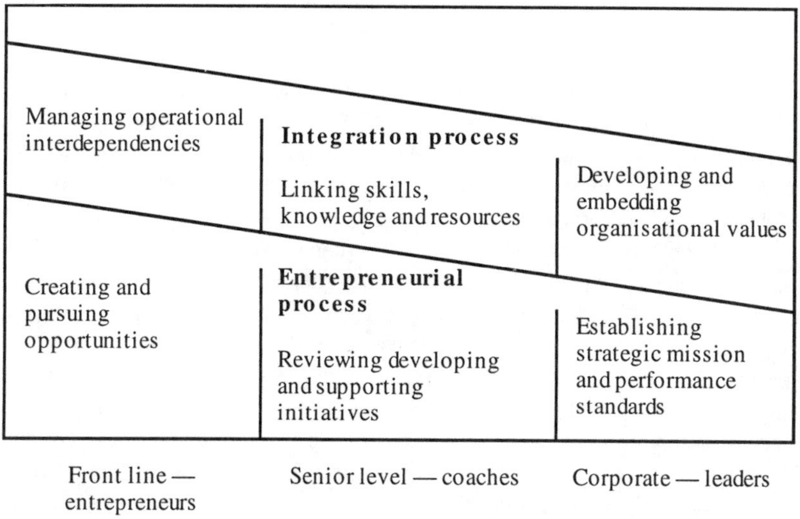

Managing operational interdependencies	**Integration process** Linking skills, knowledge and resources	Developing and embedding organisational values
Creating and pursuing opportunities	**Entrepreneurial process** Reviewing developing and supporting initiatives	Establishing strategic mission and performance standards
Front line — entrepreneurs	Senior level — coaches	Corporate — leaders

The small and relatively autonomous work units of the entrepreneurial corporation — each responsible for specific customer groups or product lines or functional competencies — create an enormous centrifugal force, which, in the absence of a countervailing centripetal force, can overwhelm the company with inconsistencies, conflicts and fragmentation. The first task in integration, therefore, is to create a glue to hold the different parts together and to align their initiatives. A set of clear and motivating organisational values provides the basis for such normative integration and the job of developing, nurturing and embedding these values becomes a key task of the management group we have described as corporate leaders.

The organisational processes of Kao are designed to foster the spirit of harmony and social integration based on the principle of absolute equality of human beings, individual initiative and the rejection of authoritarianism. Free access of everyone to all information 'serves as the core value and the guiding principle,' of what Dr Maruta describes as Kao's 'paperweight organisation': a flat structure, with a small handle of a few senior people in the middle, in which all information is shared horizontally and not filtered vertically. 'In today's business world, information is the only source of competitive advantage,' according to Dr Maruta:

> The company that develops a monopoly on information and has the ability to learn from it continuously is the company that will win, irrespective of its business. This makes it necessary to share all information. If someone has special and crucial information that others don't have, that is against human equality and will deprive us and the organisation of real creativity and learning.

These core values of human equality and free sharing of all information are embedded throughout the organisation, not only through continuous articulation and emphasis by Dr Maruta and other members of the top-management team, but also through their own behaviours and through a set of institutionalised practices.

For example, Dr Maruta and his top-management colleagues share the 10th floor of Kao's head office building, together with a pool of secretaries. A large part of this floor is open space, with conference tables, overhead projectors and lounging chairs spread around. This is known as 'decision space', where all discussions with and among the top management take place. Anyone passing, including the chairman, can sit down and join in any discussion, on any topic and they frequently do. The executive vice president in charge of a particular business or a specific territory can, therefore, be engaged in a debate on a topic that he has no formal responsibility for. The same layout and norm are duplicated in the other floors, in the laboratories and in workshops. Workplaces look like large rooms: there are no partitions, only tables and chairs for spontaneous or planned discussions in which everyone has free access and can contribute as equals.

Every director of the company and most sales people have a fax machine in their homes to receive results and news. A biweekly Kao newspaper keeps every employee informed about competitors' moves, new product launches, overseas developments and key meetings. Terminals installed throughout the company ensure that all employees can, if they wish, retrieve data on sales records of any product from any of Kao's numerous outlets, or product development at their own or other branches. The latest findings from each of Kao's research laboratories are available for all to see, as are the details of the previous day's production and inventory at every Kao plant. 'They can even,' says Dr Maruta, 'check up on the president's expense account.' The benefits from this open sharing of data outweigh the risk of leaks, the company believes and, in an environment of flux, 'leaked information instantly becomes obsolete'.

While the corporate leaders carry the principal responsibility for developing and embedding the corporate values that provide the context for integration, it is the front-line entrepreneurs who must integrate the day-to-day activities of the company by managing the operational interdependencies across the different product, functional and geographic units. This requires certain attitudes and some specific skills, but also some facilitating infrastructures and processes.

In Kao, information technology is a key element of the infrastructure and its own extensive value-added networks (Kao VANs) provide the anchors for operational integration. Fully integrated information systems link the company's marketing, production and research units. These systems control the flows of materials, products and ideas from the stage of new product development to production planning involving over 1500 types of raw materials, to distribution of over 550 types of final products to about 300 000 retail stores.

Kao's logistics information system (LIS) links the corporate headquarters, all the factories, the independent wholesalers and the logistics centres through a network that includes a sales planning system, an inventory control system and an on-line supply system. Using LIS, each salesperson at Kao's 30 wholesalers projects sales plans on the basis of a head office campaign plan, an advertising plan and past market trends. These are corrected and adjusted at the corporate level and provide the basis for the daily production schedules of each factory. The system designs the optimal machine allocation, personnel schedules for production, the actual quantities to be supplied to each wholesaler based on factory and wholesaler inventories and the transportation plans for shipping the supplies on the following day. A separate computerised ordering system, built on point-of-sales terminals installed in the retail stores and connected to LIS, allows automatic replenishment of store inventory based on the previous day's sales data.

Kao's marketing intelligence system (MIS) tracks sales by product, region and market segment. Artificial intelligence tools are used extensively on this system to develop new approaches to advertising and media planning, sales promotion, market research and statistical analysis. Another sophisticated computerised system, ECHO, codes all telephone queries and complaints about Kao's products on-line. Linked to MIS, ECHO is an invaluable 'window on the customer's mind' that allows the company to fine-tune formulations, labelling and packaging and also to develop new product ideas.

These extensive IT networks provide the tools for the front-line managers in Kao to carry much of the burden of day-to-day operational coordination and integration, which in most companies are, the key tasks of middle and senior management. But these IT networks are not seen as a replacement for face-to-face meetings. Indeed the company has one of the most extensive systems of intrafunctional, interfunctional and interbusiness meetings to facilitate exchange of ideas and joint development of new initiatives and projects. Top management, marketers and research scientists meet at regular conferences. 'Open space' meetings are offered every week by different units and people from any part of the organisation can participate in such meetings. Within the R&D organisation, the lifeblood of Kao's innovations, monthly conferences are hosted, in turn, by different laboratories to bring junior researchers together. Researchers can nominate themselves to attend any of these meetings if they feel that the discussions can help their own work, or if they wish to talk separately with someone in the host laboratory. Similarly, any researcher in the host laboratory is free to invite anyone he wishes to meet from any of Kao's several laboratories spread around the world. It is through the collaborative work triggered by such meetings that Kao developed many of its breakthrough innovations, such as a special emulsifier developed jointly by three different laboratories, which later proved to be crucial for Sofina's success. Similar processes are in place in most of the other businesses and functions and these meetings — perhaps even more than the IT linkages — provide the means for Kao's front-line entrepreneurs to build and leverage their own lateral networks within the company.

But while the leaders create the context of integration and the front-line managers link and align operational activities, it is the group of coaches in senior management who serve as the engine for linking the diverse skills, expertise and resources in different research, manufacturing and marketing units to launch the strategic thrusts of Kao and maintain their momentum over time. If the entrepreneurs are the linchpins for the entrepreneurial process, the coaches are the pivots for the integration process.

A company-wide total creative revolution (TRC) project serves as the main vehicle for the senior managers in Kao to constantly pull together teams and task forces from different parts of the company to find creative responses to emerging problems or new opportunities. In the fourth phase in a two-decade-long program that started its life in 1971 as an organisation-wide computerisation initiative (the CCR movement), and evolved into a total quality control (TQC) program in 1974 and a total cost reduction (TCR) effort in 1986, total creative revolution is aimed at making 'innovation through collaborative learning' the centrepiece of Kao's strategic thrust into the 1990s. According to Dr Maruta, 'Kao must be like an educational institution — a company that has learnt how to learn'. And senior managers are formally expected to be 'the priests' — the teachers who must facilitate this process of shared learning. Thus, when a small and distant foreign subsidiary faces a problem, it is one of these constantly traveling senior managers who helps the local management team identify the appropriate expert in Japan and sponsors a task force to find a creative solution. Similarly, when some factory employees were made redundant following the installation of new equipment, one of these coaches sponsored five of them to form a team to support a factory in the United States to install and commission a plant imported from Japan. Over time, this group became a highly valued flying squad, available to help new production units get over their teething troubles.

The success of Sofina was the result of a very similar process, albeit on a much larger scale. Sensing an opportunity to create a high-quality, reasonably priced range of cosmetics that would leverage Kao's technological strengths and emphasise the functionality of 'skin care' rather than 'image', the top management of Kao presented it as a corporate challenge. To create such a product and to market it successfully, Kao would need to integrate its capabilities both within specific functions, such as diverse technologies in emulsifiers, moisturisers and skin diagnosis lodged in different laboratories and across functions including R&D, corporate marketing and sales, production and market research.

Instead of trying to create one gigantic team involving all the people who would need to contribute to the project, a few senior managers including the head of the Tokyo Research Laboratory, the director of marketing research and a director of marketing formed themselves into a small team to coordinate the project. They created small task forces, as required, to address specific problems — such as developing a new emulsifier — but kept the lateral coordination tasks among the operating managers at the simplest possible level. When the new emulsifier created some problems of skin irritation, a different group was established to develop a moisturiser and a chemical to reduce irritation. Similarly, when the Sofina foundation cream was found to be sticky on application, they set it up as a challenge for a marketing team, who responded by positioning the product as 'the longest lasting foundation that does not disappear with perspiration', converting the stickiness into a strength. This group of senior managers continued to play this integrating and coordinating role for over a decade, as the project evolved from a vision in the early 1970s to a nationwide success in the mid-1980s.

THE RENEWAL PROCESS: MANAGING RATIONALISATION AND REVITALISATION

The historical management processes in large MNCs have been premised on the assumption that environmental changes will be relatively linear and incremental. The accounting, budgeting, planning and control systems have been designed in these companies to provide order and efficiency to an essentially vertical process of managing information. The front-line units provide data. This data is analysed by middle-level managers to create useful information. Information obtained from several different sources is combined to generate knowledge within the organisation. Finally, top management absorbs and institutionalises this knowledge to build wisdom that becomes a part of the accepted perspectives and norms within the company. In an environment of relative stability, the order and efficiency of such a linear process have allowed these companies to continuously refine their operational processes through incremental accumulation and exploitation of knowledge.

In an environment of often turbulent and unpredictable change, however, incremental operational refinement is not enough; companies now also need the ability to manage strategic renewal. They must establish mechanisms in which internalised wisdoms and established ways of thinking and working are continuously challenged. If the integration process links and leverages existing capabilities to defend and advance current strategies, the renewal process continuously questions those strategies and the assumptions underlying them and inspires the creation of new competencies to prepare the ground for the very different competitive battles the company is likely to confront in the future.

The renewal process is built on two symbiotic components. It consists, on the one hand, of an ongoing pressure for rationalisation and restructuring of existing businesses to achieve continuous improvement of operational performance. This rationalisation component focuses on resource use — the effectiveness with which existing assets are deployed — and strives for continuous productivity growth. This part of the renewal process aims to refine existing operations incrementally to achieve ever-improving current results. Rigorous benchmarking against best-in-class competitors provides the scorecard on concrete operational measures such as value-added per employee, contributions per unit of fixed and working capital, time to market for new products and customer satisfaction. This process pinpoints performance gaps and focuses organisational energy on closing those gaps.

The other part of renewal is revitalisation — the creation of new competencies and new businesses, the challenging and changing of existing rules of the game and the leapfrogging of competition through quantum leaps. Driven by dreams and the power of ideas, it focuses on 'business not as usual' to create breakthroughs that would take the company to the next stages of its ambition. Revitalisation may involve fast-paced, small bets to take the company into new business domains — as Canon is trying in the field of semiconductors — or big 'bet the company' moves to transform industries — as AT&T is trying to do in the emerging new field of infocom.

As with entrepreneurship and integration, rationalisation and revitalisation are also often viewed in mutually exclusive terms. Managers complain of the unsatiable appetite of the stockmarket for short-term results, which forces them to focus on rationalisation rather than revitalisation. Some justify poor operating results as the evidence of long-term investments. The renewal process, in contrast, emphasises the essential symbiosis between the present and the future: there is no long-term success without short-term performance just as short-term results mean little unless they contribute to building the long-term ambition. Rationalisation provides the resources needed for revitalisation — not just money and people, but also legitimacy and credibility — while revitalisation creates the hope and the energy needed for rationalisation. Amid the general bloodbath that has characterised the semiconductor business, Intel has been among the few players who have achieved steady growth together with satisfactory financial returns. While its fortunes have turned with the tide — from spectacular successes in the 1970s when it introduced, in quick succession, the 1130 DRAM, the 1702 EPROM and the 8086 microprocessor, to heavy losses in the mid-1980s when the company was forced to exit the DRAM and SRAM businesses and cut 30 per cent of its workforce, to phenomenal success again with the 80386 32-bit microprocessor in the late 1980s — Intel has so far taken most of the correct turns as it hit the forks in the road, avoiding hitting the dividers, as many of its competitors have done.

In this process, the company has continuously renewed itself, changing its products and strategies and adopting its organisation and culture, to respond to the dramatic changes in its business environment. From the 'self-evident truth' that Intel was a 'jellybean' memory company, it changed itself into a logic devices company — selling boards — and then to a systems house — providing solutions in boxes. From a heritage of manufacturing inefficiency that was almost celebrated as the evidence of creativity in product development, Intel has now become almost cost competitive *vis-à-vis* its Japanese rivals. Its marketing focus has evolved too, from selling product features to OEM customers in the early 1970s to benefits-oriented marketing in the late 1970s, to positioning-oriented marketing in the 1980s (emphasising compatibility with end-user standards), to full-fledged end-user marketing in the 1990s in direct partnership with the final customers of the company's microprocessors. To support these changes, Intel has also transformed its culture. From an organisation of and for 'bright, talkative, opinionated, rude, arrogant, impatient and very informal macho men interested only in results and not in niceties,' the company has evolved into a better balance between task focus and concern for a friendly work environment in which 'people don't have to be Milky the milk biscuit to get their work done, but then, they don't have to be Atilla the Hun either'. Intel's ability to stay one step ahead of competition — which is all that separates the winners from the losers in the semiconductor business — has been built on some demanding roles and contributions of managers at all levels of the company (see Figure 7.5). But, if the front-line entrepreneurs drive the entrepreneurial process and the senior-level coaches anchor the integration process, it is the corporate-level leaders who inspire and energise the renewal process. It is they who create and manage the tensions between short-term performance and long-term ambition, challenging the organisation continuously to higher levels of operational and strategic performance.

Until the demise of Noyce in 1990, Intel had been led by the trio of Gordon Moore as chairman, Robert Noyce as vice chairman and Andy Grove as president, who collectively formed the company's executive committee. Of these, while Noyce looked after external relations, it was Moore and Grove who guided the company internally: Moore in the role of the technology genius and architect of long-term strategy and Grove as the detail-oriented resident pragmatist. Moore has been the quiet, long-term-oriented, philosophical champion of revitalisation. Grove, on the other hand, has served as the vocal, aggressive and demanding driver of rationalisation. When Motorola's competitive microprocessor gained momentum at the cost of Intel's 16 bit 8086 chip, it was Grove who initiated 'operation crush' — an 'all out combat' plan, complete with war rooms and SWAT teams, to make 8086 the industry standard. But it was Moore who built the company's long-range planning process and provided the blueprint for technological evolution — what has since come to be known as 'Moore's law'. In essence, the two had divided the renewal responsibility between them in a way that was originally serendipitous but has since been institutionalised within the company as an unusual management concept: two-in-a-box. It has become normal in Intel for two executives with complementary skills to share the responsibilities of one role.

Whether through a combination of more than one person, as in the case of Andy Grove and Gordon Moore at Intel or Sochiro Honda and Takeo Fujisawa at Honda Motors, or singlehandedly, as Jack Welch is now attempting at GE and Jan Timmer at Philips, creating and managing this tension between the short term and the long term, between current performance and future ambition, between restructuring and revitalisation, is a key part of the corporate leader's role in the entrepreneurial corporation. In this role, the leader is the challenger — the one who is constantly upping the ante and creating the energy and the enthusiasm necessary for the organisation to accept the perpetual stretch that such challenging implies.

Personal credibility within and outside the organisation is a prerequisite for the corporate leader to play this role, but it is not enough. Charisma sustains momentum for short periods but fatigue ultimately overtakes the

Figure 7.5: The renewal process: management roles and tasks

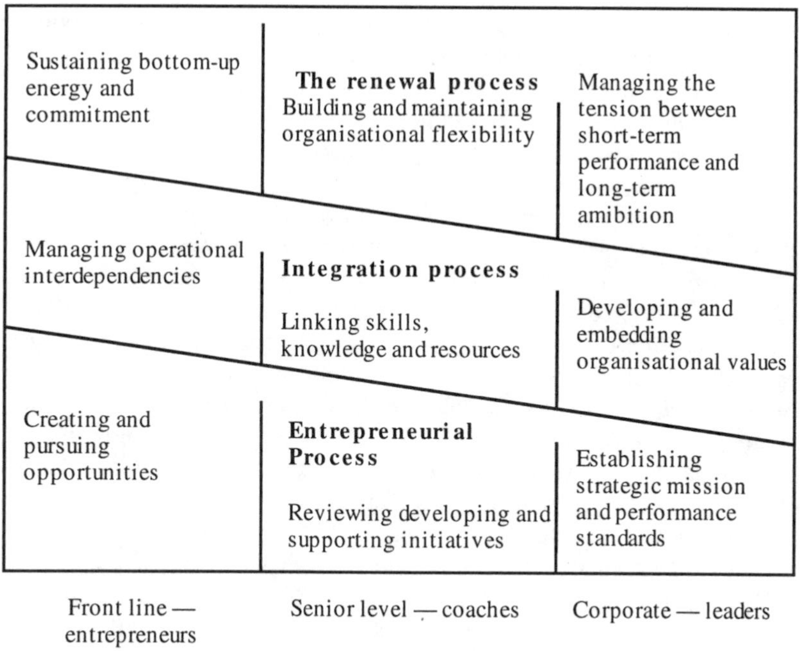

Sustaining bottom-up energy and commitment	**The renewal process** Building and maintaining organisational flexibility	Managing the tension between short-term performance and long-term amibition
Managing operational interdependencies	**Integration process** Linking skills, knowledge and resources	Developing and embedding organisational values
Creating and pursuing opportunities	**Entrepreneurial Process** Reviewing developing and supporting initiatives	Establishing strategic mission and performance standards
Front line — entrepreneurs	Senior level — coaches	Corporate — leaders

organisation that depends on individual charisma alone for its energy. To inspire self-renewal, companies must develop an inspiring corporate ambition — a shared dream about the future and the company's role in that future — and must embed that ambition throughout the organisation. Whether the ambition focuses on something as tangible as size, as in Canon's expressed desire to be a company as big as IBM and Matsushita combined, or something less tangible, such as Intel's desire to be the best in the world, what matters is the emotional commitment the leader can build around the dream. Ultimately, it is this emotional commitment that unleashes the human energy required to sustain the organisation's ability to continuously renew itself. And developing, marshalling and leveraging this energy is the key to simultaneous rationalisation and revitalisation and will perhaps be the single most important challenge for the corporate leaders of the transnational companies of the future.

While the leaders must provide the challenge and the stretch necessary for organisational self-renewal, it is the coaches who must mediate the complex trade offs that simultaneous restructuring and revitalisation imply. It is they who must manage the tension between building new capabilities and stretching existing resources and the conflict inherent in the high and unrelenting performance demands of the company. This requires enormous flexibility and an environment of mutual trust and tolerance and creating such processes and attitudes is a key element of the coach's role.

As described by Andy Grove, in the semiconductor business 'there are the quick and there are the dead'. In a highly volatile technological and market environment, the company has developed the ability to be very flexible in moving human resources as needs change. Levels change up or down at Intel all the time — people move in every direction, upwards, sideways or downwards. Careers advance not by moving up the organisation but by individuals filling corporate needs. Official rank, decision-making authority and remuneration — highly correlated in most companies — are treated separately at Intel and this separation among different kinds of rewards lies at the core of Intel's organisational flexibility. But such a system is also susceptible to gaming and needs a high level of openness and transparency in decision-making processes and mutual trust and tolerance among people to be effective. Flexibility requires not only that the organisation act fairly but also that it be seen to be acting fairly; creating and protecting such fairness — necessary in any winning team — is again a key task for the coaches.

While Intel's action-oriented and direct, if somewhat confrontative, management style has evolved in Grove's mould of aggressive brilliance, it is the senior-management group heading different operating divisions and corporate functions who have embedded the norms of transparency and openness at all levels of the company. Key decisions at Intel are typically taken in open meetings, all of which have preannounced agendas and inevitably close with action plans and deadlines. During a meeting, participants are encouraged to debate the pros and cons of a subject aggressively through what is described as 'constructive confrontation'. But once something has been decided on, Intel has the philosophy of 'agree or disagree, but commit'. As a result, everyone has the opportunity to influence key decisions relevant to themselves and to openly advocate their perspectives and views and is party to the final decisions, even though the decisions may not always conform to their preferences. The opportunity for such active participation on an equal basis in open and transparent decision processes, coupled with the norm of disciplined and fast implementation once a decision has been taken, creates the environment of trust, which, in turn, is key to the operational and strategic flexibility of the company.

The effectiveness of the renewal process ultimately depends on the ability of front-line managers to generate and maintain the energy and commitment of people within their units. The battles for efficiency and integration, for rationalisation and revitalisation, are ultimately fought at the level of the salesperson in the field, the operator in the plant and the individual research scientist or engineer in the laboratory. While the energising ambition personified by the top management and the open and transparent decision-making processes orchestrated by the senior managers provide the anchors for the grass roots-level commitment at Intel, two other elements of its organisational philosophy and practices also contribute a great deal to maintaining the enthusiasm of its front-line teams.

First, at Intel, there is not only fairness in management processes but there is also fairness in organisational outcomes. In contrast to companies that cut front-line jobs at the first sight of performance problems, Intel adopted the '125 per cent solution' to deal with the industry-wide recession in the early 1980s: instead of retrenching people, all salaried workers — including the chairman — were required to work an additional 10 hours per week without additional compensation. When the recession continued in 1982, still unwilling to lay off large numbers of people, the company proposed a 10 per cent pay cut on top of the 125 per cent solution. As the economy pulled out of the recession, returning the company to profitability, the pay cuts were first restored in June 1983 and, by November 1983, the employees who had accepted pay cuts received special bonuses. Similarly, in 1986, when the memory product bloodbath finally forced the company to reduce its workforce by 30 per cent, the cuts were distributed across all levels of the company, instead of being concentrated at the lowest ranks.

Second, at Intel, it is legitimate to own up to one's personal mistakes and to change one's mind. Gordon Moore regretfully but openly acknowledges his personal role in missing the engineering workstation revolution, even though the company was among the pioneers for this opportunity. Andy Grove, the symbol of the company's confrontative, task-oriented culture, had long insisted on not having any recreation facilities in the company. 'This is not a country club. You come here to work' he would say to all employees. But as the organisation grew and the need for supplementing the task focus with concern for friendly work environment became manifest, he gave in and made a celebration of being beaten down. At the dedication of the new facilities, he appeared in his bathing suit and took a shower under a big banner that read '"There will never be any showers at Intel" — Andy Grove'. Such open acknowledgment of errors and good-hearted acceptance of alternatives one has personally opposed creates an environment in which failures are tolerated and changes in strategy do not automatically create winners and losers. It is this overall environment that, in turn, co-opts the front-line managers into the corporate ambition and allows them to sustain energy and commitment at the lowest levels of the organisation.

A MODEL FOR THE FUTURE

Over the last decade, many observers of large corporations have highlighted some of the vulnerabilities of the traditional company's strategy and organisation described in this chapter. The specific prescriptions of needing to build entrepreneurship, integration and renewal capabilities are also not new. Academics, consultants and managers themselves have long recognised these needs to respond to a variety of changing environmental demands. Typically, however, these changing external demands and the consequent need for new internal capabilities have been studied in a piecemeal fashion, triggering ad hoc responses. Facing slowing economic growth and increasingly sophisticated customer demands, companies have attempted to decentralise resources and authority to capture the creative energy and entrepreneurship of front-line managers. But prescriptions of creating and managing chaos have ignored the need for clarity of strategy and the discipline of centralised financial control to channel bottom-up energy into a coherent corporate direction. Companies that have attempted such radical decentralisation without a centrally – managed strategic framework have soon lost their focus and their ability to leverage resources effectively and have been forced to retreat to the known devil of their old ways.

Observing the ever-increasing pace of globalisation of markets and the rising cost, complexity and convergence of technologies, managers have recognised the need to consolidate and integrate their diverse organisational capabilities. But presented typically with examples of high-tech and highly centralised Japanese companies, they have confused capabilities with technologies and integration with centralisation. Similarly, faced with the rapid enhancement of the skills and resources of once-distant competitors and the changing norms and expectations in the many societies in which they operate, companies have realised the limits of incremental improvements and the need for dramatic change. Yet, guided by prescriptions of creating dreamlike, long-term ambitions, they have allowed short-term performance to slip, thereby abandoning the long term too because of increasing resource scarcity.

In contrast to these fragmented and often contradictory prescriptions, we have presented a broad model encompassing the key capabilities we believe companies must develop to respond to the environmental demands of the 1990s. Nothing needs a theory more than practice and the lack of an integrated theory of the new organisation, we believe, has prevented companies from abandoning the old divisional model even though they have long recognised its constraints. The model of the future organisation we have presented here is intended to provide such a theory for practice.

The real challenge in building this new organisation lies in the changes in management roles we have described. The metamorphosis of front-line managers, from being operational implementers to becoming aggressive entrepreneurs, will require some very new skills and capabilities. Similarly, the transformation of the middle-management role from that of administrative controller to that of inspiring coach will represent a traumatic change. But the management group that will be most severely challenged in the new organisation will be the one currently at the top of the hierarchy. Not only will they have to change their role from that of resource allocator and political arbitrator to that of institutional leader, they will also have to create the infrastructures and the contexts necessary for the others to play the new roles demanded of them. The managers who can build the attitudes and skills appropriate for these new roles and the companies that can develop and retain such managers are likely to emerge as the future winners in the game of global competition.

8. Global Strategies for Multinational Enterprises

Alan Rugman and Alain Verbeke

THE EXTENDED GENERIC STRATEGIES FRAMEWORK OF PORTER

Porter (1980) has argued that a generic strategy consists of two major choices. First, with regard to the type of competitive advantage being pursued, the choice is between low cost and differentiation. Second is the choice of the firm's competitive scope, which reflects the breadth of its target market segments; the alternatives are a broad target, covering a whole industry, and a narrow target, including only specific segments within an industry.

Based on these two parameters, Porter (1980) has distinguished among three generic strategies: cost leadership, differentiation and focus: 'Generic strategy requires a fundamental choice, whether intended or realised, made among alternative patterns of decisions and actions, with a substantial effect on an organisation's functioning and performance'.

Porter (1986) has extended this generic strategies framework to take account of the complexities of global competition. This work suggests that there are in fact four dimensions of competitive scope: (a) segment scope (the range of segments the firm serves); (b) industry scope (the range of related industries the firm competes in with a coordinated strategy); (c) vertical scope (the activities performed by the firm versus by suppliers and channels); and (d) geographic scope (the geographic regions in which the firm operates with a coordinated strategy) (Porter 1986: 22). Porter (1986: 22) states that international strategy is seen primarily as 'an issue of geographic scope'. He then defines a global industry as one 'in which a firm's competitive position in one country is significantly affected by its position in other countries or vice versa' (1986: 18).

Rugman and Verbeke (1993a) have demonstrated that Porter's generic strategies framework needs to be extended to take into account the issue of geographic scope in a global industry. They show that his three initial generic strategies can be transformed into the set of five depicted in Figure 8.1.

132

Figure 8.1: Porter's extended generic strategies framework for global industries

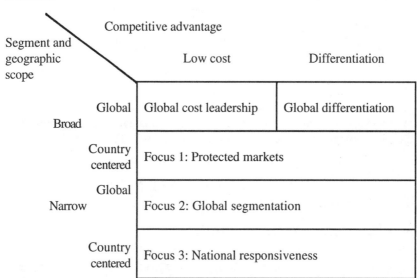

There are two key problems associated with Porter's extended generic strategies framework as shown in Figure 8.1. First, the type of competitive advantage — namely cost leadership or differentiation cannot be used to discriminate between strategies in three of the five cases: a protected market strategy, global segmentation and national responsiveness. In Porter's framework, firms may become 'stuck in the middle' if they pursue both cost leadership and differentiation simultaneously within the chosen geographic and/or market segment niche. In other words, the Porter (1980) domestic generic strategies framework is inconsistent with the Porter (1986) global framework, since cost leadership and differentiation cannot distinguish among three of the strategies in the international context.

Second, Porter's third strategy of protected markets does not fit at all with the other four extended generic strategies. Global cost leadership and global differentiation are defined as 'seeking the cost or differentiation advantages of global configuration/coordination through selling a wide line of products to buyers in all or most significant country markets' (Porter 1986: 47). Global segmentation is viewed as 'serving a particular industry segment worldwide'. National responsiveness for a firm is a 'focus on those industry segments most affected by local country differences though the industry as a whole is global' and it meets 'unusual local needs in products, channels and marketing practices in each country, foregoing the competitive advantages of a global strategy' Porter (1986: 48). In each of these four cases, efficiency, as measured by relative output/input differentials throughout the value chain, determines a firm's economic performance in terms of survival, profitability and growth.

In contrast, as Porter (1986: 48) recognises himself, 'protected markets strategies lack a competitive advantage in economic terms, their choice depends on a sophisticated prediction about future government behaviour'. This demonstrates that Porter's extended framework of generic strategies based upon two parameters (scope and type of efficiency driven competitive advantage) cannot include the protected market strategy. Again, one of the five generic strategies of Porter (1986) is inconsistent with Porter (1980).

FIRM-SPECIFIC ADVANTAGES AS GENERIC STRATEGIES

Rugman and Verbeke (1990, 1992a) have demonstrated that the development and use of firm-specific advantages (FSA), or the lack of them, reflects the truly generic strategies between which firms need to make a choice in each identifiable pattern of decisions and actions. Firm-specific advantages include both proprietary know-how (unique assets) and transactional advantages with potential cost reducing and/or differentiation enhancing effects. In a number of cases it may be difficult to assess the actual impact of an FSA, in terms of cost reduction or differentiation enhancement. Rugman and Verbeke (1991a) have suggested that, in such cases, the contribution of an FSA to 'infrastructure development' of the firm should be considered. All strategies that build upon such FSAs or aim to develop new ones are classified as efficiency based.

In contrast, strategies that do not build upon FSA to achieve a satisfactory economic performance in terms of survival, profitability, growth or any other goal considered relevant by decision-makers are classified as non-efficiency-based or 'shelter'-based. If the economic performance of a firm or set of firms does not result from FSA with cost-reducing, differentiation-enhancing or infrastructure-building characteristics, this performance must result from 'shelter-based behaviour'.

Shelter-based behaviour reflects instances where firms (a) attempt to impose 'artificial' costs or barriers to differentiation upon (foreign) rivals through government regulation (e.g. tariff and non-tariff barriers) or (b) reduce the market incentives for cost reduction, differentiation enhancement or infrastructure building themselves (e.g. collusive behaviour and cartel formation aimed primarily at exploiting the consumer) or limit the potential effects of these incentives (e.g. government subsidies). In both cases, such strategies may lead to the elimination of workable competition.

Shelter-based strategies are especially significant in the international business context, where firms located in a particular nation may convince public policy-makers that protectionist measures will lead to higher economic welfare in terms of value-added creation or to a special type of public good in terms of the creation of domestic control over strategic sectors, technological spill-over effects, etc. This occurs even where such public goods may be nonexistent or where shelter leads to a substantial reduction in consumer welfare. Rugman and Verbeke (1991b, l991c) have demonstrated that such strategies may even subvert policies aimed at achieving a level playing field and fair trade, as now frequently occurs in the United States and the European Union.

The distinction between an efficiency-based strategy and a shelter-based strategy is truly fundamental because each strategy builds upon different intellectual premises as to what constitutes the source of success. In the case of an efficiency-based strategy, consumer sovereignty ultimately determines whether or not the firm will be successful (except in the case of natural monopolies, which do not exist in international business). Strong economic performance reflects the successful creation of value for customers. In contrast, shelter-based strategies reflect behaviour that reduces value to customers, compared with the situation where efficiency-based strategies would prevail.

The importance of distinguishing between these two types of strategy results from the fact that different 'weapons' are used and different 'rules of the game' are followed in each case. More specifically, firms pursuing a conventional efficiency-based strategy, but faced with shelter-seeking rivals, may suffer in the short run, compared with a situation where all competitors would be engaged in efficiency-based behaviour. In the short run, shelter-based behaviour will reduce the possibilities for rivals not engaged in such behaviour to exploit their FSA or develop new ones. Yet, in the long run, shelter obviously works against the firms that build their economic performance on it. Rugman and Verbeke (1993b) explore the ten main reasons why shelter-based strategies may fail in the long run.

In practice, it may not always be easy for outside observers to classify a specific pattern of decisions and actions as efficiency-based or shelter-based. There are five main dimensions to consider: need; managerial intent; organisational routines; outcome; and impact on performance.

First, shelter-based strategies are used in international business only as the need arises. This occurs when there is an absence of strong FSA that would allow firms to beat rivals on the basis of the cost and differentiation characteristics of the products offered. An exception is the case of collusive behaviour when the various firms involved have strong FSA (i.e. relative to foreign rivals) but attempt to extract rents from consumers through the elimination of competition.

Second, shelter-based behaviour generally results from managerial intentions to engage in such a pattern of decisions and actions but may still contain an emerging component (Rugman and Verbeke 1991b). Third, specific organisational routines resulting in lobbying efforts may increase the probability of shelter-based behaviour. Fourth, as in the case of efficiency-based strategies, the goals pursued may not be achieved. Fifth, government may refuse to provide shelter, thus affecting the firm's performance.

The study by Cho Sung Dong and Porter (1986) on the global shipbuilding industry demonstrates the weaknesses of Porter's extended generic strategies framework. This analysis demonstrates that firms in the United Kingdom were not able to achieve a satisfactory economic performance after the mid-1950s in spite of strong government intervention in the form of subsidies. In contrast, alleged protected markets strategies in Japan after World War II led to a global cost leadership position. The main reason is that in the United Kingdom and many other European nations, government support was used to provide shelter, in other words, it was not intended to, and did not, lead to a more efficient exploitation of existing FSA or development of new ones. In other words, government support acted as an artificial substitute for strong FSA, and often resulted from firm lobbying. In contrast, Japanese government support programmes were always intended to develop new FSA and to foster the long-run cost competitiveness/differentiation position of Japanese yards. In Japan, government support was used by shipbuilding companies as a complement to their existing FSA and as a stimulus to generate new ones. These firms pursued efficiency-based strategies.

A NEW FRAMEWORK FOR GLOBAL STRATEGY

Much of the international business literature suggests that, within the efficiency-based patterns of decisions and actions, two parameters could be used to distinguish fundamental subcategories of behaviour.

The first parameter is the type of FSAs to be developed or exploited, (Rugman and Verbeke 1992b). An important distinction exists between location bound FSAs (LB-FSAs) and non-location bound FSAs (NLB-FSAs). The former benefit a company only in a particular location (or set of locations), and lead to benefits of national responsiveness. In the context of international business operations, these LB-FSAs cannot be effectively transferred as an intermediate output (e.g. a tangible or intangible asset) or embodied in the final outputs of the organisation, to be sold across borders. In contrast, NLB-FSAs are easily transferred and exploited abroad, whether in the form of intermediate outputs or embodied in final outputs. They lead to benefits of integration in terms of economies of scale and scope and exploitation of national differences. Many authors, including Bartlett (1986), Bartlett and Ghoshal (1989), Doz (1986), Ghoshal (1987), Kogut (1985a, 1985b), Prahalad and Doz (1987), and Roth and Morrison (1990), have provided the intellectual foundations that led to making this important distinction between two fundamentally different types of FSAs (see Rugman and Verbeke 1991a, 1992a, 1992b).

The second parameter is related to the number of 'home bases' used by the firm. A 'home base' is defined by Porter (1990) as the nation where the firm retains effective strategic, creative and technical control. In addition, it is considered central 'to choosing the industries to compete in as well as the appropriate strategy' (see Porter 1990: 599). Rugman and Verbeke (1993b) have demonstrated that a firm may actually have several home bases contributing substantially to the development of new FSA, so as to improve international competitiveness. It is important to distinguish between the existence of a single home base or multiple home bases in the pursuit of international competitiveness, because it reflects the impact of the country-specific advantages (CSAs) of specific locations on strategic behaviour. A single home base implies the dominating impact of one set of national 'diamond' CSAs on the firm's overall competitiveness, both now and in the future. In contrast, a firm with multiple home bases depends upon decisions and actions taken in various locations and upon the characteristics of these locations.

To the extent that the development and exploitation of NLB-FSAs requires coordination of decisions and actions across borders, a single home base implies direct, centralised control of all foreign operations. In contrast, in the case of a global subsidiary mandate for example, the 'corporate headquarters role shifts toward 'managing dispersed strategic processes, ensuring that subsidiary strategies continue to fit the overall corporation goals and providing the resources and freedom required to support the mandates' (Roth and Morrison 1992: 718). In this case, typical home base activities are concentrated in the various nations where subsidiaries have received global subsidiary mandates.

Using the above analysis, we can generate the two axes for Figure 8.2; number of home bases and either LB-FSA or a NLB-FSA. In Figure 8.2, four important categories of efficiency-based strategies in global industries are described, which, in our view, are much more fundamental than the Porter ones.

Figure 8.2: Principal categories of efficiency-based strategies

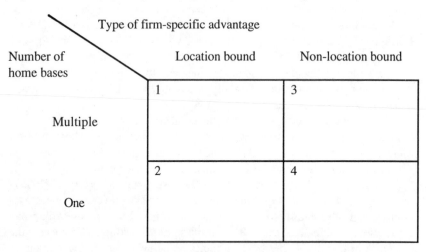

Patterns of decisions and actions in quadrant 1 are typical for so-called 'multinational' firms, as defined by Bartlett and Ghoshal (1989). Here, the different operations in various countries are viewed as largely independent and build their performance on strengths in being national responsive. In quadrant 2, competitiveness results from having only a single home base and building upon FSA that lead to benefits of national responsiveness. Here, we find uni-national firms that attempt to remain competitive *vis-à-vis* global rivals in one or a limited set of nations. Quadrant 3 reflects strategies aimed at achieving a superior economic performance through using multiple home bases, each of which builds upon NLB-FSAs. Firms with global subsidiary mandates, as described by Rugman and Bennett (1982), Poynter and Rugman (1983), Roth and Morrison (1992), typically fall in this quadrant. The main characteristic of Bartlett and Ghoshal's (1989) 'transnational solution' is the simultaneous occurrence of patterns of decisions and actions that fit into quadrants one and three of Figure 8.2.

Finally, quadrant 4 reflects behaviour typical for both the 'global firms' and the 'international firms' as defined by Bartlett and Ghoshal (1989). Global firms attempt to achieve global scale economies by producing primarily in a single country and exporting products globally as these embody the firm's NLB-FSAs. International firms pursue international scope economies and/or benefits of exploiting national differences by transferring know-how across borders and/or by coordinating dispersed activities placed in different optimal locations. The dispersion of value activities implies global rationalisation, whereby each subsidiary specialises in a narrow set of activities in the value chain (see Kobrin 1991).

These four types of efficiency-based strategies appear to reflect the various archetypal firms engaged in international business as portrayed in the relevant literature. They also represent clearly identifiable patterns of decisions and actions in the pursuit of a satisfactory economic performance. These patterns in fact constitute alternatives among which choices need to be made, for example, when reacting to an environmental change such as the EC 1992 program or the North American Free Trade Agreement (NAFTA), even within a single strategic business unit.

The framework is more relevant for strategic management purposes than the one of Porter (1986) on the configuration (geographically dispersed or concentrated) and coordination (low or high) of activities. A dispersed as opposed to a concentrated configuration of a firm's activities, in general, does not necessarily carry important strategic implications. More relevant is knowing where and how the core activities are carried out which will determine the development of new FSAs, and which may be substantially affected by CSAs of the locations where they were developed. Similarly, the framework is more relevant for coordination issues. It is more important to know what the resources of a firm and its rivals are, in terms of LB-FSAs and NLB-FSAs that will lead to either benefits of national responsiveness or benefits of integration, than to observe that some of these benefits, especially scope economies and benefits of exploiting national differences, require coordination across borders in order to be realised.

In related work, Chang Moon (1993) has shown that Porter's configuration/coordination framework is conceptually flawed. Porter (1986: 28) argues that a firm with a geographically concentrated configuration of activities and a high international coordination among these activities pursues a simple global strategy. In fact, in the extreme case, the firm with a concentrated configuration of activities is either a uni-national or an exporting firm that does not perform activities in other countries, so that there is nothing to be internationally coordinated. In other words, in Porter's matrix, the concentrated configuration/high coordination quadrant is really an empty cell. Porter argues that 'the simplest global strategy is to concentrate as many activities as possible in one country, serve the world from this home base, and tightly coordinate through standardisation those activities that must inherently be performed near the buyer'. The problem with this statement is that it suggests that some activities must always be performed near the buyer. In reality, a virtually complete concentration of activities in one country makes the international coordination issue redundant in global strategic management.

THE GENERALITY OF THE RUGMAN AND VERBEKE FRAMEWORK

This new framework, developed in greater detail in Rugman and Verbeke (1993b) is a general framework of global strategy. For example, two recent mainstream classifications of multinational strategies in the international business literature are in accordance with the framework. These are the typologies of international business strategies of Ghoshal and Bartlett (1988a, 1988b) and of Gupta and Govindarajan (1991). Both typologies are based on the role of the foreign subsidiaries in the R&D process.

Ghoshal and Bartlett's four types of R&D strategies can be fitted into Figure 8.2 based on the analysis of the preceding sections. First, the local-for-local process (quadrant 1); second, the local-for-global and global-for-global approaches (quadrant 3); third, the centre-for-global process (quadrant 4).

The Gupta and Govindarajan typology also fits in Figure 8.2. The local innovator (quadrant 1), the global innovator and integrated player (quadrant 3) and the implementor roles (quadrant 4) of the subsidiaries in the innovation process are again in accordance with our framework. It is interesting to observe that quadrant 3 of Figure 8.2 includes two types from each of the typologies. In our view, the local-for-global (or global innovator) approach is fundamentally very similar to the global-for-global (or integrated player) process, but the latter approach just reflects a more complex process of creating NLB-FSAs through multiple highly interdependent, rather than semi-autonomous home bases.

Several recent descriptions of strategic decision making patterns in MNEs suggest that many firms are now moving toward a structure that builds upon multiple home bases and requires the simultaneous development of LB-FSAs and NLB-FSAs. This allows an effective response to the dual requirements of national responsiveness and global integration. One of the main characteristics of this structure is that it can consider all factors contributing to these conflicting demands simultaneously rather than separately. This new organisational form has been given various names, including the 'transnational' (Bartlett 1986), the 'heterarchy' (Hedlund 1986) the 'multifocal firm' (Prahalad and Doz 1987) and the 'multiple headquarters system' (Nonaka 1990).

Ghoshal and Westney (1993) have identified five characteristics of this new type of firm, namely dispersion, interdependence, tight coupling of subunits, cross-unit learning and structural flexibility. The *dispersion* aspect precisely reflects the existence of multiple home bases, for example, in the area of innovation. The presence of multiple home bases implies that the MNE becomes an integrated network of *interdependent* units that must be *tightly coupled* in order to exploit NLB-FSAs across borders. The development and diffusion of new NLB-FSAs becomes a process whereby the different subunits of the network need to engage in cross-unit learning. However, in order to achieve an optimal balance between the creation and exploitation of both LB-FSAs and NLB-FSAs, structural flexibility is required. Structural flexibility means that the management process must be able to change from product to product, from country to country and even from decision to decision (Bartlett 1986).

The requirement to build upon both LB-FSAs and NLB-FSAs in order to achieve global competitive success is now well established. However, the important question remains whether individual firms require specific linkages with their environment to develop and exploit the required resource base, especially in terms of the NLB-FSAs. In other words, is it sufficient to focus on establishing an intraorganisational network with cross-unit learning or is it necessary to develop strategies regarding the management of an interorganisational network?

BUSINESS NETWORKS AND GLOBAL COMPETITIVENESS

In spite of a clear evolution in the direction of multiple home bases, a substantial number of MNEs still operate from a single home base, as is reflected in the work of Porter (1990). Given that NLB-FSAs can be initiated in one or many geographical locations, the important question arises whether their development and diffusion throughout the company requires specific linkages with outside actors.

Figure 8.3 represents this managerial focus on an intraorganisational versus interorganisational network (horizontal axis), in the situation of both a single and multiple home bases (vertical axis).

The second quadrant (focus on intra-organisational network and choice of a single home base) reflects a substantial body of primarily economics driven literature on the expansion of MNE activity. Vernon's (1966, 1979) product cycle hypothesis, Dunning's (1981) original eclectic paradigm and conventional internalisation theory as developed by Buckley and Casson (1976) and Rugman (1981) all attempt to explain the international expansion and success of MNEs building upon the premise that FSAs are developed in a single location and then diffused internationally through foreign direct investment rather than other entry modes when a number of specific internal conditions (internalisation advantages) and external conditions (location advantages) are fulfilled. Williamson's transaction cost approach (1981),

Figure 8.3: Business networks in international strategic management

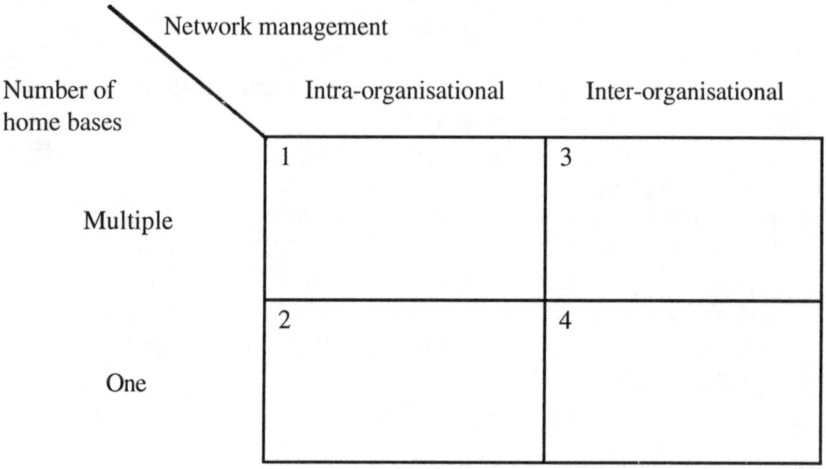

Network management		
Number of home bases	Intra-organisational	Inter-organisational
Multiple	1	3
One	2	4

building upon the work of Chandler (1962) and Tsurumi (1977), as well as its extensions (see for example, Teece 1983, 1985), is consistent with this view. The multinational, multidimensional (M) form portrayed in this work describes a very simple intraorganisational network whereby the corporate headquarters organise the firm into semi-autonomous profit units, monitor the (financial) performance of these units, allocate resources to them and engage in centralised strategic planning. A clear top-down, hierarchical structure is established and no direct interdependences are supposed to exist among sub-units.

Recent extensions of both the eclectic paradigm (Dunning 1988 and 1993a) and internalisation theory (Rugman and Verbeke 1990, 1992b) have recognised the intraorganisational implications of MNEs functioning with multiple home bases and the limits of the M-form. More specifically, in accordance with Hennart (1993), it has been suggested that coordination and control of the internal network should be performed through the use of a mix of hierarchical controls, price controls and socialisation.

Transaction costs associated with operating complex internal networks can be further reduced by introducing procedural justice elements in strategic decision-making processes (see Kim and Mauborgne 1993). Procedural justice appears to be of fundamental importance to achieve attitudes of commitment, trust and social harmony within the different sub-units of an MNE. This is consistent with the observation of Prahalad and Doz (1987) that 'due process' constitutes a necessary condition for effective strategic decision-making in MNEs.

The complexity of internal network management in the presence of multiple home bases is consistent with the concept of heterarchy as described by Hedlund (1986, 1993) and Hedlund and Rolander (1990). It also explains the rise of several sophisticated coordination and control mechanisms in MNEs (Martinez and Jarillo 1989). This focus on the intraorganisational network of the MNE is sufficient in cases whereby the social context exerts only a limited influence on the subunits located in different home bases, when they develop new NLB-FSAs.

However, the right hand side of Figure 8.3 takes into account the fact that MNEs may function in complex environments, many elements of which cannot be reduced to the five forces driving industry competition as described in the work of Porter (1980, 1985) on competitive strategy. The influence of the environment on the process of NLB-FSA development in MNEs also requires a richer analysis than the one provided by, for instance, conventional internalisation theory where the location advantages characterising alternative nations or regions are identified, especially within the context of optimal location selection, but where only limited attention is devoted to the dynamic interaction among firm specific and environmental factors (see Dunning 1993a for an in-depth discussion).

A large body of literature does exist on the creation and management of joint ventures and other types of cooperative agreements in international business (e.g. Contractor and L'orange 1988; Doz, Prahalad and Hamel 1990) and Geringer 1991). However, little has been written on the management of interorganisational networks with multiple actors in international business, notable exceptions being Dunning (1993b) and Westney (1993).

Institutionalisation theorists have argued that the appropriate level for studying interorganisational linkages is the so called 'organisational field' — 'those organisations that, in the aggregate, constitute a recognised area of institutional life: key suppliers, resources and product consumers, regulatory agencies and other organisations that produce similar services or products' (Westney 1990: 284 and 1993: 56, citing Di Maggio and Powell 1983: 148). The main characteristic of such a network is mutual recognition of the different partners involved. This mutual recognition may lead to isomorphism in cases whereby the different organisations are characterised by resource dependency. Such isomorphism can easily be given a transaction cost interpretation: 'transactions are less costly in time and effort between organisations that are similar, (Westney 1993: 70). If this resource dependency is symmetric, it may lead to the formation of clusters as described by Porter (1990). In the case of asymmetric interdependence, business networks may be formed (see D'Cruz and Rugman 1994).

Porter's (1990) clusters consist of sets of economic actors linked through the elements of the diamond of competitive advantage in a nation (factor conditions, demand conditions, industry characteristics, related and supporting industries). Porter's (1990) work is useful to study the impact of interorganisational networks on the international competitiveness of firms and industries with a single home base. Although such clusters arise largely unintentionally, as a result of the so-called 'systemic nature of the diamond' (Porter 1990: 148), mutual interactions among the various determinants of a national diamond, it is interesting to observe that Porter focuses primarily on the benefits of these clusters and not on the costs — for example, as regards the reduction of a firm's autonomy.

Building upon Porter's (1990) cluster framework, D'Cruz and Rugman (1993) have developed the concept of business network as a tool for obtaining a favourable international competitive advantage. This is different from Porter's cluster in two ways: first, the strategic intent of the partners to engage in network formation; and second, the asymmetric coordination and control of the network. In their view, a business network consists of a group of firms and non-business institutions competing globally and linked together through resource dependencies. There are five partners in the business network: the flagship firm which is typically a large multinational enterprise; key suppliers; key customers; competitors; and the non-business infrastructure. This last partner includes the service-related sectors, educational and training institutions, the various levels of government, and other organisations such as trade associations, non-governmental organisations and unions.

The business network is characterised also by the flagship firm's asymmetric strategic control over the network partners in common areas of interest. This asymmetry entails leadership and direction-setting, effectively a 'strategic hand', in setting the priorities of the partners in regard to their participation in the flagship firm's business system. Asymmetric strategic control by the flagship firm is consistent with the idea that international competitiveness demands NLB-FSAs. It is the flagship firm, typically a multinational (MNE), which has the global perspective and resources to lead a business network and to establish the global benchmarks necessary to lead the development of the network. The authors usefully applied this framework to describe international expansion strategies in the telecommunications industry (see D'Cruz and Rugman 1994). However, the important question that is not answered in either of the two frameworks described above is how the form and functioning of interorganisational networks positioned in quadrant 4 of Figure 8.3 may be altered, when firms move towards having multiple home bases.

Enright (1993) has examined the relationship between localisation (geographic concentration) and the coordination of economic activity within industries. He supports Krugman's (1991) view that there is no single progression or path along which geographically clustered industries evolve. By improving coordination and communication across firms in an industry, localisation may influence, but not solely determine, the boundaries of these firms. Enright's case studies of localised industries indicate that surviving industries change organisation and coordination mechanisms to reflect changes in the relevant task environment, be they in markets, technology, government involvement, etc. He warns that localised groups of firms will decline if they do not adapt to changing external circumstances. The move towards establishing multiple home bases obviously implies a similar challenge, with MNEs being confronted with fundamentally new environments, as compared to the initial home country environment.

In quadrant 3 of Figure 8.3 the main problem facing MNE management is that each home base may be faced with specific isomorphic pulls that may be conflicting. It is important to realise that the isomorphic pulls faced by a specific sub-unit of an MNE may be entirely unrelated to the development of LB-FSAs in order to become more nationally responsive. The 'local' patterns to be emulated may be those prevailing in subsidiaries of other MNEs or in foreign operations of firms from related and supporting industries. In any case, the process of creating and diffusing NLB-FSAs throughout the intra-organisational network of an MNE may also be influenced by variations in isomorphic pulls arising from interorganisational linkages. More specifically, in the case of conflicting isomorphic pulls, a local-for-global approach could be established. Here, mimetic isomorphism by each subunit in a home base, — that is, its emulation of behavioural patterns considered successful in its specific interorganisational network — leads to selective coercive isomorphism in the intra-organisational network.

In other words, the activities of subunits elsewhere in the firm that are dependent on transfers of NLB-FSAs from a particular home base need to conform to what is viewed as legitimate by the subunit in that home base. In contrast, in the case of complementarities among isomorphic pulls faced by subunits in the different home bases, a global-for-global approach when developing new NLB-FSAs may be adopted. Here, it should be emphasised that the relevant isomorphic pulls must not be identical but complementary. Given the existence of complementary versus conflicting isomorphic pulls that characterise the interorganisational linkages faced by the subunits in each of the multiple home bases, the question arises as to the strategies that can be pursued by the MNE in order to cope with these external forces.

More specifically, the question is, whether an MNE should simply adopt a reactive strategy — a strategy of isomorphic flexibility, whereby it attempts to adapt itself as well as possible to existing isomorphic pulls arising from the relevant organisational field in the form of coercive, normative and or mimetic isomorphism as described by Westney (1993: 55). In this case, isomorphic pulls arising from the external environment largely determine the functioning of the intra-organisational network. An alternative is to change the external network, through a so-called 'institutionalisation project' approach. In this case, the intraorganisational network attempts to alter the external network. This problem of optimal 'transnational network' management is explored further in Rugman and Verbeke (1995).

CONCLUSION

In terms of generic strategies for MNEs, the key problem with the Porter frameworks of domestic competitive strategy (Porter 1980), global strategy (Porter 1986) and the home country diamond of national competitiveness (Porter 1990) is that all of them build upon a single home base. Competitive advantage is achieved by firms using their home base as a staging ground for globalisation. Yet simple analysis of the activities of MNEs shows that they now operate across multiple home bases rather than the single home base consistent with an international product cycle approach (Vernon 1966). Porter's work is 30 years out of date when applied to an analysis of MNEs. Indeed, most of the interesting research issues in international business today stem from the complexities of organising an MNE network across multiple home bases. The new framework advanced here is a useful starting point for realistic research on MNEs and their network organisational structures.

Michael Porter's (1980) three generic strategies of cost, differentiation and focus are transformed into five generics in the Porter (1986) paper on global strategy. Unfortunately, the resulting strategies are neither global nor generic. This paper demonstrates why. One key problem is Porter's peculiar use of the concept of national responsiveness. A new framework for generic strategies is developed here in which location-bound and non–location-bound firm-specific advantages are related to the number of home bases. This generates truly generic global strategies.

The second half of the chapter develops a new organising framework to analyse the role of transnational networks in global competition. It demonstrates that the analysis of transnational networks may lead to new insights regarding the sources of sustainable global competitive advantage. Previously, mainstream conceptual models in the international business literature neglected the formation of transnational networks as a condition for global competitiveness. These models, which include the eclectic paradigm (Dunning 1993a), the transnational solution framework (Bartlett and Ghoshal 1989) and the diamond of competitive advantage model (Porter 1990), fail to recognise the major role that transnational networks can fulfil in a context of global competition. The new framework suggests a classification of transnational network strategies which can incorporate other mainstream literature in international business.

Today, most MNEs function with multiple home bases. The problems faced by these firms to create and diffuse new knowledge go far beyond questions related to solving Porter-type home country-host country conflicts and require finding a balance between developing LB-FSAs and NLB-FSAs. The process of developing NLB-FSAs in an organisational context of multiple home bases is complicated further by the fact that not only the intraorganisational network must be managed, but also the interorganisational network(s). Isomorphic pulls arising from interorganisational linkages in each home base may be conflicting or complementary. The last unresolved issue is whether the intraorganisational network should adopt a strategy of isomorphic flexibility or make an attempt to alter the external context. A related question is whether these two options can be pursued simultaneously by a single MNE engaged in transnational network management, or whether one option needs to be selected, based on the administrative heritage of the intraorganisational network.

REFERENCES

Bartlett, C.A. 1986. Building and managing the transnational: The new organisational challenge. In Michael Porter (ed.), *Competition in Global Industries.* Boston, MA.: Harvard Business School Press, pp. 367–404.

Bartlett, C.A. and Ghoshal, S. 1989. *Managing Across Borders: The Transnational Solution.* Boston, MA: Harvard Business School Press.

Buckley, P. and Casson, M. 1976. *The Future of the Multinational Enterprise.* London: Macmillan.

Chandler, A.D. 1962. Strategy, and Structure. Chapters in *The History of the Industrial Enterprise.* Cambridge, MA: MIT Press.

Cho, Sung Dong and Porter, M.E. 1986. Changing Global Industry Leadership: The Case of Shipbuilding. In Michael Porder (ed.), *Competition in Global Industries,* Boston, MA: Harvard Business School Press, pp. 539–68.

Contractor F.J. and L'orange, P. 1988. *Cooperative Strategies in International Business,* Lexington, DC: Heath and Company.

D'Cruz, J.R. and Rugman, A.M. 1993. Developing international competitiveness: The five partners model. *Business Quarterly,* 58(2), Winter: 60–72.

D'Cruz, J.R. and Rugman, A.M. 1994. Business network theory and the Canadian telecommunications industry. *International Business Review,* 3(3): 275–88.

DiMaggio, P.J. and Powell, W.W. 1983. The iron cage revisited: Institutional isomorphism and collective rationality in organisational fields. *American Sociological Review,* 48: 147–60.

Doz, Y. 1986. *Strategic Management in Multinational Companies,* Oxford: Pergamon.

Doz, Y., Prahalad, C.K. and Hamel, G. 1990. Control, change and flexibility: The dilemma of transnational collaboration. In C.A. Bartlett, Y. Doz and G. Hedlund (eds), *Managing the Global Firm,* London: Routledge.

Dunning, J.H. 1981. *International Production and the Multinational Enterprise,* London: George Allen & Unwin.

Dunning, J.H. 1988. The eclectic paradigm of international production: A restatement and some possible extensions. *Journal of International Business Studies,* 19(1): 1–31.

Dunning, J.H. 1993a. *Multinational Enterprises and the Global Economy,* New York: Addision-Wesley.

Dunning, J.H. 1993b. *The Globalisation of Business: The Challenge of the 1990s,* London and New York: Routledge.

Enright, M.J. 1993. The geographic scope of competitive advantage. Working Paper, Harvard Business School, March.

Geringer, J.M. 1991. Strategic determinants of partner selection criteria in international joint ventures. *Journal of International Business Studies,* 22(1).

Ghoshal, S. 1987. Global strategy: An organizing framework. *Strategic Management Journal,* 8(5): 425–40.

Ghoshal, S. and Bartlett, C.A. 1988a. Innovation processes in multinational corporations. In M.L. Tushman and W.L. Moore (eds), pp. 499–518, *Readings in the Management of Innovation,* 2nd edn. New York: Harper Business.

Ghoshal, S. and Bartlett, C.A. 1988b. Creation, adoption, and diffusion of innovations by subsidiaries of multinational corporations. *Journal of International Business Studies,* 19(3): 365–88.

Ghoshal, S. and Westney, D.E. 1993. *Organisation Theory and the Multinational Corporation,* New York and London: St Martins Press.

Gupta, A.K. and Govindarajan, V. 1991. Knowledge flows and the structure of control within multinational corporations. *Academy of Management Review,* 16(4): 768–92.

Hedlund, G. 1986. The hypermodern MNC: A heterarchy? *Human Resource Management,* 25: 9–35.

Hedlund, G. 1993. Assumptions of hierarchy and heterarchy with applications to the management of the multinational corporation. In S. Ghoshal and D.E. Westney (eds), *Organisation Theory and the Multinational Corporation,* London: St Martins Press, pp. 211–36.

Hedlund, G. and Rolander, D. 1990. Actions in heterarchies: New approaches to managing the MNC. In C.A. Bartlett, Y. Doz and G. Hedlund (eds), *Managing the Global Firm,* London, Routledge, pp. 15–46.

Hennart, J.F. 1993. Control in multinational firms: The role of price and hierarchy. In S. Ghoshal and D.E. Westney (eds), *Organisation Theory and the*

Multinational Corporation, New York and London: St Martins Press, pp. 157–81.

Kim, W. Chan and R. Mauborgne 1993. Procedural justice theory and the multinational corporation. In S. Ghoshal and D.E. Westney (eds), *Organisation Theory and the Multinational Corporation,* New York and London: St Martins Press, pp. 237–55.

Kobrin, S. 1991. An empirical analysis of the determinants of global integration. *Strategic Management Journal.* 12, Special Issue: 17–31.

Kogut, B. 1985a. Designing global strategies: Comparative and competitive value-added chains. *Sloan Management Review,* Summer: 15–28.

Kogut, B. 1985b. Designing global strategies: Profiting from operational flexibility. *Sloan Management Review,* Fall: 27–38.

Krugman, P. 1991. *Geography and Trade,* London: MIT Press.

Martinez, J. and Jarillo, J.C. 1989. The evolution of research on coordination mechanisms in multinational corporations. *Journal of International Business Studies,* 20(3), Fall: 489–514.

Moon, C. 1994. A revised framework of global strategy: Extending the coordination–configuration framework. *The International Executive,* 36(5): 557–73.

Nonaka, I. 1990. Managing globalisation as a self-renewing process: Experiences of Japanese MNCs. In C.A. Bartlett, Y. Doz and G. Hedlund (eds), *Managing the Global Firm.* London: Routledge, pp. 69–94.

Porter, M.E. 1980. *Competitive Strategy: Techniques for Analyzing Industries and Companies,* New York: Free Press.

Porter, M.E. 1985. *Competitive Advantage: Creating and Sustaining Superior Performance*, New York: Free Press.

Porter, M.E. 1986. *Competition in Global Industries,* Boston, MA: Harvard Business School Press.

Porter, M.E. 1990. *The Competitive Advantage of Nations,* New York: Free Press.

Poynter, T.A. and Rugman, A.M. 1983. World product mandates: How will multinationals respond? *Business Quarterly,* 47(3): 5–61.

Prahalad, C.K. and Y. Doz 1987. *The Multinational Mission: Balancing Local Demands and Global Vision,* New York: The Free Press.

Roth, K. and A.K. Morrison 1990. An empirical analysis of the integration-reponsiveness framework in global industries. *Journal of International Business Studies,* 21(4): 541–64.

Roth, K. and A.K. Morrison 1992. Implementing global strategy: Characteristics of global subsidiary mandates. *Journal of International Business Studies,* 23(4).

Rugman. A.M. 1981. *Inside the Multinationals: The Economics of Internal Markets,* New York: Columbia University Press.

Rugman, A.M. and Bennett, J. 1982. Technology transfer and world product manufacturing in Canada. *Columbia Journal of World Business,* 18(4): 58–62.

Rugman, A.M. and Verbeke, A. 1990, Strategic Capital Budgeting Decisions and the Theory of Internalisation, *Managerial Finance,* 16 (2) Spring, pp. 17–24.

Rugman, A.M. and Verbeke, A. 1991a. Environmental change and global competitive strategy in Europe. In A.M. Rugman and A. Verbeke (eds), *Research in Global Strategic Management, Vol 2: Global Competition and the European Community.* Greenwich, Conn.: JAI Press, pp. 3–27.

Rugman, A.M. and Verbeke, A. 1991b. Mintzberg's intended and emergent corporate strategies and trade policies. *Canadian Journal of Administrative Sciences,* 8(3): 200–208.

Rugman, A.M. and Verbeke, A. 1991c. Trade barriers and corporate strategy in international companies. *Long Range Planning,* 24(3): 66–72.

Rugman, A.M. and Verbeke, A. 1992a. Shelter, trade policy and strategies for multinational enterprises. In A.M. Rugman and A. Verbeke (eds), *Research in Global Strategic Management Vol. 3: Corporate Response to Global Change,* Greenwich, Conn.: JAI Press, pp. 3–25.

Rugman, A.M. and Verbeke, A. 1992b. A note on the transnational solution and the transaction cost theory of multinational strategic management. *Journal of International Business Studies,* 23(4): 761–71.

Rugman, A.M. and Verbeke, A. 1993a. Generic strategies in global competition. In A.M. Rugman and A. Verbeke (eds), *Research in Global Strategic Management, Vol. 4: Global Competition: Beyond the Three Generics,* Greenwich, Conn.: JAI Press, pp. 3–15.

Rugman, A.M. and Verbeke, A. 1993b. Foreign subsidiaries and multinational strategic management: An extension and correction of Porter's single diamond framework. *Management International Review,* 33(1), Special Issue: 71–84.

Rugman, A.M. and Verbeke, A. 1995. Transnational networks and global competition: An organizing framework. In A.M. Rugman and A. Verbeke (eds), *Research in Global Strategic Management, Vol. 5: Beyond the Diamond,* Greenwich, Conn.: JAI Press, pp. 3–24.

Teece, D. 1983. A Transaction Cost Theory of the Multinational Enterprise. In M. Casson (ed.), *The Growth of International Business,* London: Allen & Unwin.

Teece, D. 1985. Multinational enterprise, internal governance and economic organisation. *American Economic Review,* 75: 233–38.

Tsurumi, Y. 1977. *Multinational Management,* Cambridge, Mass: Ballinger.

Vernon, R. 1966. International investment and international trade in the product cycle. *Quarterly Journal of Economics* 80(2): 190–207.

Vernon, R. 1979. The product cycle hypothesis in a new international environment. *Oxford Bulletin of Economics and Statistics,* 4: 255–67.

Westney, D.E. 1990. Internal and external linkages in the MNC: The case of R & D Subsidiaries in Japan. In C.A. Bartlett, Y. Doz and G. Hedlund (eds), *Managing the Global Firm.* New York and London: Routledge, pp. 279–302.

Westney, D.E. 1993. Institutionalisation theory and the multinational corporation. In S. Ghoshal and D.E. Westney (eds), *Organisation Theory and the Multinational Corporation,* New York and London: St Martins Press, pp. 237–55.

Williamson, O.E. 1981. The modern corporation: Origins, evolution, attributes. *Journal of Economic Literature,* 19 (December): 537–68.

9. An Invisible History, a Competitive Future: Women Managers in a Worldwide Economy[1]

Nancy Adler and Dafna Izraeli[2]

> The best reason for believing that more women will be in charge before long is that in a ferociously competitive global economy, no company can afford to waste valuable brainpower simply because it's wearing a skirt. (Fisher 1992: 56)

World business has become intensely competitive. Top-quality people allow corporations to compete. Yet, while outstanding human resource systems provide competitive advantages, companies worldwide draw from a restricted pool of potential managers. Although women represent over 50 per cent of the world population, in no country do women represent half, or even close to half, of the corporate managers. Even in the United States, where many believe the proportion of female executives to be outstanding, reality belies the belief: whereas half of the American workforce is female, women constitute only 3–5 per cent of the expatriate managers (Moran, Stahl and Boyer 1988), 3 per cent of the senior executives (Ball 1991; Segal and Zellner 1992) and less than half of a per cent of the highest paid officers and directors (Fierman 1990).

CROSS-NATIONAL COMPARISONS

Until the late 1970s, women were virtually invisible as managers and their absence was generally considered a non-issue (Antal and Izraeli 1993). Since then, women managers have become increasingly visible in many countries where broad societal forces during recent decades have resulted in more women entering lower level managerial positions.

In the economically developing and recently industrialised countries, a shift took place between the 1950s and early 1970s from agrarian towards intensive industries, primarily by multinational corporations, created a demand for cheap labour that brought many women into the urban labour force. Governments saw increasing women's labour force participation as essential for national economic growth and development and therefore encouraged women's economic activity. These governments, however, had no special interest in women's promotion into management. Moreover, the traditional male ethos associated with manufacturing industries made industrial firms less friendly towards women managers than the next wave of service sector firms would be.

In both the industrialised and industrialising worlds, the expansion of the public and service sectors, along with the increased importance of staff positions, became major factors promoting women's initial breakthrough into management. The expansion of banking and other financial services opened opportunities for women in lower and middle level management positions. In most countries in the 1970s and 1980s, the growing public sector also absorbed the growing population of educated women into lower level managerial positions. As new jobs were created, women moved into management and men moved up the hierarchy. Reference to positive stereotypes — such as recognising Asian women's traditional experience managing family finances and regarding women as more honest and trustworthy than men — helped employers rationalise women's presence in what had previously been a male domain (see Chan and Lee 1994; Cheng and Liao 1994; Siengthai and Leelakulthanit 1994; and Steinhoff and Tanaka 1994, among others).

Economic growth and increasing global competition also heightened the demand for top quality managers in both the industrialised and industrialising worlds. Economic enterprises began to take advantage of the growing availability of qualified women to fill the new positions. In each country, however, the specific processes used to bring about change differed.

In the United States, powerful women's groups used the political process and the courts to help establish regulations that held employers responsible for implementing equal opportunity within their organisations (see Fagenson and Jackson 1994). Such political and legal changes made it in organisations' self-interest to open their doors to women for lower level managerial positions. However, neither the political nor the legal changes were sufficiently powerful to counter resistance to women entering the most senior levels.

In France, legislation passed in the 1980s gave unions responsibility for negotiating equal opportunity on behalf of women. Progress, however, was very limited. The French unions appear to have lacked sufficient motivation to effect the previously legislated societal changes. Many French observers believe that the union leaders, most of whom are men, share management's prejudicial attitudes against women (Serdjenian 1994).

In Hong Kong, where government intervention in commerce has been purposefully minimal and sex discrimination in employment continues to be legal, the proportion of women among corporate managers remains negligible (see De Leon and Ho 1994).

In the social welfare states of Western Europe and Israel, social democratic parties created large public service bureaucracies that became the major employers of women and therefore provided a major channel for women moving into management. Not surprisingly in these countries, gender segregation emerged along sectorial lines, with women managers concentrated in the public sector and men in the private sector (see, for example, Hanninen-Salmelin and Petajaniemi 1994; and Izraeli 1994).

Under communist rule, Eastern European countries and the former Soviet Union set quotas for women in local level management. However, women remained highly under-represented in more senior and national positions. In the former Yugoslavia, for example, opportunities for women managers depended on the political interests of the Communist Party (see Kavcic 1994). Women's chances for promotion were best during periods of economic growth and political calm. However, during the times when political unrest was greatest, the proportion of women promoted into and within management dropped. At those times, the Communist Party allocated positions either to men known to be loyal to the Party or to men whose loyalty it needed to secure. In Poland, since women rarely filled managerial positions in state enterprises, few now have sufficient experience to draw upon for managing in the new market-oriented economy (see Siemienska 1994). The large women's organisations in certain former communist countries, such as Poland and Russia, operated essentially as extensions of the Communist Party. As such, they served primarily a social control function for the Party, rather than an advocacy role for women (see Puffer 1994; and Siemienska 1994).

Countries recently freed from communist rule appear to be experiencing a male backlash against many of the policies that were supportive of women's employment, professional advancement and general freedoms (Moghadam 1992). For example, high unemployment has increased competition, including for managerial positions, most often to women's detriment.

In addition, due to a lack of funds, most former communist countries have chosen to severely reduce the extensive network of childcare services, thus further increasing unemployment among women managers forced to quit working because too few acceptable childcare options remain available. Moreover, the belief that a woman's place is in the home is replacing the quota system that guaranteed women's representation in lower and middle level management in most former communist countries. For example, under pressure from the Catholic Church, the Polish parliament recently passed a severely limiting anti-abortion law. In Russia, Poland, Eastern Germany and parts of former Yugoslavia, women face a difficult struggle ahead to maintain or regain their previous representation in the economy (see Antal and Krebsbach-Gnath 1994; Kavcic 1994; Puffer 1994; Siemienska 1994). Only now are women in these transitional economies beginning to organise to advance their professional and political status and interests (Moghadam 1992).

Other countries, such as Singapore, Malaysia, Indonesia and Zimbabwe, have only recently emerged from extended periods of colonial rule. Colonialism's impact on women differed in important ways from its impact on men. For example, in colonial Indonesia, the Dutch recruited upper class men for roles in the civil service and reinforced women's exclusion from public life (see Wright and Crockett-Tellei 1994). Moreover, the Dutch in Indonesia did not develop an educational system for the local people. In contrast, the Americans introduced universal education in the Philippines, thus giving Philippine women a decided advantage in urban labour markets compared with women from many other post-colonial countries. In Zimbabwe, where white men control the private business sector and black men control family life, black women continue to face a double challenge, both as women and as black women (Muller 1994; also see Erwee 1994 for similar patterns in South Africa).

In most post-colonial countries, women participated in the struggle for liberation. A number of them later became members of their country's new government, thus providing role models for other women. However, because they were brought into government positions only by these unusual circumstances, the token women leaders did not necessarily become harbingers for succeeding women's continued involvement in the centers of economic or political power. More commonly, they emerged as exceptions to a pattern that generally continues to exclude women from power (see Muller 1994). This exclusion has most frequently reasserted itself with the passing of the original leadership.

To date, there is no systematic research on the few executive women of almost every nationality who have succeeded in assuming very senior positions: however, they appear to come from the same societal groups as do male executives. For example, in cultures in which executives are drawn primarily from the upper classes, such as from the Javanese Priyayi in Indonesia, the few female executives, like their male counterparts, are most likely to come from elite families in which family connections smooth the way for business success (Wright and Crockett-Tellei 1994). Similarly, in cultures such as Hong Kong in which the dominant enterprise structure is the family business, senior women, like their male counterparts, are most likely to run their family's business (De Leon and Ho 1994). In such cultures, executives generally view themselves as working in the service of their family. However, for a woman, being an executive in a family business is not necessarily recognised as qualifying her to assume an executive position in a non-family enterprise. For example, in the Malaysian province of Kelantin, where women have traditionally dominated both business activity and family finances while men worked primarily in agriculture, the proportion of women who have been promoted into upper-level managerial positions in non-family enterprises and government organisations remains negligible (Mansor 1994).

WOMEN AS SENIOR EXECUTIVES AND EXPATRIATE MANAGERS

Until recently, a single theme dominated questions about women managers worldwide: the concern for understanding their under-representation, under-utilisation and skewed distribution among the levels of domestic and international management. Only in the 1990s has the question of global competitiveness and transnational efficacy begun to transform and complement these equity-based concerns.

While the proportion of women managers increased significantly in recent years in all countries for which data are available, the anticipated breakthrough into the centres of organisational power seems even less likely today than it did twenty years ago, when the groundbreaking book *Breakthrough: Women into Management* noted: 'it's when and how, not if women move up. The groundwork has been laid (Loring and Wells 1972: 15).'

This optimism was reflected in many of the countries described in our earlier book, *Women in Management Worldwide* (Adler and Izraeli 1988), the first to provide a multinational perspective on women in management. We were cautioned, however, that we must analyse the gains carefully to separate myth from reality (Keller Brown 1988).

Whereas the optimism about women's movement into management appears to have been well-grounded, the optimism about women moving into the international arena or up into the executive suite now appears to have been premature. Conditions that we, like other observers, expected would remove the barriers to women's progress throughout the profession of management, left most women well below the glass ceiling, where they could glimpse the executive suite but not quite enter it. Similarly, it left most women in domestic positions while power was shifting to the global market

(Calas and Smircich 1993). Women's increased investment in higher education and greater commitment to management as a career, as well as new equal opportunity legislation and the shortage (or anticipated shortage) of high quality managers, did not result in a significant breakthrough either into international management or into the executive suite. Regardless of the proportion of women managers at lower levels, women in every country remain only a tiny fraction of those sent on international assignments and of those who make it to senior positions (Segal and Zellner 1992). According to *Business Week*, at the current rates it will be 475 years before women reach equality in the executive suite (Spillar 1992:76).

MYTHS ABOUT WOMEN MANAGING ACROSS BORDERS

As cross-border business becomes pervasive and more firms become multinational and transnational, global assignments form an increasingly important component of the new definition of managerial roles (see Adler and Bartholomew 1992). Within this context, the issue of women as expatriate managers grows in importance (see, for example, Izraeli and Zeira 1994). Given the historical scarcity of local women managers in almost all countries, the majority of firms have questioned if women can succeed in cross-border managerial assignments. They have believed that the relative absence of local women managers formed a basis for accurately predicting the potential for success, or lack thereof, of expatriate women. To predict the salience of women's roles in management in the twenty-first century, it is important to investigate the underlying assumptions that firms make about the role of women in international management.

Given the importance of these questions to future business success, a multi-part study was conducted on the role of women as expatriate managers. Research revealed a set of assumptions that managers and executives make about how foreigners would treat expatriate women, based on their beliefs about how foreign firms treat their own local women. The problem with the story is that the assumptions have proven to be false. Moreover, because the assumptions fail to accurately reflect reality, they are inadvertently causing executives to make decisions that are neither effective nor equitable.

Three beliefs about women's unsuitability for international assignments are widely held to be true, although not supported by the facts of the case. Because they are held to be true, however, they become true in their consequences and serve to limit women's opportunities in international management.

The three most commonly held 'myths' about women in international management are:

- Myth 1: Women do not want to be international managers.
- Myth 2: Companies refuse to send women abroad.
- Myth 3: Foreigners' prejudice against women renders them ineffective, even when interested in foreign assignments and successful in being sent.

These assumptions are labelled myths because, although widely believed by both men and women, their accuracy had never been tested until the 1980s (Adler 1984a, 1984b, 1987, 1994).

Myth 1: Women Do Not Want to Be International Managers

Is the problem that women are less interested than men in pursuing international careers? The study tested this myth by surveying more than a thousand graduating MBAs from seven top management schools in the United States, Canada and Europe (see Adler 1984b, 1986). The results revealed an overwhelming case of no significant difference: female and male MBAs display equal interest, or disinterest, in pursuing international careers. More than four out of five MBAs — both women and men — want an international assignment at some time during their career. Both female and male MBAs, however, agree that firms offer fewer opportunities to women than to men and significantly fewer opportunities to women pursuing international careers than to those pursuing domestic careers.

Although there may have been a difference in the past, women and men today are equally interested in international management, including in expatriate assignments. The first myth — that women do not want to be international managers — is false; it is, in fact, a myth.

Myth 2: Companies Refuse to Send Women Abroad

If the problem is not women's disinterest, is it that companies refuse to select women for international assignments? To test if the myth of corporate resistance was true, human resource vice-presidents and managers from 60 of the largest North American multinationals were surveyed (see Adler 1984a). Over half of the companies reported that they hesitate to send women abroad. Almost four times as many reported being reluctant to select women for international assignments as for domestic management positions. When asked why they hesitate, almost three-quarters reported believing that foreigners were so prejudiced against women that the female managers could not succeed even if sent. Similarly, 70 per cent believed that dual-career issues were insurmountable. In addition, some human resource executives expressed concern about the women's physical safety, the hazards involved in travelling in underdeveloped countries and especially in the case of single women, the isolation and loneliness.

Many of the women who succeeded in being sent abroad as expatriate managers report having confronted some form of corporate resistance before being sent abroad. For some, their firms seemed to offer them an expatriate position only after all potential male candidates had turned it down. Moreover, although most of the women were sent in the same capacity as their male expatriate colleagues, some companies demonstrated their hesitation by offering temporary or travel assignments rather than regular expatriate positions.

These findings concur with those of 100 top line managers in Fortune 500 firms, the majority of whom believed that women face overwhelming resistance when seeking managerial positions in international divisions of US firms (Thal and Cateora 1979). Similarly, 80 per cent of US firms report believing that women would face disadvantages if sent abroad (Moran, Stahl and Boyer 1988). Thus the second myth is true: firms are hesitant, if not outright resistant, to sending female managers abroad.

Myth 3: Foreigners' 'Prejudice' Against Female Expatriate Managers

Is it true that foreigners are so prejudiced against women that they could not succeed as international managers? Would sending a female manager abroad be neither fair to the woman nor effective for the company? Is the treatment of local women the best predictor of expatriate women's potential to succeed? The fundamental question was and remains, whether the historic discrimination against local women worldwide is a valid basis for predicting expatriate women's success as international managers.

To investigate this third myth — that foreigners' prejudice against women renders them ineffective as international managers, over 100 women managers from major North American firms who were on expatriate assignments around the world were surveyed. Fifty-two were interviewed while in Asia or after having returned from Asia to North America (Adler 1987; Jelinek and Adler 1988). Others were interviewed during or following assignments in Africa, Europe, Latin America and the Middle East. Since most of the women held regional responsibility, their experience represents multiple countries rather than just their country of foreign residence.

Who Are the Female Expatriate Managers?

The women were very well educated and quite internationally experienced. Almost all held graduate degrees, the MBA being the most common. Over three-quarters had had extensive international interests and experience prior to their present company sending them abroad. On average, the women spoke two or three languages, with some fluently speaking as many as six. In addition, they had excellent social skills. Nearly two-thirds were single and only very few had children.

Firms using transnational strategies sent more women than did those using other strategies, with financial institutions leading all other industries. On average, the expatriate assignments lasted two-and-a-half years, with a range from six months to six years. The women supervised from zero to 25 subordinates, with the average falling just below five. Their titles and levels within their firms varied: some held very junior positions — assistant account manager — while others held quite senior positions — for example, regional vice-president. In no firm did a female expatriate hold her company's number one position in the region or in any country.

The Decision to Go

For most firms, the female expatriates were 'firsts': only 10 per cent followed another woman into her international position. Of the 90 per cent who were 'firsts', almost a quarter represented the first female manager the firm had ever sent abroad.

Others were the first women sent to the region, the first sent to the particular country, or the first to fill the specific expatriate position. Clearly, neither the women nor the companies had the luxury of role models or of following previously established patterns. Except for several major financial institutions, both the women and the companies found themselves experimenting, in hope of uncertain success.

Most women described themselves as needing to encourage their companies to consider the possibility of assigning international positions to women in general and to themselves in particular. In more than four out of five cases, the woman initially suggested the idea of an international assignment to her boss and company. For only six women did the company first suggest the assignment.

Since most firms had never considered sending a female manager abroad, the women used a number of strategies to introduce the idea and to position their careers internationally. Many explored the possibility of an international assignment during their original job interview and eliminated companies from consideration that were totally against the idea. Other women informally introduced the idea to their boss and continued to mention it at appropriate moments until the company ultimately decided to offer her an expatriate position. A few women formally applied for a number of international assignments prior to actually being selected and sent.

Many women attempted to be in the right place at the right time. For example, one woman who predicted that Vietnam would be her firm's next major growth area arranged to assume responsibility for the Vietnam desk at headquarters, leaving the rest of Asia to a male colleague. The strategy paid off: within a year, the company elevated the importance of their Vietnamese operations and sent her to Asia as one of their first female expatriate managers.

Most women claimed that their companies had failed to recognise the possibility of selecting women for international assignments, rather than having thoroughly considered the idea and then having rejected it. For the majority of the women, the obstacle appeared to be the company's naivete, not malice. For many women, the most difficult hurdle in their international career involved getting sent abroad in the first place, not — as most had anticipated — gaining the respect of foreigners and succeeding once sent.

Did it Work? The Impact of Being Female

Almost all of the female expatriate managers (97 per cent) reported that their international assignments were successful. This success rate is considerably higher than that reported for North American male expatriates. While the women's assessments were subjective, objective indicators support that most assignments, in fact, succeeded. For example, the majority of the firms — after experimenting with their first female expatriate manager — decided to send more women abroad. In addition, most companies promoted the women on the basis of their foreign performance and/or offered them other international assignments following completion of the first one.

Advantages

Given the third myth, the women would have been expected to experience a series of difficulties caused by their being female and, perhaps, to create a corresponding set of solutions designed to overcome each difficulty. This was not the case. Almost half of the expatriates (42 per cent) reported that being female served as more of an advantage than a disadvantage; 16 per cent found it to be both positive and negative; 22 per cent saw it as being either irrelevant or neutral; and only 20 per cent found it to be primarily negative.

The women reported numerous professional advantages to being female, including high visibility, accessibility and memorability. Most frequently, they described the advantage of being highly visible. Foreign clients were curious about them, wanted to meet them and remembered them after the first encounter. The women therefore found it easier for them than for their male colleagues to gain access to foreign clients' time and attention.

Similarly, contrary to the third myth, the female managers discovered a number of advantages based on their interpersonal skills, including that the local men could talk more easily about a wider range of topics with them than with their male counterparts. Many women also described the high social status accorded local women and found that such status was not denied them as foreign women. The women often received special treatment that their male counterparts did not receive. Clearly, it was always salient that they were women, but being a woman was not antithetical to succeeding as a manager.

In addition, most of the women described benefiting from a 'halo effect'. Few of the women's foreign colleagues and clients had ever met or previously worked with a female expatriate manager. Similarly, the local community was highly aware of how unusual it was for North American multinationals to send female managers abroad. Hence the local managers assumed that the women would not have been sent unless they were 'the best', and therefore expected them to be 'very, very good'.

Disadvantages

The women also experienced a number of disadvantages in being female expatriate managers. Interestingly enough, the majority of the disadvantages involved the women's relationship with their home companies, not with their foreign colleagues and clients.

As noted earlier, a major problem involved the women's difficulty in obtaining an international position in the first place. Another problem involved home companies initially limiting the duration of the women's assignments, or labelling the assignment as temporary. While short-term or temporary assignments may appear to offer companies a logically cautious strategy, in reality they create an unfortunate self-fulfilling prophecy. When the home company is not convinced that a woman can succeed (and therefore offers her a temporary, rather than a permanent, position), it communicates the company's lack of confidence to foreign colleagues and clients as a lack of commitment. The foreigners then mirror the home company's behaviour by also failing to take the woman manager seriously. Assignments become very difficult, or can fail altogether, when companies demonstrate a lack of initial confidence and commitment.

A subsequent problem involved the home company limiting the woman's professional opportunities and job scope once she was abroad. Many female expatriates experienced difficulties in persuading their home companies to give them latitude equivalent to that given to their male counterparts, especially initially. For example, some companies, out of supposed concern for the woman's safety, limited her travel (and thus the regional scope of her responsibility), thus excluding very remote, rural and underdeveloped areas. Other companies, as mentioned previously, initially limited the duration of the woman's assignment to six months or a year, rather than the more standard two to three years.

A few companies limited the women to working only internally with company employees, rather than externally with corporate clients, suppliers and government officials. These companies often implicitly assumed that their own employees were somehow less prejudiced than were outsiders. In reality, the women often found the opposite to be true. They faced more problems from home country nationals within their own organisations than externally from local clients and colleagues.

Managing foreign clients' and colleagues' initial expectations was one area that proved difficult for many women. Some found initial meetings to be 'tricky', especially when a male colleague from their own company was present. Since most local managers had never previously met a North American expatriate woman who held a managerial position, there was considerable ambiguity as to who she was, her status, her level of expertise, authority and responsibility and therefore the appropriate form of address and demeanour toward her.

Since most North American women whom local managers had ever met previously were expatriates' wives or secretaries, they naturally assumed that the new woman was not a manager. Hence, they often directed initial conversations to male colleagues, not to the newly arrived female manager. Senior male colleagues, particularly those from the head office, became very important in redirecting the focus of early discussions back toward the women. When this was done, old patterns were quickly broken and smooth ongoing work relationships were established. When the pattern was ignored or poorly managed, the challenges to credibility, authority and responsibility became chronic and undermined the women's effectiveness.

As mentioned earlier, many women described the most difficult aspect of the foreign assignment as getting sent abroad in the first place. Overcoming resistance from the North American home company frequently proved more challenging than gaining local clients' and colleagues' respect and acceptance. In most cases, assumptions about foreigners' prejudice against female expatriate managers appear to have been exaggerated: the anticipated prejudice and the reality did not match. It appears that foreigners are not as prejudiced as many North American managers had assumed.

The Gaijin *Syndrome*

One pattern is particularly clear: first and foremost, foreigners are seen as foreigners. Like their male colleagues, female expatriates are seen as foreigners, not as local people. A woman who is a foreigner (a *gaijin) is* not expected to act like the local women. Therefore, the societal and cultural rules governing the behaviour of local women that limit their access to managerial positions and responsibility do not apply to foreign women. Although women are considered the 'culture bearers' in all societies, foreign women are not expected to assume the cultural roles that societies have traditionally reserved for their own women.

It seems that most corporate representatives have confused an adjective, *foreign,* with a noun, *woman,* in predicting foreigners' reactions to expatriate women. We expected the most salient characteristic of a female expatriate manager to be that she is a *woman* and predicted her success as based on the success of the local women in each country. In fact, the most salient characteristic is that expatriates *are foreign* and the best predictor of their success is the success of other foreigners (in this case, other North Americans) in the particular country. *Local managers see female expatriates as foreigners who happen to be women, not as women who happen to be foreigners.* The difference is crucial. Given the uncertainty involved in sending women managers to all areas of the world, our assumptions about the greater salience of gender (female/male) over nationality (foreign/local) have caused us to make false predictions concerning women's potential to succeed as executives and managers in foreign countries.

The third myth — that foreigners' prejudice precludes women's effectiveness as international managers — is false; it is, in fact, a myth. Of the three myths, only the second myth proved to be true. The first myth proved false: women are interested in working internationally. The third myth proved false: women do succeed internationally, once sent. However, the second myth proved to be true: Companies are hesitant, if not completely unwilling, to send women managers abroad. Given that the problem is caused primarily by the home companies' assumptions and decisions, the solutions are also largely within their control.

CONCLUSION

Global competition and the need for top quality managers are making women's promotion into global responsibility and senior management a business issue, rather than strictly an issue of equity. Global competition, already intense in the 1990s, will not diminish in the twenty-first century.

Can corporations risk not choosing the best person just because her gender does not fit the traditional managerial profile? Needs for competitive advantage, not an all-consuming social conscience, may answer the question, if not in fact define it. Successful companies will select both women and men to manage their domestic and cross-border operations. The option of limiting senior and global management positions to men has become an archaic 'luxury' that no company can afford. The only remaining question is how quickly and effectively each company will increase the number and use of women in their worldwide managerial workforce. Some observers already argue that the 'number of qualified women will soon be so great that ignoring them will be bad business' (Segal and Zellner 1992: 76). While this may well be true, those in power are only now beginning to recognise the broader economic and competitive advantages of sharing the executive ranks with more women.

The intensification of global competition has become a major influence compelling executives to view women managers as a competitive advantage rather than as a legislated necessity. Global competition challenges corporations to maximise the effectiveness of their human resources. The successful performance of growing numbers of women managers offers firms an opportunity to out-perform their more prejudiced competitors by better using women's talents. A number of leading transnational firms have already accepted this reality and begun to act accordingly (see Adler 1994 and 1987).

NOTES

[1]   This chapter is based on Nancy J. Adler and Dafna N. Izraeli's (eds) 1994.
[2]   Authors names are listed in alphabetical order.

REFERENCES

Adler, Nancy J. 1984a. Expecting international success: Female managers overseas. *Columbia Journal of World Business*, 193: 79–85.
Adler, Nancy J. 1984b. Women do not want international careers and other myths about international management. *Organizational Dynamics*, 132: 66–79.
Adler, Nancy J. 1986. Do MBAs want international careers? *International Journal of Intercultural Relations*, 103: 277–300.
Adler, Nancy J. 1987. Pacific Basin managers: A gaijin, not a woman. *Human Resource Management*, 262: 169–91.
Adler, Nancy J. 1994. *Competitive frontiers: Women managers in the Triad*, International Studies of Management and Organisation. In press.
Adler, Nancy J. and Bartholomew, Susan 1992. Managing globally competent people. *Academy Of Management Executive*, 63: 52–65.

Adler, Nancy J. and Izraeli, Dafna N. (eds) 1988. *Women in Management Worldwide*, Armonk, New York: M.E. Sharpe.

Adler, Nancy J. and Izraelik Dafna N. (eds) 1994. *Competitive Frontiers: Women Managers in a Global Economy,* Cambridge, Oxford: Blackwell Publishing.

Antal, Ariane Berthoin and Izraeli, Dafna N. 1993. Women managers from a global perspective: Women managers in their international homelands and as expatriates. In Ellen A. Fagenson (ed.), *Women in Management: Trends. Perspectives and Challenges*, 4, Newbury Park: California, Sage.

Antal, Ariane Berthoin and Krebsbach-Gnath, Camilla 1994. Women in management in Germany: East, West, and reunited in Adler and Izraeli (1994).

Ball, Karen 1991. Study finds few women hold top executive jobs. *Washington Post*, 26 August: A–11.

Calas, Marta B. and Smircich, Linda. 1993. Dangerous liaisons: The feminine-in-management meets globalization. *Business Horizons*, March–April: 73–83.

Chan, Audrey and Lee, Jean 1994. Women executives in a newly industrialized economy: The Singapore scenario, in Adler and Izraeli (1994).

Cheng, Wei-Yuan and Liao, Lung-li 1994. Women managers in Taiwan, in Adler and Izraeli (1994).

De Leon, Corrina and Ho, Suk-Ching 1994. The third identity of modern Chinese women: Female managers in Hong Kong, in Adler and Izraeli (1994).

Erwee, Ronel 1994. South African women: Changing career patterns, in Adler and Izraeli (1994).

Fagenson, Ellen and Jackson, Janice J. 1994. The status of women managers in the United States in Adler and Izraeli (1994).

Fierman, Jaclyn 1990. Why women still don't hit the top. *Fortune*, 30 July: 40–62.

Fisher, Anne B. 1992. When will women get to the top? *Fortune*, 21 September: 44–56.

Hanninen-Salmelin, Eva and Petajaniemi, Tulikki 1994. Women managers, the challenge to management: The case of Finland in Adler and Izraeli (1994).

Izraeli, Dafna N. 1994. Outsiders in the promised land: Women managers in Israel in Adler and Izraeli (1994)..

Izraeli, Dafna N. and Zeira, Yoram 1994. Women as managers in international business: A research review and appraisal. *Business and the Contemporary World*, 53, Summer: 35–46.

Jelinek, Mariann and Adler, Nancy J. 1988. Women: World-class managers for global competition. *Academy of Management Executive*, 21: 11–19.

Kavcic, Bogdan 1994. Women in management: The case of the former Yugoslavia in Adler and Izraeli (1994).

Keller Brown, Linda 1988. Female managers in the United States and in Europe: Corporate boards, MBA credentials, and the image/illusion of progress. In Nancy J. Adler and Dafna N. Izraeli (eds), *Women in Management Worldwide*, Armonk, New York: M.E. Sharpe, pp. 265–74.

Loring, Rosalind and Wells, Theodora 1972. *Breakthrough: Women into Management*. New York: Van Norstrand Reinhold.

Mansor, Norma 1994. Women managers in Malaysia: Their mobility and challenges in Adler and Izraeli (1994).

Moghadam, Valentine M. 1992. *Privatization and Democratization in Central and Eastern Europe and the Soviet Union: The Gender Dimension*, Helsinki: WIDER Institute of the United Nations University.

Moran, Stahl and Boyer, Inc. 1988. *Status of American Female Expatriate Employees: Survey Results*, Boulder, Col: International Division.

Muller, Helen J. 1994. The legacy and opportunities for women managers in Zimbabwe in Adler and Izraeli (1994).

Puffer, Sheila 1994. Women managers in the former USSR: A case of too much equality in Adler and Izraeli (1994).

Segal, Amanda Troy and Zellner, Wendy 1992. Corporate women: Progress? Sure. But the playing field is still far from level. *Business Week*, 8 June: 74–78.

Serdjenian, Evelyne 1994. Women managers in France in Adler and Izraeli (1994).

Siemienska, Renata 1994. Women managers in Poland: In transition from communism to democracy in Adler and Izraeli (1994).

Siengthai, Sununta and Leelakulthanit, Orose 1994. Women managers in Thailand in Adler and Izraeli (1994).

Spillar, K. 1992. Quoted in Segal, Amanda Troy and Zellner, Wendy 1992. Corporate women: progress? Sure. But the playing field is still far from level. *Business Week,* June 3: 74–78.

Steinhoff, Patricia and Tanaka, Kazuko 1994. Women executives in Japan in Adler and Izraeli (1994).

Thal, N. and Cateora, P. 1979. Opportunities for Women in International Business. *Business Horizons,* 22(6): 21–27.

Wright, Lorna and Crockett-Telli, Virginia 1994. Women in management in Indonesia in Adler and Izraeli (1994).

10. The Ties that Bond?

Mark Casson, Ray Loveridge and Satwinder Singh

INTRODUCTION

As Buckley (1994) has noted, the long–term dominance of multinational enterprises (MNEs) in world production and trade has brought about a growing convergence between the literature of international business and the more prescriptive writings of authors on strategic management. Both traditions recognise that relations between the parent firm and its overseas subsidiaries are critical in exploiting worldwide economies of internalisation (Buckley and Casson 1976; Teece 1981; Casson 1990). For example, strategic theorists, such as Bartlett and Ghoshal (1989), argue that overseas subsidiaries can be important sources of innovation and of corporate responsiveness to local market needs, provided they are allowed sufficient autonomy in their operations by headquarters.

This shared concern for better control over both internal and external factors has been taken further by a growing body of theorists from several disciplines who have emphasised the strategic benefits of an entrepreneurial corporate culture (Williamson 1981; Wanous 1992; Casson 1995). Employee commitment towards a collective mission and a set of goals formulated by corporate management is advanced as the most important source of 'sustainable competitive advantage' (Barney 1986; Schoemaker 1990). The advantages that are claimed include reduced strategic uncertainty and greater honesty, loyalty and effort by employees. Corporate culture is thus seen as a potentially valuable asset that is unique to the organisation.

The historical context for this radical return to the analysis of intangible sources of comparative advantage is associated with the emergence firstly of Japan and then of other ASEAN countries as competitors for global market positions hitherto held by Western countries (Ouchi 1981; Ohmae 1985). However the mixed results obtained by Western firms' attempts to achieve the cultural bases for 'excellence' described by Peters and Waterman (1982) in their influential analysis of 'world–class performance' has brought about a more circumspect view among management writers of the benefits of engineering cultural symbols in the manner recommended by the latter authors (Trice and Meyer 1993). Short–term revolutions in corporate culture are no substitute for long–term continuity in establishing the ideational and institutional bases for employee compliance, as several regional and national studies of economic development have emphasised (Bendix 1956; Maurice and Sellier 1979; Sorge and Warner 1986). Indeed, the success of 'late developing' nations such as Japan and other ASEAN economies is partly due, it is claimed, to their selective retention and reinforcement of a range of traditional (pre–industrial) attitudes, practices and symbolic forms within the national corporate environment (Dore 1973).

The institutional complementarity between the firm and its national context has been given even greater significance by the concept of the 'national business system' (NBS) (Whitley 1992). Evolutionary and institutional economists such as Nelson (1993), Mowery (1992) and Lundvall (1992) represent national configurations of institutions as varying in adaptive capability and therefore assess them as 'national innovation systems'. Porter (1990) assesses the 'national competitive advantage' of such systems in terms of relatively tangible factors such as the competitiveness of domestic markets for new products, but others, most notably Chandler (1990) and Lodge and Vogel (1987), argue that competitive advantages arise out of the associational cultures of cooperative capitalism or 'communitarianism'. Thus the dramatic success of some MNEs located in the Newly Industrialising Countries (NICs) is seen not to have been associated with direct government intervention in any uniform way across those new nations, but in their selective preservation of various institutionalised modes of inter–firm association and of individual commitment to adapted forms of traditional, hierarchically disposed relationships.

An obvious tension exists between these rival culturally based explanations of economic performance. One asserts the hegemony of corporate norms and of the socialising process by which they are fashioned, while the other emphasises the national or regional context and the distinctive orientations provided by local communities. This tension exists in the actual operations of the MNE, as evidenced by the conflicting role norms and subsequent experiences of stress among expatriate managers (Gregersen and Black 1992). Moreover, in his classic study of international management, Hofstede (1980) has demonstrated wide differences in nationality–related value orientations among managers employed worldwide by IBM. (This 1980 study gained significance from the fact that IBM had practised an elaborate programme of screening and socialisation of its staff in the manner of a 'total institution' since the early years of this century (Rodgers 1971).)

By the same token, it is clear that the strategies pursued by MNE parents themselves reveal the cultural and institutional effects of their national location. Perlmutter's (1969) influential taxonomy of corporate styles of MNE management suggested a predominance of ethnocentric, or domestically influenced, approaches to strategic control. Attempts at geocentric or universalistic standards or polycentric, devolved modes of management can themselves be related to the history of the company and its national context. This association can, indeed, be extended to the manner in which the domestic origins of the MNE have affected patterns of trade and inter–firm relations within sectors or industries. Thus the development of Shell/BP in petro chemicals and Unilever within food processing cannot easily be detached from the colonial history of Britain and the Netherlands, while that of Ford, GM and Chrysler reflects their access to a domestic market that has exceeded the overseas markets tapped by their early 'overspill' operations (Porter 1990; Loveridge 1994).

THE SAMPLE

The evidence presented in this paper derives from an UK government–funded (ESRC) survey of Fortune 500 firms involving postal questionnaires and interviews with their senior personnel executives. The purpose of the study was to explore the relationship between HRM practice and the stances adopted by senior management towards other strategic issues. The research design allowed for differences between parent (or head office) views and those held in overseas subsidiaries or affiliates.[1]

The survey has been described in detail elsewhere (Casson, Loveridge and Singh 1996a) and only a brief account will be given here. The sample included thirteen parent countries in which firms were headquartered, together with twelve host countries in which they operated. Some 200 affiliates and 50 parents responded to our postal questionnaire and a total of 47 firms were subsequently interviewed *in situ* using semi–structured approaches. Some countries such as France are represented by parents only, while others, such as Brazil, are represented only as host countries.[2]

Non–respondents were typically smaller firms and those that appeared to be most heavily affected by managerial delayering, restructuring or the effects of recent acquisition and merger. In telephone follow–up interviews with non–respondents, it became clear that many personnel managers were involved in large scale destaffing exercises which they found professionally demoralising. In this context the subject of our enquiry took on added significance and provoked a disbelief by respondents about its random nature.

The overall response of 17 per cent is therefore reflective of the current preoccupations of the senior personnel executives to whom it was addressed.

A separate questionnaire was sent to parents and affiliates but considerable commonality was maintained in the substance of the questions to allow the responses of parents and affiliates to be compared. The emphasis in this paper is on the responses from the affiliates. The format for both consisted of five sections. The first ascertained the formal objectives of the organisation and the strategies adopted in their pursuit. The second part focused on the organisation and responsibilities of the HRM function and of the director or senior executive in charge. This concern extended to the third section, which explored the company's policies and attitudes to recruitment, training and retention of staff. Part four addressed issues concerning the rewards, incentives and motivation of company employees, while the final section refocused on corporate culture and relations between parent and affiliate. It is this latter section that provides most of the data used in this paper.

The basic statistical method used to analyse the responses to questions on job security, career, business objectives, strategy and corporate culture was multiple linear regression. Responses were regressed on the industry in which the affiliate was based as well as on the parent country and the host country. The roles of industries and countries were captured using dummy variables. In constructing these dummy variables, the paper industry was used as the control industry, while the United States was used as the control for both the parent country and the host country.[3] The paper industry was chosen because it is a relatively homogenous industry with a medium level of technological sophistication and one for which a reasonable number of responses were available. Some writers prefer to use 'other manufacturing' as the control industry, but the drawback to this is that, because the industry is so heterogeneous, it is difficult to know exactly what is being compared with what when the regression coefficients for industry dummy variables are being interpreted.

It was evident from the responses to the questions about the organisation of HRM that the size of the affiliate was an important factor and to allow for this, the size of the affiliate was incorporated as an explanatory variable in all the regressions. The results have been reported in a separate paper. All the regressions were estimated by ordinary least squares (OLS) and where appropriate, by tobit and logit regressions. The different methods seem to have made hardly any difference to the results and so, on the grounds of their simplicity and robustness, only the OLS results are reported here.

JOB SECURITY AND CAREER

To illustrate how this methodology works in practice, a typical set of results is reported in Table 10.1. The five main categories of variable — industry, parent country, host country, firm–specific objectives and firm–specific strategies are listed down the left–hand side. Two separate regressions are shown for purposes of comparison. The first analyses the responses to a question about job security whilst the second analyses views on career prospects. The degree of congruence between answers to related questions provides reassurance that the responses are meaningful ones. Conflicts are revealed, as are anomalies that require explanation.

For each regression, two columns of figures are shown. The left–hand column shows the estimated coefficient. The important thing here is whether the sign is positive or negative — to interpret the magnitude it is necessary to refer to the scale on which the dependent variable is measured, as described in the footnote to the table. In the case of Table 10.1, both dependent variables are measured on a five–point Likert scale. It can be seen that the sizes of the main coefficients are quite large. Magnitude does not, however, guarantee statistical significance, as the right–hand columns make clear. These columns report the significance level associated with the coefficients; an asterisk indicates those cases where significance is greater than 10 per cent. The overall significance of the various groups of dummy variables is indicated at the bottom of the table by the F–statistics. The overall significance of the entire regression is also shown, together with the number of responses to the particular question involved. Because not all respondents answered all questions, this number is normally less than the 200 who replied altogether.

The results in Table 10.1 give the first indication that the national archetypes set out in the NBS scenario might receive confirming evidence from our survey data. Japanese–owned affiliates regard job security as far more significant for their employees than do United States–owned affiliates. It seems that Japanese foreign investors also export to their affiliates the need to emphasise job security in their local employment policies. In Japan itself, foreign–owned affiliates also report that job security is important to their employees, reinforcing the view that this is still an important component of the employment relationship in Japan. But Japan is not the only host country where job security is emphasised. The NICs — Brazil, India and Taiwan — all rate it as important, as does Italy. (In the latter case, this is strongly reinforced by legal restrictions on dismissal.)

It might be expected that the responses to the second question — on career prospects —would be similar to the first, in the sense that companies that rate job security highly would also emphasise career progression. This is not the case. Despite the emphasis on job security in Japan, for example, the results show that Japanese–owned firms do not attach significantly more weight to career prospects than their United States counterparts. British–owned firms, by contrast, do indeed downplay the role of career prospects in retaining key staff. The explanation for this apparent incongruence derives in part from the interview data and is confirmed in classical studies such as that of Dore (1973), quoted earlier. The Japanese promotion system has traditionally been related to length of service and has been largely disengaged from incentives offered to the younger managers occupying key roles in project teams. Amongst older managers, the 'window watcher' benefits from job security, even though he or she enjoys no career progression. The reason why career progression is considered unimportant in British–owned firms may be that their economic performance is relatively weak and their weaknesses are being addressed by delayering and downsizing. This means that HRM managers cannot honestly offer career progression even to their key staff.

Canadian, French and Dutch parents continue to see career prospects as an attraction to staff within their sector. This could be because they are, on average, performing better and so have been able to afford to stick to a more traditional hierarchical view of the firm.

The role of national differences should not be overstated, however, because there is evidence of systematic firm–specific differences too. Thus job security, but not career progression, is emphasised by firms which make special efforts to maintain good relations with customers and suppliers. These strategies are typical of firms producing industrial products, often as subcontractors to other large firms. This emphasis on managerial job security could therefore reflect the importance to the firm of the manager building long–term personal relationships with his or her 'opposite numbers' in other firms along the supply chain.

BUSINESS OBJECTIVES

The national archetypes receive further qualified support from Table 10.2. Both Japanese–owned affiliates and foreign firms operating in Japan attach less weight to current profitability than do their United States counterparts. German–owned firms are less likely to emphasise objectives that are difficult to measure, such as reputation or contribution to communal well–being. Like those of the Japanese, the Swedes and the Finns, German–owned firms also report less concern with the share price than their United States counterparts. The explanation for this offered by NBS theorists is that all these countries have a strong tradition of industrial banking and until recently, had relatively under–developed equity markets.

The relatively low regard for corporate reputation and for communal well–being expressed by personnel directors in Swedish multinationals could be attributed to the small size of our sample. One particular parent MNE laid considerable importance on the quantification of financial performance among its affiliates. However, in answer to a question on stake–holder priorities, even this Swedish parent company put its local community interest above that of other shareholder interests. These responses have to be understood in the context of the recent traumas experienced by Swedish parents through their fairly sudden exposure to external market forces caused by the erosion of both formal and informal regulation within their parent country.

STRATEGY AND HUMAN RESOURCES MANAGEMENT

In practice senior personnel staff appeared to have little direct influence on corporate strategy inspite of their claim to prioritise organisational design over all other activities (Casson, Loveridge and Singh 1996b). Their technical input into the design of recruitment, appraisal and records systems and structures was clearly significant, especially in larger multinationals. However, even here the use of a specialist subordinate — usually female — and external consultants in preparing advice to the board appeared normal. Taken in the wider sense, however, most corporations seemed to possess a coherent HRM approach which resulted from the traditional relationships within and towards their affiliations, or strategic business units and the general style of their senior executives. It is worth noting that customers, suppliers and equity shareholders ranked more highly as stakeholders than employee interests across the whole of this sample of personnel directors, with national interest last. However, in the socialisation of new management staff the inculcation of corporate values of respectability ranked more highly than that of a work ethic overall (see Table 10.3).

In general, companies valuing investment in traditional products and growth through aggressive acquisition appear most likely to encourage ambition in management recruits while those looking for growth through increased sales of their own products tend to prioritise the respectable exemplification of company image in their recruits. National differences are displayed in the importance attached to socialisation into company life by Japanese parents and upon loyalty by German multinationals Table 10.4. By way of contrast, French parents emphasise ambition combined with respectability in their meritocratic recruiting to their hierarchical and centrally controlled organisations. Affiliates in Japan and Sweden, as well as in India, Taiwan and Brazil, also mention a traditional emphasis upon the social integration of recruits while those in Britain and Germany seem less concerned with either the work ethic or corporate reputation (respectability). In both cases the responses of affiliates appear to reflect a realistic assessment of the career ceilings presented to local recruits by ethnocentric inward investors.

The approach of most corporate directors to the employment contract was that of accepting it as a 'formal expression of mutual obligations' (mean response: 0.63) as against the more extreme positions of either 'specifying the actual duties that the employee is required to perform' (mean response: 0.16) or as a 'document drawn up by lawyers which is of little practical use' (mean response: 0.13). Table 10.5 demonstrates that companies in the aircraft and electrical engineering sectors and in the newly reorganised motor vehicle industry were most likely to reject a formalistic view as — perhaps surprisingly — were French and Swiss respondents. These views appear to be related to an emphasis on long–term reputation and good relations with customers and suppliers instead of product innovation. However, in the context of local networks in Japan, Taiwan, Germany and Sweden and foreign investors in Britain, mutual obligation was also strongly emphasised.

HEADQUARTERS–SUBSIDIARY RELATIONS

When offered the options set out in Table 10.6, personnel directors in both parents and affiliates were generally inclined to give most weight to a traditional strategic tactical division of responsibility in which headquarters determines long–term strategy and affiliates determine short–term tactics. This was most significant among affiliates in Brazil, while managers of affiliates based in Britain appeared to express their individuality by rejecting the arbitrary authority of their parent significantly more than their counterparts in the United States. The Dutch appeared to favour a more consultative style of management, as did all MNEs in the food industry, in which Dutch and British multinationals are strongly represented. The Dutch also preferred to offer their affiliates considerable autonomy in developing strategies of their own rather than laying down the strategies at headquarters. The fact that personnel directors in German–owned multinationals also reported that they were allowed considerable autonomy comes as something of a surprise but with an important caveat suggested by our interviews — that it is subject to the constraints of keeping to budget and that if this becomes a problem then a comprehensive audit will be undertaken by headquarters without delay.

When asked about modes of communicating across cultural boundaries the most usual response (Table 10.7) is that of 'regular visits'. In practice such visits tend to vary in regularity and purpose from the monthly or quarterly routine meetings familiar in German multinationals to the rather more impulsive visitations that senior executives in Anglo–Saxon firms pay upon subsidiaries at times of crisis or reward (Loveridge 1994). The effect of the timings and styles of such visits upon the quality of information communicated and the uses to which it may be put is, of course, quite critical for strategic outcomes. In the context of a horizontally integrated MNE, frequent visits from one subsidiary to another may be associated with international benchmarking, in which managers from lower–performing subsidiaries visit higher performing subsidiaries to see how they operate. In the context of a vertically integrated MNE, visiting between subsidiaries may be associated with the decentralisation of the responsibility for intermediate product trade and the consequent need for face–to–face negotiations between affiliates that trade with each other.

It is interesting to note that British parents, along with the Japanese, expressed a significantly higher commitment than their competitors to the long–term recruitment of 'global managers' (Table 10.8). In Britain, as in Taiwan, Germany and Italy, affiliates also sought to develop internationally oriented managers. Language and cultural appreciation also figured highly in India, Switzerland and Other European contexts. One British respondent wrote that the most significant step taken towards internationalisation in recent years was the CEO's achievement of a 'decent level of spoken French'.

Overall, however, it appears that, even in industries that have developed in a global context, such as aircraft manufacture, or that have acquired multinational status in recent decades, like food processing, steps towards the development of a global class or profession of management are surprisingly small. Only in the latter sector was foreign experience believed to be significantly important to the board of directors (see Table 10.9). Perhaps surprisingly, this was most likely in German and Swiss companies, whose reputation for nationally closed business associations obviously belies their strong export orientation.

It is, perhaps, not surprising that the major cause of cross–cultural problems within the MNEs in our sample arose from 'different assumptions about the context in which information is to be interpreted' (Table 10.10). This problem outweighed those of substance such as the 'desirability of change and innovation' or style of communication such as the use of formal documentation. These and other factors listed as options in Table 10.8 clearly interacted, but it is the frustrations caused by differences in operational circumstances across time, space and culture that cause most problems.

Language difficulties faced by foreign affiliates in the United States appear to be greater than the language difficulties experienced by foreign affiliates in India, Canada, United Kingdom and Italy. This may be due to the different composition of foreign investment by country of origin and needs to be investigated further. Local operational conditions do appear to reveal significant differences in basic understanding between parent and affiliates in a number of industries including, once more, high–technology globally networked sectors such as aircraft, pharmaceuticals and motor vehicles (see Table 10.11). The implications for the internalisation of technology transfer advanced by several authors as the most important source of competitive advantage possessed by the multinational are, to say the least, interesting!

Reverting to the data contained in Table 10.9, it is interesting that the HRM directors of British–owned firms, who were significantly more tolerant of intra–firm cultural diversity than their United States counterparts, experienced significantly more 'procedural problems caused by different customs and rituals' (Table 10.11). The causal nature of this juxtaposition is confirmed in the rather aspirational approach our British informants revealed in interviews, operating with an idealised view of the company and reluctant to confront practical issues. Evidently both Japanese and British parents have difficulty in adjudging the degree of formal control to be exercised over subsidiaries through procedurally documental means. This appears to reveal itself in difficulties encountered in the establishment of collaborative relationships in cross–national joint ventures and alliances (as suggested by the interview evidence). Two contrasting responses to the management of change and innovation are revealed in responses from French and Swedish parents, the latter being significantly less likely to experience opposition to change, the former significantly more so. Interestingly it is affiliates in Japan and Taiwan who express most frustration with their parents' views on the need for innovation.

CONCLUSION

This paper has identified a number of attitudes to HRM within the MNE which, though they do not imply a formal policy or strategy in the personnel function, nevertheless seem to have a consistency of belief and action that might be described as an 'ideology in use' (Argyris and Schon 1978). To this extent it is possible to say that a congruency exists between overall corporate beliefs and actions and those operationalised in HRM. As Purcell (1989) has suggested, it is generally more likely that HRM management is shaped by business strategy than the reverse.

The generalisation of normative commitment appears more possible within certain national settings than others. These are generally ones in which the wider institutions of socialisation — those of school and family, for instance — are more congruent with the objectives of business. MNEs with affiliates in other countries evidently experience difficulty in understanding both the institutional boundaries they encounter and the attitudes to work and trading that shape them. Perhaps more might be accomplished with appropriate recruitment of foreign experienced board members or through teaching the CEO to speak decent French! However, the redesign of management structures and accompanying career structures to ensure better local representation might improve the development of MNEs' core competencies in the long run.

Table 10.1: Response to the questions: 'How important are the social and psychological benefits of job security to a manager working for your company?' and 'How important are better career prospects than those of other firms in the same industry in retaining key staff?'

	Job security		Career prospects	
Explanatory variable	Coefficient	Significance	Coefficient	Significance
Industry				
Aircraft and electrical engineering	+0.12	0.79	−0.46	0.31
Chemicals	+0.78	0.09*	−0.36	0.44
Coal and petroleum	+0.24	0.65	−0.25	0.64
Food, drink and tobacco	+0.56	0.25	−0.48	0.33
Mechanical engineering	+0.46	0.36	−0.23	0.66
Non–metals	+0.46	0.40	−0.36	0.53
Office equipment	+0.28	0.62	−0.05	0.94
Pharmaceuticals	+0.67	0.17	+0.01	0.99
Other manufacturing	+0.69	0.19	+0.10	0.85
Metals	+0.65	0.19	−0.10	0.84
Motor vehicles	+0.81	0.12	−0.06	0.91
Parent country				
Japan	+0.65	0.05*	−0.03	0.92
Canada	−0.67	0.25	+1.00	0.09
UK	−0.24	0.40	−0.61	0.04*
Germany	+0.28	0.36	+0.02	0.95
Sweden	+0.06	0.89	+0.66	0.16
Finland	−0.60	0.32	+1.02	0.10*
France	+0.75	0.20	+1.13	0.06*
Switzerland	−0.30	0.54	+0.43	0.39
Netherlands	+0.09	0.85	+0.85	0.08*
Other Europe	+0.06	0.90	−0.54	0.26
Host country				
Brazil	+1.44	0.00*	+0.60	0.09*
India	+1.00	0.04*	+0.71	0.14
Japan	+1.18	0.01*	+0.16	0.72
Taiwan	+0.39	0.01*	+0.59	0.27
Canada	+0.28	0.42	+0.24	0.51
UK	+0.29	0.36	+0.49	0.13
Germany	+0.57	0.15	+0.36	0.38
Switzerland	−0.23	0.67	+1.13	0.04*
Italy	+0.79	0.04*	+0.70	0.07*
Other Europe	+0.57	0.56	−0.96	0.34

Table 10.1 cont'd

Explanatory variable	Job security		Career prospects	
	Coefficient	Significance	Coefficient	Significance
Objectives				
Growth of total sales	−0.08	0.51	−0.03	0.83
Growth of market share	−0.00	0.99	+0.04	0.74
Profitability	+0.11	0.37	+0.09	0.45
Maximise share price	+0.04	0.62	+0.03	0.73
Company reputation	−0.29	0.02*	+0.15	0.24
Communal well-being	−0.01	0.91	+0.31	0.00*
Strategies				
Product innovation	−0.02	−0.86	+0.01	0.92
Investment in traditional products	+0.25	0.02	−0.01	0.96
Basic research	+0.10	0.20	+0.03	0.67
Relations with customers and suppliers	+0.57	0.00*	+0.19	0.28
Sophisicated advertising	+0.01	0.87	−0.04	0.64
Competitive prices	+0.00	0.96	−0.08	0.38
Aggressive acquisitions	+0.12	0.19	+0.02	0.84
Joint ventures and cooperation	+0.06	0.50	+0.08	0.41
Size of firm	−0.35	0.01*	+0.08	0.57
Intercept	+0.61	0.58	+0.35	0.76
Mean	+3.44		+3.90	
R^2	0.47		0.48	
F industry	0.71	0.73	0.47	0.92
F parent	1.14	0.34	2.44	0.01*
F host	3.08	0.10	1.20	0.30
F overall	1.98	0.00*	1.97	0.00*
Number of responses	148		146	

Note: Size of firm is measured by the logarithm of employment in the affiliate. The control industry is paper. The control country is the United States. Responses to both questions are on a scale from 1 (not important) to 5 (very important).

Table 10.2: Responses to the question: 'What are the main business objectives of the company?' (scale 1–5)

Objective	Mean	Standard deviation	Industry	Parent	Host	R^2	N
Profitability (post-tax rate of return on assets)	4.52	0.78		– Japan (0.00) – Italy (0.05)	– Japan (0.00) – Italy (0.01)	0.29	172
Growth of total sales	4.35	0.75		– Canada (0.08) – Finland (0.03)		0.19	172
Growth of market share	4.19	0.87	Coal and petroleum (0.07) Non-metals (0.07)	– Switzerland (0.06)		0.25	171
Maintain or improve reputation within the industry	4.03	0.99		– Germany (0.02) – Sweden (0.05)	– Germany (0.01) – Italy (0.05)	0.30	168
Contribute to communal well-being	3.33	1.14		– Germany (0.05) – Sweden (0.02)	+ Brazil (0.07)	0.26	167
Maximise the share price	3.06	1.39		– Japan (0.05) – Germany (0.00) – Sweden (0.05) – France (0.01	+ Brazil (0.04) – Canada (0.02) – Germany (0.06) + Other European (0.04)	0.35	161

Note: The regressions control for the affiliate's size, as measured by the number of employees (in logarithms). Control industry is paper. Control country is United States.

Table 10.3: Responses to the question: 'When explaining the company ethos to a new management recruit, what values would you emphasise most?'

Value	Mean response	Standard deviation
Respectability: You must exemplify corporate values in your everyday conduct so that, as you become more senior, you are a good role model for others.	3.90	0.93
Loyality: The greatest rewards go to those who make the greatest long–term commitment to the company.	3.47	1.03
Work ethic: Work carries priority over personal and social commitments.	3.22	1.18
Ambition: You must want to get to the top.	3.19	0.97
Calculation: You must submit to hard–headed appraisal and in due course administer such appraisal to your own subordinates.	2.89	1.01
Socialisation: You must integrate fully into company life, no only during normal hours but after hours as well.	2.36	1.16

Note: The number of respondents is 150. The responses are on a scale of 1 (not necessary) to 5 (very necessary).

Table 10.4: Regression analysis of responses to the question: 'When explaining the company ethos to a new management recruit, what values would you emphasise most?'

	Objectives and strategy	Industry	Parent	Host	R^2y
Work ethic. Work carries priority over personal and social commitments.	+ Competitive prices (0.03)			– UK (0.03) – Germany (0.08) – Italy (0.04	0.36
Ambition. You must want to get to the top.	– Communal well-being (0.03) + Investment in traditional products (0.08) + Aggressive acquisitions (0.06)		+France (0.06)		0.36
Calculation. You must submit to hard-headed objective appraisal and in due course administer such appraisal to your own subordinates.	+ Growth of market share (0.06)			+ India (0.02) + Other (0.08)	0.38
Socialisation. You must integrate fully into company life, not only during normal hours but after hours as well.		+ Non-metals (0.05) + Office equipment (0.11)	+ Japan (0.01) – Other Europe (0.07)	+ Brazil (0.01) + India (0.01) + Japan (0.03) + Taiwan (0.070 + Sweden (0.01)	0.43

Table 10.4 cont'd

	Objectives and strategy	Industry	Parent	Host	R^2y
Respectability. You must exemplify corporate values in your everyday conduct so that, as you become more senior, you are a good role model for others.	+ Growth of total sales (0.01)	+ Food (0.08) +Pharmaceuticals (0.04) + Metals (0.08) + Motor Vehicles	– Canada (0.08) + France (0.08)	– UK (0.06) – Germany (0.06)	0.39
Loyalty. The greatest rewards go to those who make the greatest long-term commitment to the company.	+ Sophisticated advertising (0.05)		+ Germany (0.01)*	+ Brazil (0.03) + Japan (0.04) + Taiwan (0.04) + Italy (0.05)	0.38

Note: The results control for the size of the firm (as measured by the logarithm of the number of employees).
*Japan is positive and significant at 0.10 level.

Table 10.5: Regression analysis of responses to the question: 'How is the contract of employment interpreted in your company?'

	Objectives and strategy	Industry	Parent	Host	R^2y
It specifies the actual duties that the employee is required to perform and the way their reward is determined.		+ Aircraft (0.09) − Motor vehicles (0.07)	− Switzerland (0.06)	− Germany (0.08) − Sweden (0.09)	0.29
It is a document drawn up by lawyers which is of little practical use unless there is a very serious disagreement.	− Company reputation (0.05) + Relations with customers and suppliers	− Aircraft (0.09) + Other manufacturing (0.02)	+ France (0.04) + Switzerland (0.02)	+ Italy 0.33	0.33
It is a formal expression of the mutual obligations of employer and employee.	+ Company reputation (0.01) + Communal well-being (0.09) − New products (0.09) − Relations with customers and suppliers (0.08)			+ Japan (0.09) + Taiwan (0.05) + UK (0.00) + Germany (0.01) + Sweden (0.03)	0.37

Note: The regressions control for the size of the responding firm (as measured by the logarithm of the number of employees). The respondent was asked to indicate just one of the alternatives, which carries a unit value. Alternatives not selected receive a zero value.

184

Table 10.6: Responses to the question: 'What best describes headquarters–subsidiary relations?'

Objective	Mean	Industry	Parent	Host	R^2	N
Headquarters determines long-term strategy and subsidiaries determine short-term tactics within this framework	0.51		– Netherlands (0.03)	+ Brazil (0.06)	0.16	173
Headquarters gives instructions to subsidiaries and subsidiaries report regularly to headquarters	0.21			– UK (0.07)	0.21	173
Headquarters coordinates a network of subsidiaries as a 'first among equals'.	0.17	+ Food (0.07)	+ Netherlands (0.06)		0.18	173
Subsidiaries decide for themselves how much support they need from headquarters.	0.11		+ Germany (0.04) + Netherlands (0.03)		0.17	173

Note: The regressions control for the affiliate's size as measured by the number of employees (in logarithms). Control industry is paper. Control country is US.

The respondent was asked to indicate just one of the alternatives, which carries a unit value. Alternatives not selected receive a zero value.

185

Table 10.7: Responses to the question: 'What measures does your company employ to facilitate cross–cultural communications between managers?'

Measure	Mean response (yes/no)
Regular visits to other foreign subsidiaries	0.51
Regular conferences on 'neutral ground'	0.41
International career development involving a number of expatriate assignments	0.37
Requiring managers to take language courses and/or cultural appreciation courses	0.35
Recruiting junior managers who have a strong international outlook	0.21

Note: Number of responses is 153. Responses are either 0 or 1.

Table 10.8: Regression analysis of responses to the question: 'What measures does your company employ to facilitate cross-cultural communications between managers?'

Objective	Objectives and strategy	Industry	Parent	Host	$R^2 y$
Regular conferences on neutral ground				+ UK (0.05)	0.27
Regular visits to other foreign subsidiaries	– Investment in traditional products (0.05) – Sophisticated advertising (0.09) + Competitive prices (0.06)	– Aircraft (0.07)		+ Italy (0.09)	0.29
International career development involving a concession of ex-patriate arrangements	+ New products (0.01) – Food (0.08)				0.33
Recruiting junior managers who have a strong international outlook	+ Maximise share price (0.03) – Basic research (0.08)	– Food (0.09) – Other manufacturing (0.09) – Metals (0.05)	+ Japan (0.02) + UK (0.06)	+Taiwan (0.01) + UK (0.02) + Germany (0.01) + Italy (0.01)	0.36

Note: the regression control for the size of the responding firm (as measured by the logarithm of employment)

187

Table 10.9: Regression analysis of responses to the questions: 'Do you agree that it is desirable that main board directors should have had experience of managing one of the company's foreign operations?' and 'Do you agree that it is important to standardise corporate culture across different countries?'

	Foreign experience		Standardised culture	
	Coefficient	Significance	Coefficient	Significance
Industry				
Aircraft and electrical engineering	+0.39	0.52	–0.09	0.89
Chemicals	+0.48	0.43	–0.51	0.42
Coal and petroleum	+0.63	0.38	–0.66	0.38
Food, drink and tobacco	+1.15	0.09*	–0.40	0.56
Mechanics engineering	+0.92	0.17	–0.73	0.30
Non–metals	+0.97	0.21	–0.27	0.74
Office equipment	+0.38	0.62	+0.39	0.62
Pharmaceuticals	+0.82	0.21	–0.85	0.21
Other manufacturing	–0.22	0.75	–0.91	0.21
Metals	–0.44	0.53	–0.10	0.89
Motor vehicles	+0.40	0.57	–0.81	0.27
Parent country				
Japan	+0.41	0.33	–0.51	0.24
Canada	+0.28	0.70	–0.55	0.46
UK	–0.01	0.97	–0.76	0.05*
Germany	+0.72	0.06*	+0.61	0.12
Switzerland	+1.37	0.02*	–0.03	0.96
Finland	–0.39	0.60	+0.22	0.78
France	+0.91	0.21	–1.20	0.11
Switzerland	+0.18	0.80	–0.99	0.12
Netherlands	–0.31	0.59	0.37	0.54
Other Europe	+0.21	0.72	+0.06	0.93
Host country				
Brazil	+0.16	0.72	+0.95	0.04*
India	–0.67	0.28	+0.99	0.11
Japan	–0.06	0.91	+0.23	0.69
Taiwan	+0.41	0.53	+1.36	0.05*
Canada	–0.81	0.07*	–0.37	0.43
UK	0.79	0.05	+0.50	0.24
Germany	0.35	0.47	+0.90	0.08*
Switzerland	–0.37	0.57	+0.50	0.45
Italy	–0.18	0.71	+0.94	0.06*

Table 10.9 cont'd

	Foreign experience		Standardised culture	
	Coefficient	Significance	Coefficient	Significance
Other Europe	+0.08	0.96	0.79	0.54
Objectives				
Growth of total sales	+0.07	0.64	+0.21	0.20
Growth of market share	−0.06	0.72	−0.26	0.12
Profitability	+0.13	0.40	−0.11	0.4B
Maximise share price	+0.10	0.30	+0.17	0.10
Company reputation	−0.16	0.28	+0.05	0.73
Communal well-being	−0.17	0.19	+0.16	0.21
Strategies				
Product innovation	+0.11	0.43	+0.06	0.69
Investment in traditional products	−0.06	0.61	+0.11	0.39
Basic research	+0.02	0.82	+0.07	0.48
Relations with customers and suppliers	+0.17	0.41	+0.06	0.79
Sophisticated advertising	−0.07	0.51	−0.13	0.26
Competitive prices	+0.03	0.74	+0.21	0.06*
Aggressive acquisitions	−0.14	0.22	−0.13	0.26
Joint ventures and cooperation	+0.12	0.29	−0.09	0.43
Intercept	2.15	0.03*	1.35	0.38
Mean	3.43		2.87	
R^2y	0.36		0.44	
F industry	0.92	0.53	0.62	0.81
F parent	1.12	0.36	2.43	0.01 *
F host	2.24	0.01*	2.71	0.01*
F overall	1.2	0.22	1.74	0.01*

Note: Number of responses is 148.
*denotes significance at the 10 per cent level. Dependent variables are on a scale from 1 (strongly disagree) to 5 (strongly agree). The regressions control the size of the responding firm (as measured by the logarithms of the number of employees).

Table 10.10: Responses to the question: 'What are the principal causes of cross–cultural problems in your organisation?'

Cause	Mean response	Standard deviation
Misunderstandings caused by different assumptions about the context in which information is to be interpreted	3.33	1.01
Different attitudes to the desirability of continual change, innovation and renewal	3.32	1.18
Disagreements over the degree of formality and the amount of documentation required for decision–making	2.95	1.10
Conflict stemming from different views of the nature and legitimacy of authority within the company	2.95	1.13
Procedural problems caused by different customs and rituals	2.91	1.20
Misunderstandings caused by different nuances in the same language	2.76	1.19
Misunderstandings caused by errors in translation between languages	2.50	1.22
Different value systems stemming from different religious and ethical traditions	2.23	1.17

Note: Number of responses is 149. Responses are on a scale from 1 (not significant) to 5 (very significant).

Table 10.11: Regression analysis of responses to the question: 'What are the principal causes of cross-cultural problems in your organisation?'

Objective	Objectives and strategy	Industry	Parent	Host	R^2y
Misunderstandings caused by errors in translation between languages	– Competitive prices (0.09)			– India (0.9) – Canada (0.04) – UK (0.01) – Sweden (0.08) – Italy (0.09)	0.39
Misunderstandings caused by different nuances in the same language	– Growth of total sales (0.06) – New products (0.03)	+ Non-metals (0.09) +Office equipment (0.06)		– Brazil (0.03) – India (0.03) – Canada (0.01) – UK (0.03) – Italy (0.04)	0.37
Misunderstandings caused by different assumptions about the context in which information is to be interpreted	– Competitive prices (0.01)	+Aircraft (0.00) +Non-metals (0.05) +Pharmaceuticals (0.02) +Metals (0.02) +Motor vehicles (0.03)	– Finland (0.03)	+ Taiwan (0.08) + Sweden (0.04) + Other European (0.02)	
Procedural problems caused by different customs and rituals	– Aggressive acquisitions (0.01) + Joint ventures and cooperation (0.00)		+ UK (0.06) + Switzerland (0.06)	+ Japan (0.09) + Other Europe (0.06	0.43

191

Table 10.11: Cont'd

Objective	Objectives and strategy	Industry	Parent	Host	R²y
Disagreements over the degree of formality and the amount of documentation required for decision-making	Sophisticated advertising (0.06) + Joint ventures and cooperation (0.00)		+ Japan (0.01) + UK (0.07)		0.31
Conflicts stemming from different views of the nature and legitimacy of authority within the company	+Growth of total sales (0.02) −Company reputation (0.01) −Sophisticated advertising (0.09)	+Food (0.08) +Mechanical engineering (0.09) +Office equipment (0.03) +Motor vehicles (0.06)	−Netherlands (0.02)		0.32
Different value systems stemming from different religious and ethical traditions		+Mechanical engineering (0.09) +Non-metals (0.03) +Metals (0.03)	−Switzerland (0.06) −Netherlands (0.09)	−Brazil (0.03)	0.35
Different attitudes to the desirability of continual change, innovation and renewal	− Competititve prices (0.01)	+Metals (0.05)	−Sweden (0.02) +France (0.07)	+Japan (0.01) +Taiwan (0.03)	0.37

Note: The regressions control for the size of the regarding time (as measured by the logarithm of employment)

192

NOTES

[1] This is a subject that has been touched upon in several recent monographs and articles but one complicated by two characteristics of the methodological frames deployed. North American authors usually adopt a managerial perspective on organisational control and personnel planning issues while, under the same HRM subject title, European scholars tend to focus on work-related issues within an industrial relations or labour-process frame. A further difficulty is that HRM is sometimes defined by researchers as being synonymous with the adoption of devolved modes of work organisation and of a high-commitment management style. In this case our questions become, firstly, how far HRM exists within the MNE at all and secondly, if it does, whether or not it has been orchestrated by managers in the personnel function. Our approach has been to focus on the extent and manner by which the functional elements of personnel management are carried out, whilst testing ideological dispositions that informants display towards these elements. 'Written in' references to organisational restructuring constituted the single most important set of answers to open-ended questions.

[2] (a) Countries participating in the survey were: Parent locations: Canada, Finland France, Germany, Japan, Netherlands, Other European, Sweden, Switzerland UK, US (used as control); Host locations (affiliates): Canada, Brazil, India, Italy, Japan, Other European, Switzerland Taiwan, UK, US (used as control).

(b) Industrial categories used in placing respondents: Aircraft and electrical engineering, Chemicals; Coal and petroleum; Food and drink; Mechanical engineering; Motor vehicles; Metal manufacturing; Non-metal manufacturing; Office equipment; Pharmaceuticals; Paper and related products (used as control); Other Manufacturing.

[3] The methodological significance of using the United States as control has not escaped us, nor indeed have the problems associated with the interpretation of language by respondents to a cross-national postal questionnaire survey (Garfinkel 1967). Most of the managerial concepts addressed in this survey originated within US business literature and are familiar to personnel professionals as part of a US archetype. However, at least one of our British non-respondents was not aware of the meaning of the initials HRM and was therefore unsure as to whom the questionnaire should be addressed!

REFERENCES

Argyris C. and Schon, D. 1978. *Organizational Learning,* Reading, MA: Addison Wesley.

Barney, J.B. 1986. Organizational Culture: can it be a source of sustained competitive advantage? *Academy of Management Review,* 1(1): 656–65.

Bartlett, C. and Ghoshal, S. 1989. *Managing Across Borders,* Boston, MA: Harvard Business School Press.

Bendix, R. 1956. *Work and Authority and Industry,* New York: Wiley.

Buckley, P.J. 1994. International Business Versus International Management? International Management from the Viewpoint of Internalisation Theory. *Journal of the Economics of Business,* 1(1): 95–104.

Buckley, P.J. and Casson, M. 1976. *The Future of the Multinational Enterprise.* London: Macmillan.

Casson, M. 1990. *Enterprise and Competitiveness,* Oxford: Clarendon Press.

Casson, M. 1995. *Entrepreneurship and Business Culture,* Aldershot: Edward Elgar.

Casson, M., Loveridge, R. and Singh, S. 1996a. The ethical significance of corporate culture in large multinational Enterprises. In F.N. Brady (ed.), *Ethics in International Business,* Berlin: Springer Verlag 1996 forthcoming.

Casson, M., Loveridge, R. and Singh, S. 1996b. Corporate culture in Europe, Asia and North America: Implications for global competition. In A.M. Rugman and G. Boyd (eds), *Europe Pacific Investrnent and Trade.* Aldershot: Edward Elgar

Chandler, A.D. 1990. *Scale and Scope: the Dynamics of Industrial Capitalism.* Cambridge, Mass.: Belknap Press.

Dore, R. 1973. *British Factory: Japanese Factory.* London: Allen & Unwin.

Garfinkel, H. 1967. *Studies in Ethnomethodology,* Englewood Cliffs, NJ: Prentice Hall.

Gregersen, H.B. and Black, J.S. 1992. Antecedents to Commitment to a Parent Company and a Foreign Operation. *Academy of Management Journal,* 35(1):65–90.

Hofstede, G. 1980. *Culture's Consequences.* Beverley Hills, CA: Sage.

Lodge, G.C. and Vogel, E.F. 1987. *Ideology and National Competinveness – An Analysis of Nine Countries Competitiveness,* Boston, Mass.: Harvard Business School Press.

Loveridge, R. 1994. Sponsoring World Class Players. *Proceedings of the Academy of International Business,* 21st UK Conference, Manchester.

Lundvall, B.A. 1992. Introduction. In B.A Lundvall (ed.), *National Systems of Innovation, Towards a Theory of Innovation and Interactive Learning,* London: Pinter.

Maurice, M. and Sellier, F. 1979. A societal analaysis of industrial relations. *British Journal of Industrial Relations,* 17(3): 322–36.

Mowery, D.C. 1992. 'The US innovation system: origins and prospects for change, *Research Policy,* 21:125–44.

Nelson, R.R. 1993. *National Innovation Systems – A Comparative Analysis,* Oxford: Oxford University Press.

Ohmae, K. 1985. *Triad Power,* New York: Free Press.

Ouchi, W.G. 1981. *Theory Z: How American Business can Meet the Japanese Challenge,* Reading: Addison–Wesley.

Perlmutter, H.V. 1969. The tortuous evolution of the multi–national corporation. *Columbia Journal of World Business,* 4 (January–February): 9–19.

Porter, M.E. 1990. *The Competitive Advantage of Nations,* London: Macmillan.

Purcell, J. 1989. The impact of corporate strategy on Human Resource Management. In J. Storey (ed.) *New Perspectives on Human Resource Management,* London: Routledge.

Rodgers, W. 1971. *Think: a biography of the Watson and IBM,* London: Panther Books.

Schoemaker, P.J.H. 1990. Strategy, complexity and economic rent. *Management Science,* 36:1178–92.

Sorge, A. and Warner, M. 1986. *Comparative Factory Organization,* Aldershot, UK: Gower.

Teece, D.J. 1981. The market for know–how and the efficient international transfer of technology. *The Annals of the American Academy of Political and Social Scicnce,* 285–305.

Trice and Meyer, J.M. 1993. *The Cultures of Work Organization,* Englewood Cliffs, NJ: Prentice Hall.

Wanous, J.P. 1992. *Organisational Entry: Recruitment, Selection, Orientation and Socialization of Newcomers* (2nd edn) Reading, MA: Addison–Wesley.

Whitley, R. 1992. *Business Systems in East Asia*, London: Sage.

Williamson, O.E. 1981. The economics of organization: the transaction cost approach. *American Journal of Sociology.* 87 (November): 548–77.

PART FOUR

Future Directions in IB Education and Research

11. The Compleat Executive[1]: The State of International Business Education and Some Future Directions

Farok Contractor

To complete their academic education, do business executives need to study International Business (IB)? Does student interest in the subject reflect merely a dilettantish and romanticised appeal, in much the same way that young English gentlemen in the eighteenth century would take a 'grand tour' of continental Europe and the Mediterranean to see exotic foreign lands such as Italy or Egypt, returning laden with bric a brac, antiquities and pictures of the natives? Moreover, if much of the world that the executive deals with has homogenised or 'globalised', then is there any more reason to study International Business than for an American to take a course in Interstate Commerce? Today, with only narrow economic and cultural differences between states of the United States, few bother to study Interstate Commerce and there are virtually no academic departments devoted to that purpose.

VIVE LES DIFFERENCES

A broadening of the mind as part of education, in itself, provides sufficient justification for international studies at the undergraduate level, as it did in the eighteenth century. But today's practice of global management goes far beyond romanticism into the hard realities of competition and profit. A number of studies show that firms that are represented in several country markets are more competitive and do better than companies operating in one or a few markets. Moreover, if differences across countries persist, the manager must study how to overcome them, arbitrage across them and take advantage of the uneven economic landscape.

The leveling of the cultural and economic landscape, on a trans–continental scale, is still very much a phenomenon that is peculiarly American (and possibly Australian). The notion of cultural convergence (Levitt 1983), or the idea of democratic equality, are far from becoming the 'universal and irresistible ... governing power(s) in the world's affairs', even though a century and a half have passed since Toqueville (1840) wrote those words about the American scene and prophesied its extension to the rest of the world.

True, a flood of potent images spews over the planet from the US media and from advertising agencies in other nations that closely imitate the American model. The young, in most cultures, are sympathetic. Their elders have put up a brisk resistance, from the officially sanctioned lexicon of the French Ministry of Culture, to the banning of satellite dishes in some countries, to the fulminations of the Ayatollah Khomeini who described the United States as 'The Great Satan' — not so much because of its military might, but because of the perceived threat of American ideals. On the one hand we have the vision of McWorld; on the other we have the vision of Jihad as depicted by Barber (1995). Barber describes the opposite pulls of globalised consumerism and the search for identity thus: 'Belonging by default to McWorld, everyone is a consumer; seeking a repository for identity, everyone belongs to some tribe'. By 'Jihad', Barber does not mean actual guerrilla warfare (although multinational companies from Bougainville to Bogota have encountered guerrilla action in the not so distant past). Rather, he is referring to a general resistance and resentment against the 'spiritual poverty of markets' as an organising paradigm for societies. This resistance continues to be expressed by groups as diverse as French union members loath to relinquish their bourgeois privileges to the dictates of European monetary convergence, the millions in Poland and Russia who vote Communist and the employees of Indian and Chinese state enterprises. The countervailing forces of protectionism and cultural identity are strong and will persist for the indefinite future.

Borders persist. Barriers remain even in the nascent European Union. In 1995 an English motor driving school was offering its services in Germany and Denmark. An example of post–1992 reduction of intra–EU barriers? Possibly. The curious fact was that several Germans, Danes and other continental Europeans bore the costs of travel to Britain, lodging and food for ten days to a fortnight, paid the English driving school (for instruction on the 'wrong' side of the road) — and still came out ahead financially, compared with the cost of obtaining a driver's licence in their own countries.[2] The extraordinary fact was not that Germany and Denmark were now willing to accept United Kingdom certification. Rather the most extraordinary fact, for International Business educators, is that such arbitrage opportunities continue to exist in thousands upon thousands of examples, in a wide range of industries, within the EU. The EU represents a far more uneven economic and cultural landscape than the United States. No surprise then, that Arpan, Folks and Kwok (1993) report that European business schools had far more internationalised curricula and faculty compared with US schools. European schools were 'more than three times as likely' to want functional field international courses at the undergraduate and PhD levels and 'more than four times as likely' as their US counterparts, at the masters level. As the American economy becomes more internationalised from its currently low level,[3] it is likely that, in this respect, US school curricula will tend towards the European pattern, rather than vice versa.

The foreign exchange markets provide another glaring illustration of the persistence of deviations from parity. Despite floating rates in the context of efficient exchange markets, the US dollar continued for a decade to be grossly undervalued against the yen and several European currencies, for reasons that were not always strongly connected with inflation or interest rate differentials.[4] An understanding of exchange rate theories and the persistence of deviations is a key ingredient in the tool kit of the compleat executive. However, the shocking fact remains that many business majors continue to receive their diplomas without encountering the PPP or interest parity theories. Vital nuggets of their education are missing. How can this be? The introduction of International Business curricula is still spotty, even in major state–supported universities. And unless the instructor in the introductory International Business (IB) course covers this topic, it is entirely possible that a non–finance major may graduate without encountering such ideas, vital to the general practice of global management. The problem may be even deeper and endemic as described in Arpan, Folks and Kwok's (1993) survey of 557 institutions (including 87 schools in Europe and 27 in Asia). For the overall sample they report that 'students receiving no or minimal international business education (were) 62 per cent at the undergraduate level, 57 per cent at the master level and 59 per cent at the doctoral level'.[5] The European subsample did considerably better.

International differences will continue to exist for a very long time. Hence one justification for International Business studies which trains managers how to identify these differences, overcome them and arbitrage and rationalise across them.

IS INTERNATIONAL BUSINESS A DISCIPLINE?

A large acquaintance with particulars often makes us wiser than the possession of abstract formulas, however deep.

— William James
The Varieties of Religious Experience

Some prefer to use the word 'discipline' to describe business 'functions' such as Finance, Marketing or Management Information Systems (MIS). But each of these, in turn, draws on concepts and principles developed elsewhere. For example, Marketing can be deconstructed into areas such as consumer psychology, statistics and the economics of pricing. MIS can be deconstructed into computer science, accounting and so on. Finance and managerial economics have a larger proportion of concepts developed from within, compared with other business functions. But all have borrowed freely. The study of management is the study of eclectic concepts.

It may be time to abandon the notion that the general practice of management is a science. The study of management necessitates a balance between models or theories and the examination of particular facts. In the United States, several schools have been accused of having models and theories occupy too large a proportion of the curriculum, to the detriment of real–life complexities and integrative, cross–functional learning such as an IB course provides.[6]

So, is international business a 'discipline' or a 'theme'? At the heart of the IB literature exist some theories and concepts that are not found anywhere else.[7] But the teaching of International Business, as well as research reflected in the content of the apex journal *Journal of International Business Studies*, has a preponderant cross–functional and eclectic content. But so do most other areas of management, albeit to a lesser extent. International Business has as much legitimacy to be classified as a theme or focus area as Marketing or Management Information Systems.

The organisation of companies into departments, as well as the thematic classification of curricular concepts into headings such as Marketing or International Business is, to some extent, a matter of administrative convenience and perceived importance of the function at that particular time. For example, production management and R&D are as vital pieces of the value chain as is marketing. Yet virtually every business school has a Marketing department; hardly any have departments devoted to Production. Another example: in the early evolution of American companies into foreign markets, many created separate International Divisions at that time, only to fold foreign operations back into individual 'Global Product Divisions' at a later stage, as the firms became internationally experienced (Dymsza 1987). (At this stage in the evolution of many American management schools, a separate IB department may indeed be desirable — this issue is tackled later in this chapter.)

But the need for global management concepts and expertise remains. Whether International Business operations are grouped into a separate department or performed separately in a company's product divisions is less important than having managers with the requisite International Business concepts in the first place. Similarly, it is less important whether schools of management have a separate IB department than to ensure that students, somewhere in the curriculum, secure the requisite set of tools needed for the practice of international management. What then are the key concepts and tools for the practice of international management?

THE TOOL KIT OF THE COMPLEAT EXECUTIVE

What should the well–educated manager know about global management? The international dimensions of business amplify, even more, the eclectic nature of business studies. The list is therefore necessarily disparate and its boundaries ill–defined. Table 11.1 is only an illustration. There will rarely be unanimity on what should be included or deleted from such a list. But in curricular design it is desirable that we start with the components and only then decide how to assemble the pieces into academic departments (as opposed to the normal practice where entrenched 'functional' departments offer their own partisan agendas so that many key IB concepts end up being missed by students). At the least, a list such as the one in Table 11.1 can identify what is missing in a curriculum. Some comments are in order on the pedagogical implications of Table 11.1. The extent of coverage of topics is, after all, a function of whether the programme is undergraduate or postgraduate. The thematic content is also likely to be influenced by the school's location and mission.[8] Kedia and Cornwell (1994) describe several institutions that have adopted a country or regional focus as part of their IB curriculum. Some have focused on a secondary language capability as their internationalisation theme (Rich–Duval 1995). In such cases, the study of a country or a language can become the unifying theme for an internationalised business curriculum.

Some topics involve pure theory (e.g. PPP theory or International Transfer Pricing Models). Others mainly deal with practice (e.g. export mechanics or differences in distribution methods across countries). Many draw from the so–called functional areas of Marketing, Management, Accounting

Table 11.1 Some examples of key concepts that every executive should know about international management

(Disclaimer: The following list is for illustrative purposes only and contains concepts in no particular order, until ordered by a rational curriculum design depending on the pedagogic logic and circumstances of a particular school.)

- International expansion options (modal choice)
- Evolution of the firm and FDI theory
- 'Globalisation': What exactly does it mean in practice?
- Rationalisation models in the context of international logistics and Global production
- Cultural differences and the practice of management
  How are 'their' business practices different from 'ours'?
  Impact on HR and personnel costs
  Managing a multi–ethnic workforce and conflict resolution
  Negotiating agreements across the cultural divide
- International aspects of strategic alliances
- The continuing role of governments
  Market segementation
  Protectionism
  Regional clusters and created advantage
  Strategic trade theories
  Political risk: defining, assessing and managing it
- Alternative organisation designs for the multinational firm
- Purchasing power parity
- Covered interest parity
- Forwards, futures and options in foreign exchange
- Basic foreign exchange hedging techniques
- Economic exposure (cash flow)
- Translation exposure (balance sheet)
- Basics of international taxation
- International transfer pricing (simple models)
- Differences in international markets and distribution
- Basic mechanics of exporting
- Pricing and price discrimination in international markets
- Theory of optimal pricing in imperfect competition in the context of multiple currencies
- Social responsiveness and managing the external relations function in a multinational context
- International aspects of business ethics
- Intellectual property protection internationally

or Finance and may involve international extensions of existing material in such departments. But several topics are uniquely International Business (e.g. fdi Theory, Globalisation or Political Risk Analysis).

Finally, one can identify a large sub–set of topics where teaching expertise is unlikely to be found in the traditional functional academic departments (except at a few of the best schools), even though the topics nominally 'belong' to those functional areas. For example, it is only the rare accounting department that can boast expertise in international taxation. It is only a small minority of management departments that can boast expertise in cross–cultural business negotiations. For management schools as a whole, it is rare to find competence in international intellectual property protection. Yet such topics need to be covered by all students at the postgraduate level, at an introductory level, at least. Often, such topics, as well as topics that are uniquely International Business, fall by the wayside unless the school has a separate IB department, brings in external instructors, or holds specialised seminars.

Plugging the holes in the curriculum may require patchwork responses. Better yet is a policy of concerted organisational and curricular change. The next section examines alternative methods for achieving the objective of internationalising business school teaching.

APPROACHES TO INTERNATIONALISING BUSINESS EDUCATION: THE MODELS AND THE CLAY

In a study sponsored by the Academy of International Business and AACSB (American Assembly of Collegiate Schools of Business) on internation–alisation of business education, Arpan, Folks and Kwok (1993) reported 'low levels of achievement' and a 'general dissatisfaction with the current level of curriculum internationalisation'. This was nineteen years after 1974 when the AACSB suggested that United States schools increase resources to internationalise the curriculum. Over this nineteen-year period, business schools, in the United States and worldwide, have tried various organisational approaches and incentives to further this objective. They mainly fall into four archetypes shown in Table 11.2. In each instance, the purported advantages of the model are described, together with some illustrations of how the clay (faculty) has actually behaved in the hands of the master potter (dean or administration). The overall work is very much in progress.

The 'Infusion' Approach

Since International Business is a theme that transcends and infuses all the traditional functional departments, it would be ideal if international business concepts were 'infused' into each functional area's teaching and research materials. Various incentives have been proposed to bring this about, such as reductions in teaching load to develop internationalised curricula, preferential allocation of funds for research with an international aspect and incremental travel funds to attend overseas conferences. The handful of schools fortunate enough to have received external grants to set up Centres for International Business have been able to provide such funds. Alas, in most schools the money has been absent, or merely been a smattering. Overall, the financial incentives to internationalise curricula and research across all departments have been grossly inadequate in most schools. Directors and deans can exhort and some have done this well, but the carrot has not been appealing enough to most faculties. A few deans have used the stick of promotion and tenure to foster internationalisation. But this approach can only go so far, since it is only in a minority of schools that deans hold the preponderance in tenure or promotion applications. For the most part, in the better schools, the kind of teaching and research that faculty members choose to do is driven by the example and recommendation of peers in their functional field. And it has only been in the 1990s that some of the academies such as the Academy of Management or the American Marketing Association have finally heard the clarion call.[9]

'Infusing' international business into traditional functional areas has proven therefore to be a very protracted and incomplete method. This model, where the international content of the curriculum is left to each department, is appropriate only at the end of a long evolutionary process of internationalisation — when other drivers such as separate IB departments are no longer needed to perform this evolutionary task. This is analogous to the early international expansion of companies which concentrate foreign market expertise and resources in a separate International Division. Later, when the firm is internationally experienced, the international functions may be split and allocated back to each product division which now has a global mandate.

The fact that a slight majority of schools in the United States (and a slight minority in Europe) follow this approach (see Table 11.2) hardly suggests that these schools have evolved and that their curricula are permeated with international business content. On the contrary, the explanation for the large percentages in this category is that many of them have not even begun the process and simply remain content with the traditional curricula and

Table 11.2: Approaches to organising the International Business function within schools of management

	Actual Incidence from AIB Survey		
	Total sample	Europe subsample (Percentages)	US subsample
Traditional functional departments (with varying incentives for internationalising teaching and research)	54	47	57
An international business centre or institute departments (joint affiliation of some or all faculty with the centre)	3	3	2
Identified IB specialists within functional (or occasionally a sub-department for IB)	29	29	30
International Business department	7	11	4
Other/unspecified	7	10	7

Source: Arpan, Folks and Kwok (1993)

departments. Some continue to assert that, just as globalised companies no longer need a separate IB division, since global functions are performed separately by each product division, a functional departmental structure for schools of management is all that is needed. But such magisterial assertions typically tend to come from academics at the best business schools who do not realise how large a body of smaller and less well–endowed schools exists below them — including schools where the internationalisation process has barely begun. Arpan, Folks and Kwok (1993) conclude:

One of the most telling criticisms of infusion is that European business schools, long held to be exemplar of the infusion process because of the multinational nature of their core courses, are more likely to offer and require separate international business courses and generally tend to accord international business greater stature as a separate academic discipline.

International Business Centres

An International Business Centre or Institute, separate from other faculty departments, is an excellent vehicle to foster internationalisation. Often headed by a full– or part–time director, it signals serious intent by the allocation of significant money and serves as a focal point for the promotion of curricular change, study abroad or student exchange programmes, internationally oriented research and external relations with multinational firms. In many universities, such centres have also provided links between the business school and International Relations, Political Science, Language and other schools or departments in the university. In a few instances, some individual faculty members in the school are formally given a joint affiliation, with their departments and with the centre. The record of such centres towards fostering international business education is fairly good, but at considerable expense.

IB centres can usually only be afforded by affluent schools, or schools fortunate enough to have received external grants for this purpose. This is the principal explanation for the low percentages in this category in Table 11.2. By being distinct from the traditional departments, the centres have to work hard to overcome the disadvantage of being disconnected from the rest of the school. Joint or matrix affiliation of the faculty with the centre may go well beyond symbolic value. But, to the extent that promotion and tenure rewards continue to remain with the traditional departments, the willingness of faculty to change will remain weak. Centre directorships, especially those on a full time basis, sometimes tend to be non–academic appointments.

Identified International Business Specialists within Functional Departments (or a Sub–Department for International Business)

Designating IB specialists within a department gives responsibility for internationalising the department's teaching to specific persons and provides the school with a focal point for research on international business topics. The incremental costs of this approach are relatively small (although some management schools have had to explicitly reorient their recruitment to acquire IB specialists within functional areas — something that has not been easy until recently, because the bulk of even the recent PhD dissertation topics have not been internationally oriented). As a result of the small incremental cost, a large proportion of schools shown in Table 11.2 claim in the survey response have adopted this approach. The actual extent to which they have implemented this policy and its effectiveness, remain unknown.

An International Business Department

A separate IB department can perform several distinctive functions — to teach the compulsory introductory IB course required at many schools; to serve as a logical point of curricular integration since international business offers a logical rubric for multi–functional material; to cover core IB theory and specialised topics which would not be treated by the traditional functional departments (e.g. exporting or US–Mexico Trade); and as a home for language or country–related portions of the curriculum. In theory, these functions could be carried out by an IB centre, or even by traditional functional departments. But, in practice, do they? Left only to exhortation, IB topics are the proverbial Chapter 35, that never gets covered in a 14–week semester. International Business Centres, in the handful of schools fortunate enough to have them, often provide the icing of conferences, foreign travel and exchange programmes, but fail to tackle the tougher meat of thoroughgoing curricular change.

A separate International Business Department can be very effective. But it also has limitations. First, it is expensive to maintain an additional administrative unit. Schools whose constituencies include a large number of multinational companies, or those located near major ports, justify this expense. But many smaller institutions, located away from major international business centres may not find this model worthwhile.

Second, in very turf–conscious institutions where departments operate with a high degree of autonomy, creating a separate IB department may occasionally retard, rather than foster, the objective of internationalising the content of the entire curriculum. True, required or elective IB courses would be offered, to reduce the likelihood of students graduating without at least encountering some international material. But this may stultify initiative to internationalise in the other departments.

Third, because of their subject's eclectic nature, IB scholars tend to have more disparate interests than most other traditional functional areas. Defining the boundaries of the field remains an issue.[10] (So–called 'Management' departments may possibly be the one case of even greater variation across their sub–specialties than IB. Incidentally, this provides another point in favor of the viability of separate IB departments — if so diverse a group as 'organisation and management' scholars can coexist in a department, then surely IB can as well.) Variety in scholarly endeavors is something that is desirable. 'Let a hundred flowers bloom', wrote Mao Zedong. But then he proceeded to mow them down, once they had bloomed. In the United States at least, the rigors and narrow–mindedness of the tenure and promotion process at many research–intensive schools makes membership in IB or Management departments a trifle riskier than membership in more narrowly demarcated functional areas such as Accounting or Finance. And, in the minds of older faculty who have not encountered the currently rigorous standard of IB scholarship, the old prejudices and stigmas remain.

Table 11.3: Does the IB label carry a stigma?

Being known as the 'international' person within a department sometimes carries with it privileges and a touch of glamour. But in some schools it continues to be suspect, even though the teaching capabilities and research of the person are at the cutting edge of the functional field. Why?

Thirty–five years after the formation of the Academy of International Business and despite the accumulation of a body of empirical research and theory of its own, the field of International Business continues to suffer a mild case of an identity crisis. This is principally because the subject matter of IB is even more eclectic than, say, Marketing or Management Information Systems. Birds of many feathers have roosted under its umbrella. There is no getting around the fact that, in its early years, the field attracted more than its share of academic charlatans and dilettantes. The situation is now corrected, of course. The *Journal of International Business Studies* and other IB journals uphold as rigorous a standard as any in other fields. But the old memories linger. Thirdly, the field of IB is, to some extent, going to be a victim of its own missionary success. Having preached the gospel of International Business studies in the wilderness for three decades, new converts have suddenly flocked to the Academy of International Business, the AMA and the International Division of the Academy of Management and swelled membership to record levels. All of this is good news — except that the new converts are prone to making claims on and appropriating subject areas that were hitherto researched only by relatively few IB scholars, thereby eventually threatening to reduce the core competencies and distinctiveness of IB studies.[11]

For the most part, being identified as an 'IB person' in a department or school is desirable, even glamorous. It is being part of a necessary trend or movement sanctioned by deans, chancellors and accrediting bodies. But a few of the old questions linger.

The choice of an organisational model is, as always, a function of a school's location, environment, resources, stakeholders, degree of evolution, a school's heritage of existing faculty and its culture and history. We should also remember that there is a large gap between organisational patterns actually adopted and ones that they wished they had adopted, or deem desirable. This gap is seen in comparing Table 11.2 which shows the incidence of organisational modes actually adopted, with desires expressed by respondents in Arpan, Folks and Kwok's (1993) survey. While 'US business schools ranked an international business department the least desirable organisational form, European respondents placed it second, behind the functional department with recognised international specialists' which was deemed the best. Again, in terms of desirability, 'European business schools rejected the functional department structure as the worst organisational form' — this despite the fact that this was the single most common form adopted in Europe, as shown in Table 11.2. In general, European business schools give a higher degree of formal recognition to International Business by formally designating faculty and by a greater desire for, as well as a greater actual incidence of, separate IB departments.

THE STUDENT OR CONSUMER'S PERSPECTIVE AND THE FUTURE OF INTERNATIONAL BUSINESS EDUCATION

The market for international business education is evolving new niches which will become more important in the future. We have the traditional organisation of management education divided into undergraduate, postgraduate and doctoral levels. We must now add to these, niches such as specialised certificate programmes, international business 'finishing schools' and IB programmes designed from the perspective of managers in emerging and developing countries.

Undergraduate International Business Studies

Interest in IB studies at the undergraduate level appears to be rising, although hard data are lacking. 1994 was the first year in which UCLA's Higher Education Research Institute even included the International Business major as part of its annual survey (AACSB Newsline 1995). But already, almost ten per cent of American freshmen who indicated an interest in majoring in business indicated their preference for International Business as a concentration.[12] Arpan, Folks and Kwok (1993) report that, worldwide, the percentage of schools requiring at least one international business course sharply increased over five years, from 6 per cent to over 22 per cent.

The adage that business studies at the postgraduate level should have a vocational character, but at the undergraduate level they should have an educational character, fits in well with the IB theme. Unlike, say, Accounting, whose course content is essentially similar at postgraduate and undergraduate levels, IB courses should have a much broader philosophical, cultural, geographical and historical content at the undergraduate level. At the postgraduate level, in a crowded MBA curriculum, there is often no time to deeply contemplate issues such as the evolution of the nation state, the growth of multinational enterprises in the industrial revolution, the influence of Confucianism on business relations, or comparative ethical standards in different cultures. Unlike other business functions, International Business lends itself very well to organising, under its rubric, a broad education that integrates concepts from diverse fields such as Political Science, Religion, International Relations, Sociology and so on.

Many liberal arts colleges have followed this approach and added to the broad educational mix, language studies and country specialisations, accompanied by study–abroad programmes (Rich–Duval 1995), often in conjunction with partnerships with foreign institutions (Cavusgil, Schechter and Yaprak 1992).

Master's Level

A general trend at the Master's level has been the growing modularisation of the curriculum, which tends to reduce the number of required credits in the overall programme. This increases the likelihood of students opting for elective IB courses. But no data are available on whether this has actually happened, or whether reducing the required core has eliminated an IB requirement which, for many students, is the only IB course they will take towards their Master's degree. This trend does increase student's ability to have dual majors or concentrations, where previously this was difficult. The following extract provides a discussion of the desirability of a dual major.

In the largest sense, the promulgation of the IB major has a long way to go from a very low base with only 14 per cent of US schools as yet offering such a concentration (Rich–Duval 1995).

The Doctoral Level

The findings of the AIB/AACSB survey *vis–à–vis* the doctoral level of business studies are mildly disquieting. Since doctoral degree holders will be future instructors in schools of business, one would have expected higher levels of internationalisation, as well as greater desires to at least introduce international aspects of their functional fields to doctoral students. On virtually every criterion, be it a required IB course, or a menu of IB courses, or introducing the international dimension in the business core courses, responses were lower than the Masters or the undergraduate level. Paradoxically, the same respondents expressed a slightly higher degree of dissatisfaction with the 'current level of internationalisation of the current curriculum' for doctoral studies, as opposed to Masters or undergraduate studies — as if to say that they saw the need to internationalise, but that rigidities and orthodoxies in the organisation of doctoral studies retarded progress. This once again suggests that the models for academic success, tenure, promotion and peer–evaluation remain tradition–bound.

Table 11.4: An IB major and the job market

How desirable is an International Business major for the job market? International Business is not a field easily defined. When employers ask, 'What is it?' a short answer is not easy, as would be the case for an accounting or marketing major. In a business culture such as the United States, where many firms are driven by fragmented specialisation and immediate utilisation of graduates, the broader, generalised skills of an IB major may be judged by some employers to be of lesser immediate use for entry level positions. Hence many advisors counsel American students to be cautious about IB concentrations at the Masters level.

However, there are several circumstances where an IB major is highly regarded by the job market: (1) at the undergraduate level where the emphasis (even in the United States) is on a broad education rather than narrow specialisation; (2) when an IB major is combined with a 'functional' major in a dual concentration at the Master's level. Such combinations are highly valued by firms, as they signal both narrow and broad capabilities; (3) at elite schools of business where admission into the programme is a sufficient signal of quality to employers. Moreover, the graduates of elite programmes are more likely to be groomed for top–level management positions requiring broad, rather than specialist capabilities; (4) for middle managers (whether in Executive MBA or regular programmes) who already possess business experience in a functional field and are now ready to broaden into general management functions; (5) for students expected to return to their home in emerging or developing nations;[13] (6) for students that have been promised foreign assignments upon their graduation.

As for PhDs in the field of International Business itself, AACSB Newsline (1995) showed the 'Average Growth in Openings Per Business School Doctoral Graduate' to be the highest for IB compared with other functional fields or business areas. IB also had one of the highest ratios of unfilled positions to doctorates granted. But the job market for doctorates in IB *per se*, remains rather small (only specialties such as Insurance, Industrial Relations and Real Estate Management are smaller), for reasons we detailed earlier.

THE FUTURE OF INTERNATIONAL BUSINESS EDUCATION: NICHES AND TRADITIONAL DEGREE PROGRAMMES

Business education in the United States via the traditional degree programmes is a super–saturated market. It is not merely because of demographic reasons that enrolments are declining. (And the decline would be worse, were it not for the continued growth in Asian student enrolment in the United States.) The decline is also because US companies are somewhat disenchanted with traditional educational approaches or at least, question the cost effectiveness of acquiring human resources via normal degree channels. Perceptions in the United States have polarised in companies facing levels of competitive pressure unknown to them in the past: on the one hand, for positions requiring highly specialised skills, cost pressures are forcing some companies to seek immediate results, so that many are not willing to invest the year or two of training which would previously have been afforded new MBA and Bachelor's degree holders to acquire the depth of specialisation needed.[14] On the other hand, for generalist management positions, companies are now questioning why expensive MBAs are needed, or why they should pay a Bachelor in Business any more than, say, a graduate in History. For generalist positions all will require extensive grooming, which can be provided by in–company programmes and experience. The situation in Europe is very different, with business education likely to remain on a growth curve into the next century. And the potential in emerging economies can only be described as a coming boom.

What role can international business education play in the overall picture? IB courses, as well as the internationalisation of functional area courses, will continue to increase worldwide, even in the saturated US market. This may be a reasonably cautious prediction given the declared level of dissatisfaction with the current level of internationalisation of curricula in the AIB/AACSB survey and since it involves growth from a small base. The use of International Business at the undergraduate level, as a unifying rubric for a broad–based education, accompanied by more study–abroad programmes and internships in international firms, is likely to be a growth area in the United States. A variation on the above theme may be seen in a few 'Masters in International Business' programmes (such as the one offered by Thunderbird in Arizona) which include language, internship and study–abroad components. Educators and students, as well as firms, profess satisfaction with this trend. In all the above cases, it is more likely that US business education will tend towards European levels of internationalisation than vice versa.

The modularisation trend in business curricula is also reflected in the growth in specialist certification and mid–career retraining programmes lasting only weeks or months in duration. Certificate programmes in 'Foreign Exchange Risk Management', or 'Managing the Multinational Workforce', or 'Logistics of Global Production', or 'International Taxation' are likely to proliferate. Moreover, there is no intrinsic reason why such programmes should be restricted to working managers. Enrolment can come simultaneously from full–time students of business — provided their degree curricula have been made flexible and freed from past constraints. One can visualise MBA programmes where only half the curriculum, the core, needs to be taken at the home university. For the remainder the student would be free to earn modular credits from approved certificate programmes, be they offered in Paris or Paraguay.

A final niche, which is just over the horizon, is business education geared to the needs of managers in emerging and developing nations — from their cultural perspective and from their companies' perspectives as net buyers of information and knowledge. From Chile to Nepal, a large number of new programmes have been established in the 1990s. For the most part, their curricula have been imported, without much adaptation, from the Anglo–American or Western European model. The contribution that International Business educators can make to this coming boom market is not only related to its large size, but in adapting educational materials to the local setting. The consumers of business education have so far been content to purchase the existing American model. Accredited US educational institutions maintain a standard that is a beacon to the world and education as a whole is one of the country's leading invisible exports. But in the assertion of local business cultures and identity, it is inevitable that curricula will need to be customised to business practices in each region.

International business educators in Europe and the United States therefore have three broad missions for the future: a continuation of their internationalisation task at home institutions; global integration of fragmented and modularised course offerings into overall coherent programmes and evolution of new materials for the emerging business cultures in *nouveau riche* nations.

NOTES

1. After a famous book *The Compleat Angler*, by Izaak Walton (1593–1683). The peculiar spelling of 'compleat' continues to denote, in educated and literary circles, a polished mastery over a subject and a thorough education.

2. For example, in 1995 the total cost of obtaining a driver's license in Denmark was estimated to be between DKK 6000 and DKK 10 000 due to complex regulations and punitively high taxes on automobiles.

3. The ratio of exports over GDP in the United States is of the order of 0.1 compared with approximately 0.25 for Germany. Despite the far smaller size of its economy, the aggregate level of German exports has rivaled that of the United States.

4. According to some estimates the overvaluation of the yen and deutschmark against the dollar approached as much as 50 per cent in the first half of 1995.

5. The questionnaire categorised the levels of International Business education as None; Minimal; Moderate; and Advanced. The 'None' category was surprisingly large with 29 per cent (undergraduate); 26 per cent (masters); and 31 per cent (PhD).

6. Faculty members who are highly proficient in mathematical modeling or the stylised facts of their subject areas have made considerable contributions to our understanding of management and their work provides the backbone to our understanding of business processes. However, while providing the backbone, such faculty ignore the much larger corpus of management studies which requires an eclectic, multi-functional approach.

7. Examples include topics such as FDI Theory, Political Risk Analysis, International Joint Ventures and Alliances or Cross-Cultural Management and Negotiations which first gained currency in IB literature. The fact that the other so-called functional areas have encroached upon and even appropriated some of this literature should be regarded as a mark of success and legitimacy. Moreover, the transmigration of the centre of gravity of interest and publication is hardly unique. For example, Transactions Cost Theory, which came out of Economics a decade or more ago, now finds a new avatar in Management which may have more articles based on the theory.

8. Not all schools have mission statements (only 77 per cent in Europe and 84 per cent of US schools) according to Arpan, Folks and Kwok (1995). And only 57 per cent of their sample of 557 schools 'had written mission statements which included specific references to international or global business'.

9. No longitudinal studies exist on the percentage of papers presented at academic conferences with an international content or theme. Most observers would agree that it is only after the late 1980s that one can detect a perceptible increase.

10. Ironically, while some are concerned with defining these boundaries, other pundits preach the virtues of the 'boundaryless' corporation and 'across-functional' management skills. By its eclectic nature international business courses provide a natural rubric under which students can be taught interfunctional and integrative approaches to management. But the teaching of integrative courses cannot be the only justification for creating a separate department.

11. This is, of course, only the sentiment of the existing AIB priesthood which sees its role potentially diminished and not that of the new converts who are gleefully appropriating some of the scriptures into wider circulation into their own functional fields.

12. This was in the context of an overall decline in enrolments in the United States.

13   Such students are more likely to assume broad management responsibilities in their countries and more likely to immediately handle international business assignments.

14   Competitive pressures on American industry have come from globalisation and the growth of imports and foreign direct investment in the United States.

REFERENCES

AACSB Newsline 1995. The Enrolment Pipeline: Little Light in the Tunnel. 25(3), Spring: 6–8.

Arpan, J., Folks, W. and Kwok, C. 1993. *International Business Education in the 1990s: A Global Survey*, Columbia, SC: The American Assembly of Collegiate Schools of Business.

Barber, B. 1995. *Jihad vs. McWorld*, New York: Times Books.

Cavusgil, T., Schechter, M. and Yaprak, A. (eds) 1992. *Internationalising Business Education*, Michigan State University, East Lansing, Michigan.

Dymsza, W. 1987. Global strategic planning: A model and recent developments. In W. Dymsza and R. Vambery (eds), *International Business Knowledge: Managing International Business Functions in the 1990s*, New York: Praeger, pp. 257–71.

Kedia, B. and Cornwell, T. 1994. Mission based strategies for internationalising U.S. business schools. *Journal of Teaching In International Business*, 5(3): 11–29.

Levitt, T. 1983. The globalization of markets. *Harvard Business Review*, May–June: 92–102.

Rich–Duval, C. 1995. Practical globalization of the business curriculum. *AMA Marketing Educator*, Summer: 1–2.

Toqueville, A. 1840; 1990 reprint. *Democracy In America*, New York: Vintage Books.

Walton, I. 1653; 1906 edition. *The Compleat Angler: Or the Contemplative Man's Recreation*, London: J.M. Dent & Co.

This chapter is being simultaneously published as a journal article. Details available from the author.

12. Trends in International Business Research: The Next 25 Years

Peter Buckley

INTRODUCTION

As the sage says 'the past is always changing, while the future remains the same'. The constant reinterpretation of the past contrasts with an unknown, and largely unknowable, future. It is a salutary thought that in 25 years, someone will be able to pick up this book and know just how wrong I could be! However, being wrong has never prevented me from carrying on in the past, so why change the habit of a lifetime?

This chapter begins by reviewing developments in international business theorising. It then provides a brief review of where we stand today (1996). Several key problematiques are introduced and speculations given as to where the subject of international business will be in all our tomorrows.

I should begin by noting that (rashly) I have attempted a similar exercise twice before (Buckley 1991a, 1991b); I have endeavoured not to repeat what I wrote on those occasions.

A GLANCE BACK IN ORDER TO LOOK FORWARD

It has been said that international business theorising 'could be characterised as sitting right at the crossroads of two extremes, an innovative managerial discipline on the one hand and a stagnant by–product of traditional economics on the other.' (Macharzina and Engelhard 1991: 24). I beg to differ. Much of the provenance of international business theory has been from economics, but it has also been strongly empirical and has drawn from the most innovative streams of economics. It has also received considerable impetus from its problem centred, interdisciplinary approach and has been much less hidebound than its functionally proscribed near neighbours, such as international marketing or international finance. Moreover, international business theory has passed a very severe test of credibility in that it has fed back concepts into the core disciplines rather than being a mere borrower of basic concepts (Lessard 1991).

The origins of international business are frequently traced back to Stephen Hymer's MIT dissertation of 1960 (Hymer 1976). In fact, Hymer was fortunate in being able to draw on the work of John Dunning, whose outstanding review of foreign investment in British industry (Dunning 1958) was a milestone in the development of the subject. Before Dunning, some key empirical findings were presented by Cleona Lewis (1938), and outstanding works whose contribution is regarded as primarily empirical, such as Phelps (1936), Frankel (1938), Gull (1943), Rippy (1944), Jenks (1946) and Lewis (1948), contained the germs of the modern analysis of the multinational enterprise.

Hymer demolished a straw man (a stagnant by–product of traditional economics, perhaps) in showing that foreign direct investment (fdi) belonged more to the theory of industrial organisation than to a crude theory of international finance where capital moved according to a simplistic rate of interest differential at the national level. It is debatable whether anyone at the time actually believed that foreign direct investment responded to nominal national interest rate differentials. Rather more to the point was the fact that there was little explicit attention paid to foreign direct investment, carried out by corporations in order to control foreign activities. Hymer, moreover, directed attention to the package of resources transferred under the aegis of direct investment and put the multinational enterprise at the forefront of the analysis as a key economic institution.

Hymer thus put the multinational enterprise into a framework amenable to analysis under Joe Bain's (1956) structure–conduct–performance model. The growth of the firm, too, required explanation. Edith Penrose's classic 1959 analysis (Penrose 1959) had, in part at least, been inspired by attention to the international expansion of firms (Penrose 1956) and her more managerialist explanation was to come more to the fore as 'international management' emerged from business policy to refertilise international business theory at a later point (Buckley 1996). Kindleberger (1969) and Dunning (1993) both developed distinctive approaches, using Hymer's work as a key input, but also deriving inputs from location theory, international trade theory and empirical insights.

The dynamic element in international business theory has always been a concern. It was from 'modern trade theory' that Raymond Vernon developed his justly famous 'product cycle hypothesis' (Vernon 1966), which provided a neat overview of United States investment in Europe and 'offshore production' in cheap labour countries. Although the product cycle was troublesome to fit into the multi–investor world, its emphasis on changing locations of production, driven by dynamic comparative advantage, its attention to technological developments, and its close emphasis on the interaction of the supply side and the demand side in determining the make–up and location of international production, made it a seminal contribution to the development of theory.

A second major thread in the development of the theory came with the internalisation approach to the growth of multinational enterprises (Buckley and Casson 1976). This approach allowed transaction cost economics to focus on an empirical reality — the spread of firms across national boundaries. The incorporation of concepts from Coase (1937) and Williamson (1975) provided a major impetus for theorising in international business. Contributions written both before and after the mid–1970s demonstrate the importance of this sea–change.

A rather regrettable consequence of this shift in emphasis was the view that the two approaches deriving from Hymer, based on the oligopolistic market power of firms, an alternative to the internalisation–transactions cost paradigm, based on the substitution of more perfect internal markets for intermediate goods and services for imperfect external ones. Not only are the two approaches not substitutes, they are complements, as I have tried to show elsewhere (Buckley 1990). The interaction of the two key variables — market power in external final goods markets and internalisation of imperfect intermediate goods markets — makes for a very satisfying synthesis.

The existence of large, powerful and long–standing firms did not go unnoticed by business historians. Alfred Chandler's work (1962, 1977) inspired a whole set of theoretical and empirical studies in what became business policy (later international business policy and international management). Notable contributions following this. For example, Stopford and Wells (1972) set up a fruitful liaison with organisational theory. The business historians drew on, and contributed to, the development of international business theory through the access point of Chandler's seminal contribution and their close ties with the long–run strategy of business have considerably enriched the field (Wilkins 1970, 1974, 1989; Jones 1995).

Another major work of synthesis is the project undertaken by John Dunning to encompass international business under an 'eclectic paradigm' (Dunning 1993). This approach concentrates on three main explanatory forces: locational advantages (L), internalisation advantages (I) and ownership advantages (O). Thus the internal (I), external (L) and strategy variables (O) are aggregated in a single explanation of international production. Despite theoretical doubts about the framework, notably problems with the time–dimension of the variables and with double counting (Buckley 1983; Casson

1987), many researchers and practitioners have found this a useful framework for organising their thoughts.

The integration of international management theorising poses a problem to which I will return. For now, suffice it to notice that the contributions of Porter (1980, 1985, 1986), Bartlett and Ghoshal (1989), Doz, Hamel and Prahalad have provided another rich tradition of theorising, which although aimed primarily at practising managers, provides a number of insights into managerial practices and processes requiring further attention.

This, then, is the corpus of theorising that many would regard as the core of international business. This is perhaps too narrow a focus, as it ignores many important contributions from outside economics and management. Organisation theory, and its broader parent, economic sociology, have contributed significantly to international business, though their impact, as Ghoshal and Westney (1993) note, has not been as strong as it could have been. The major sequence of thought runs from the 'Carnegie Tech' school of Simon, Cyert and March and behavioural theories through Aharoni's (1966) *The Foreign Investment Decision Process*, a book which is still offers a fresh insight today. The key issue here concerns the role of management and — very fashionably today — the role of information and its potential distortion within the firm's structures.

A second underrated influence is that arising from the 'international political economy', where analysis of the processes of globalisation would be better integrated with international business if more cognisance were taken of international relations and political elements in business activities (Boddewyn 1992; Boyd 1995).

A third influence which is hardly underrated is that of the role of culture. It is only in the late 1990s that international business has begun to look in the right place for inspiration on culture — towards social anthropology.

Finally, the sister disciplines of international marketing and international finance have been under–exploited, perhaps because they have been more concerned with their mainstream colleagues than with attempting to reach out towards the concerns of an international business constituency.

THE STATUS QUO, CIRCA 1996

I believe it can be taken as read that a core theory which takes in both Hymer's oligopolistic analysis and the internalisation approach is generally accepted. The key deficiency of this framework is its lack of attention to dynamics, most specifically its underplaying of technological advances (both endogenous and exogenous to the firm) and of management learning. These presumed deficiencies lie in the realm of the theory's attachment to equilibrium solutions, which both technological change and learning destroy.

The issue then becomes (as we shall see again below with the challenge of social anthropology and/or economic sociology) whether we can retain the rigour and explanatory power whilst incorporating these elements.

Three key empirical issues, all of which have theoretical implications face international business analysis at the present time. They are:

1.   the growth of international alliances amongst multinational firms;
2.   the issue of globalisation;
3.   the introduction of an explicit role for management decision–taking, more generally including the social context of international business.

These three issues require approaches which build from the core theory but the last one has perhaps the most radical implications of all for future theorising.

Alliances

Alliances between multinational firms have been seen as a challenge to the core theory of international business (Parkhe 1993). The recent analysis by Buckley and Casson (1996) attempts to analyse alliances entirely within the core framework. The key issue is that alliances represent an intermediate solution — between internalisation and externalisation of activities and so are not amenable to theoretical or empirical techniques which emphasise and analyse extreme values of explanatory variables. Alliances are the solution chosen at middling values of market size and external volatility (largely arising from rapidly changing technology). 'Moderation in all things' accurately describes the position where alliances are the optimum solution. The analysis does, however, show that there are combinations of market size and volatility where alliances represent the optimum choice for a rational, profit maximising company pace. Porter (1990) asserts that 'alliances as a broad–based strategy will only ensure a company's mediocrity, not its international leadership'.[1]

It is worthy of comment that the analysis of alliances (and joint ventures) has been the driving force behind the introduction of novel concepts into international business theorising. The notions of trust, joint action defined by the exercise of 'mutual forbearance', commitment and reciprocity have all found their way into theoretical models via alliances (Buckley and Casson 1988). The central notion of business culture (Casson 1991) has come to play a major role in international business theory — although we await the grand synthesis between the economistic analysis of this concept and the notions of culture derived from social anthropology and social psychology (which are not themselves easily integrated).

Globalisation

The obvious question when this term arises is 'globalisation of what?' My own answer to this issue resides in the simple model shown as Figure 12.1. The central question (and concern) seems to be that different markets exhibit differential degrees of international integration. The capital and financial markets are effectively fully integrated at world level. Markets in goods and services are often integrated at the regional level (i.e. European Union (EU) and North American Free Trade Agreement (NAFTA). But labour markets remain segmented by national boundaries.

There are a number of ways in which this simple analysis sheds light upon issues in the world economy. First, the framework shows the power, and the potential power, of multinational firms, which have the ability to raise and disburse capital where it is most effective, to gain advantages of economies of scale from regional integration in previously fragmented goods and services markets and to locate their activities so as to optimise differences in wage rates. Second, the limitations of government policy action are brought into focus. Governments are attempting to regulate labour markets as if they were separate (and separable) from other markets. They are not. Consequently, conflicts exist between the needs of regional market integration in goods and services and the constraints exercised by the global market for capital (over 'independent exchange rate' policies, for instance) on the one hand and national regulations, attempting to reduce unemployment or control inflation on the other. Third, we can attempt to make this analysis more realistic and dynamic by examining the relative pace of change of integration in different types of markets and in different regions. For instance, integration in the EU is proceeding more rapidly than elsewhere, whilst NAFTA is extending and strengthening; moves towards an Asia–Pacific Economic Community (APEC) are now also beginning in earnest. Our picture of the world and of the crises of markets needs constant revision.

Management Decision–taking

The role of management in international business theory has been a major focus of attention (Buckley 1996), not least from the point of view of integrating business culture and entrepreneurship (Casson 1982) as crucial determinants of the success of multinational firms. Much has recently been

Figure 12.1: Internationalisation of firms — Conflict of markets

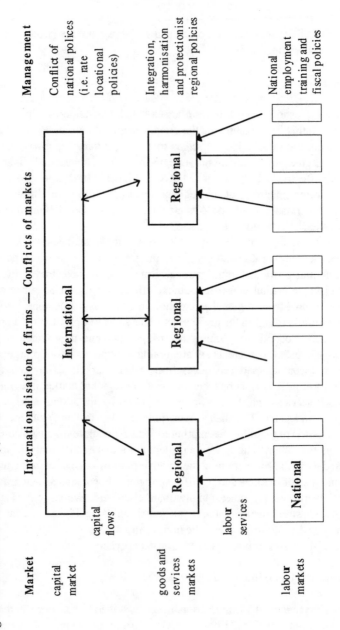

Market	Internationalisation of firms — Conflicts of markets	Management

capital market

capital flows

International

Conflict of national polices (i.e. rate locational policies)

goods and services markets

labour services

Regional

Regional

Regional

Integration, harmonisation and protectionist regional policies

labour markets

National

National employment training and fiscal policies

made of the role of 'tacit knowledge' in management decision–taking (Kogut and Zander 1992). However, it is plain that tacit knowledge can be codified and made explicit at a price. Contracts can be drawn which allow the transfer of knowledge which is difficult to codify (Casson 1979) and contingent contracts enable knowledge to be transferred under pre–specified circumstances. Much of the tacit knowledge issue comes down to societal relationships and, in particular, to trust and differential degrees of trust (insiders versus outsiders). There remains considerable progress to be made in unifying the treatment of these intangible, but vital, determinants of managerial action.

The future

Future theorising will attempt to capture the fluidity of the international business environment without losing determinancy. This is not an easy task. If we take a standard model and relax one or more of its key assumptions in turn, we may achieve new insights. If we attempt to rewrite the whole model and vary lots of parameters, the result could be an unsatisfying muddle. Much progress has been made and a great deal of this progress can be truly called interdisciplinary.

As the world economy becomes more volatile, efforts to capture volatility must be increased. This requires renewed attention to dynamics. There are essentially three ways in which dynamic change can be captured. The first (prospective) is to specify a model, give the initial conditions and drivers of change (which may include time or a time–related variable) and work through the model. The second (concurrent) means is to conduct a longitudinal study in real time, using ethnographic techniques. The third way is retrospective, to work back in time from the current position, using techniques to avoid or reduce bias and rewriting history. In attempting to capture process, it is important to avoid a collapse into categorisation.

Within the fluid international economy, the multinational firm will remain the most important institution, but its nature will inevitably change. There has been much talk of 'hollow companies', 'virtual corporations' and the like, but none of this should surprise international business theorists whose stock–in–trade has long been the changing boundaries of the firm. Although often described as 'internalisation theory', the approach could equally well be termed 'externalisation theory' (Buckley and Casson 1976). The firm will continue to face three key issues. The first is governance, the process of investment in rent-creating assets and their management. The management of rent–creating assets has an internal aspect in which attention to the economics of teams is central (Buckley and Carter 1996) and the signalling of ownership to external bodies is also vital. This signalling can be achieved, for instance, by patenting and branding (L'orange 1996). The second issue concerns the transactional properties of exchange. The issue of knowledge transfer both within and outside the firm is central here, especially given the social construction of knowledge and the way that new knowledge is generated both as an individual and as a collective project. Transaction cost economics is a start in this direction, but one whose agenda needs to be widened to take in managerial perceptions (Buckley and Chapman 1996). Finally, the market process and competition remain crucial. Competitive games are becoming more subtle and varied. The analysis of competition in future needs to take us far beyond mere price and quality competition into the management of relationships, consumer perceptions and control of key assets (inputs, brands, images, technology). The role of voice as well as exit needs to be made much more explicit (Hirshman 1970). The notion of 'core competences' needs to be extended to cover integrity, scope and image. The role of information, and its management, is likely to become more pronounced (Casson 1996) and the importance of information protection and control will achieve salience as the primary issue in the international political economy.

NOTES

[1]   Contrast this with Ken-ichi Ohmai 'Globalisation mandates alliances, makes them absolutely essential to strategy' (1989: 143).

REFERENCES

Aharoni Yair 1966. *Foreign Investment Decision Process*, Boston, Mass.: Graduate School of Business Administration.
Bain, J.S. 1956. *Barriers to New Competition,* Boston, Mass.: Harvard University Press.
Bartlett, C. and Ghoshal, S. 1989. *Managing Across Borders The Transnational Solution,* Boston, Mass.: Harvard Business School Press.
Boddewyn, J. 1992. Political Behaviour Research. In Peter J. Buckley (ed.) *New Directions in International Business; Research Priorities for the 1990s,* Cheltenham: Edward Elgar.
Boyd, G. (ed.) 1995. *Competitive* and *Cooperative Macromanagement,* Cheltenham: Edward Elgar.
Buckley, P.J. 1983. New theories of international business: some unresolved issue. In Mark Casson (ed.) *The Growth of International Business,* London: George Allen & Unwin.

Buckley, P.J. 1990. Problems and developments in the core theory of international business. *Journal of International Business Studies*, 21(4): 657–65.

Buckley, P.J. 1991a. The frontiers of international business research. *Management International Review*, 31 (Special Issue): 7–22.

Buckley, P.J. 1991b. Developments in International Business Theory in the 1990s. *Journal of Marketing Management.*,7(1) 15–24.

Buckley, P.J. 1996. The role of management in international business theory. *Management International Review*, 36 (Special Issue): 7–55.

Buckley, P.J. and Carter, M.J. 1996. The economics of business process design. *International Journal of Economics of Business*, 3(1): 5–25.

Buckley, P.J. and Casson, M. 1976. *The Future of the Multinational Enterprise*, London: Macmillan.

Buckley, P.J. and Casson, M. 1988. A theory of cooperation in international business. In Farok Contractor and Peter Lorange (eds). *Cooperative Strategies in International Business*, Lexington Mass.: Lexington Books.

Buckley, P.J. and Casson, M. 1996. An economic model of international joint ventures. *Journal of International Business Studies*, 27(5).

Buckley, P.J. and Chapman, M. (1996). The perception and measurement of transaction costs. University of Leeds, Mimeo.

Casson, M. 1979. *Alternatives to the Multinational Enterprise*, London: Macmillan.

Casson, M. 1982. *The Entrepreneur: An Economics Theory*, London: Macmillan.

Casson, M. 1987. *The Firm and the Market*, Oxford: Basil Blackwell.

Casson, M. 1991. *The Economics of Business Culture*, Oxford: Oxford University Press.

Casson, M. 1996 The Nature of the Firm Reconsidered: information synthesis and entrepreneurial organisation. *Management National Review*, 36 (Special Issue).

Chandler, A. 1962. *Strategy and Structure*, Cambridge Mass.: MIT Press.

Chandler, A. 1977. *The Visible Hand: the Managerial Revolution in American Business*, Cambridge Mass.: Harvard University Press.

Coase, R.A. 1937. The nature of the firm. *Economica*, (new series), 4: 386–405.

Dunning, J.H. 1958. *American Investment in British Manufacturing Industry*, London: George Allen and Unwin.

Dunning, J.H. 1993. *The Globalization of Business*, London: Routledge.

Frankel, S.H. 1938. *Capital Investment Africa; Its Course and Effects*, Oxford: Oxford University Press.

Ghoshal, S. and Westney, W.E. 1993. *Organisation Theory and the Multinational Enterprise*, London: Macmillan.

Gull E.M. 1943. *British Economic Interests in the Far East*, Oxford: Oxford University Press.

Hirshman, A. 1970. *Exit, Voice and Loyality*, Cambridge, Mass.: Harvard University Press.

Hymer, S. 1976. *The International Operations of National Firms; A Study of Foreign Direct Investment*, Cambridge Mass.: MIT Press. (Original Ph.D. written in 1960.)

Jenks, L.H. 1946.*The Migration of British Capital to 1875*, London: Jonathan Cape.

Jones, G. 1995. *The Evolution of International Business*, London: Routledge.

Kindleberger, C.P. 1969. *American Business Abroad.* New Haven: Yale University Press.

Kogut, B. and Zander, U. 1992. Knowledge of the firm, combinative capabilities and the replication of technology. *Organization Science,* 3: 383–97.

Lessard, D. 1991. Ownership. AIB Conference, 1991. Florida: Miami.

Lewis, Cleona (1938) *America's Stake in International Investments,* Brookings Institution: Washington DC.

Lewis, C. 1948. *The United States and Foreign Investment Problems,* Washington DC: Brookings Institution.

Lorange, P. 1996. Branding and Cooperative Strategies. JIBS, Conference Lausanne Mimeo.

Macharzina, K. and Engelhard, Johann 1991. Paradigm shift in international business research: from partist and eclectic approaches to the GAINS paradigm. *Management International Review,* 31 (Special Issue): 23–43.

Ohmae, K. 1989. *The Borderless World,* New York: Free Press.

Parke, A. 1993. Messy research, methodological predispositions, and theory development in international joint ventures. *Academy of Management — Review,* 18(2): 227–68.

Phelps, D.M. 1936. *Migration of Industry to South America,* New York: McGraw Hill.

Penrose, E.T. 1956. Foreign investment and the growth of the firm. *Economic Journal,* 66: 230–35.

Penrose E.T. 1959. *The theory of the growth in the firm,* Oxford: Basil Blackwell.

Porter M.E. 1980. *Competitive strategy,* New York: Free Press.

Porter M.E. 1985. *Competitive Advantage,* New York: Free Press.

Porter, M.E. (ed.) 1986. *Competition in Global Industries,* Boston Mass.: Harvard Business School Press.

Porter M.E. 1990. *The Competitive Advantage of Nations,* New York: Free Press.

Rippy, J.F. 1944. *Latin America and the Industrial Age,* Westport Conn.: Greenwood Press.

Stopford, John M. and Wells, Louis T. Jr. 1972. *Managing the Multinational Enterprise: Organization and Ownership of the Subsidiaries,* New York: Basic Books, Inc.

Vernon, R. 1966. International investment and international trade in the product cycle. *Quarterly Journal of Economics,* 80: 190–207.

Wilkins, M. 1970. *The Emergency of Multinational Enterprise: American Business Abroad from the Colonial Era to 1914,* Cambridge Mass.: Harvard University Press.

Wilkins, M. 1974. *The Maturing of Multinational Enterprise: American Business Abroad from 1914 to 1970,* Cambridge Mass.: Harvard University Press.

Wilkins, M. 1989. *The History of Foreign Investment the United States Before 1914,* Cambridge, Mass.: Harvard University Press.

Williamson, O.E. 1975. *Markets and Hierarchies,* New York: Free Press.1.

13. Current Issues in International Business: An Overview

Stephen Young

It was a great privilege to be asked to prepare this overview chapter on *Current Issues in International Business*, the purpose of which is to provide a summary and synthesis of the writings in the volume. The chapter contributions all come from leading academic figures in the field, a number of whom indeed were the original pioneers in international business (although certainly not the charlatans and dilettantes identified by Farok Contractor, p. 199). And with the new millennium looming, it is an appropriate moment to review the state of international business as an academic subject, and its span and contributions, and to ponder on the future.

THE STATE OF THE SUBJECT

International Business is a fairly young, eclectic area of inquiry, with the Academy of International Business (AIB) set up in 1959 and the journal *Management International Review* launched in 1960 (the *Journal of International Business Studies* was started later — in 1969) (Boddewyn and Iyer 1996). It is inevitable, therefore, that one important current issue concerns the dimensions of IB as an academic subject. International Business is not a discipline (and here I take issue with Ken Simmonds in this volume), but nor are other business subjects. Nevertheless, the apparently simple question of 'what is international business'? turns out to be a rather complex but also extremely important one for future inquiry. Toyne suggests that, unlike other fields, 'IB inquiry lacks coherence, a single defining paradigm and a central theory' (p. 35); because of this it may be categorised as a 'fragmented adhocracy', represented by a body of research that is personal and idiosyncratic. Clarification of the boundaries of the field is clearly a necessary first step in any attempts to provide this coherence and generality. It was interesting to read Stefan Robock's observation that the 1960s consensus was that the focus of IB should be the unique issues arising when business crosses national boundaries. And many people would be content with a definition in which international business is regarded as the outcome of economic–driven firm–level activity, undertaken across borders and influenced by environmental factors such as government. The difficulty with this or any such a definition is that the higher the proportion of business that becomes international, the less the subject area of 'international business' can lay unique claim to the field. At what point, for example, will business across boundaries in the EU be regarded as domestic as opposed to international business by EU companies (given that it already is formally in terms of trade and trade statistics)? While Contractor observes that the EU presents a much more diverse economic and cultural landscape than the United States, overcoming the barriers is accepted as a normal part of doing business by many continental European firms at least.

Toyne and Nigh (1996) have presented a new paradigm in which international business is seen as a 'multi–level, hierarchical process that evolves over time as a consequence of the interaction of two or more socially embedded, multi–level business processes' (p.42). By this definition, all levels of a society's hierarchical business process — from the suprasocietal to the individual as consumer or producer — are central to IB inquiry. This recognises the complexity of IB and the wide range of potential interactions, and appreciates the requirement to utilise knowledge from the sciences of anthropology, political economy and sociology as well as economics. The problem is that the wider international business is defined, the less likely it is that IB will be recognised by the academic community as a subject in its own right.

It is, nevertheless, important to clarify the boundaries of the subject, for a variety of reasons:

- Once the boundaries are set, the root disciplines can be identified. Study of these is critical to provide rigour to the subject area of IB. Without this background, the teaching of IB (like Marketing indeed) can be descriptive and lightweight.
- A major positive contribution of IB inquiry and education should be to facilitate multi–disciplinary, cross–functional thinking. Christopher Bartlett and Sumantra Ghoshal in this volume describe the large company in terms of entrepreneurial, integrative and renewal processes, as compared with a formal structure comprising business, geographic or functional units. The subject of international business is ideally suited to

provide the know–how and skills to facilitate such new trends. However, because IB education will always overlap with functional areas of study, it must be seen to be adding value and hence needs to be specific and identifiable in terms of areas of inquiry.

- Without clearly identified boundaries, the field may not be attractive to other than a small core of IB scholars (especially outside the United States). Arpan, Folks and Kwok (1993) have reported that European business schools had far more internationalised curricula and faculty than US schools. Despite this, continental European membership of the AIB or the European International Business Academy is quite small. In part this may be because of the perception that the United States–led field of IB emphasises the multinational enterprise mode as opposed to other methods of market–servicing, such as exporting, which may be more important in some countries. Scholars may then see a more natural affiliation with Marketing and, say, the European Marketing Academy. Contractor actually sees the reverse problem in the USA: since IB has been promoted heavily, there has been an influx of new academic entrants to the field which threaten 'to reduce the core competencies and distinctiveness of IB studies' (p. 210).

The boundaries of the subject could be set, according to this author's perspective, in terms of: explanations for, the management of and the societal dimensions of international business at multiple levels. In order to promote the associated multi–disciplinary study, more requires to be done to encourage good scholars from non–traditional IB fields to attend international business conferences and publish in IB journals. It is this pragmatic approach together with a clearer specification of the subject boundaries which will permit the development (even survival?) of the international business area of inquiry. In this respect Tom Brewer's chapter on the intersection of international political economy and international business strategy is very welcome. The discussion focuses upon two research areas, namely the interests and power of MNEs, particularly in relation to national governments and the interaction of international public policy regime change and MNEs' strategies. There is no question that each can enrich the other for the intellectual advancement of both. The ideas on new directions for interdisciplinary research could be widened to include other concerns at the intersection of international political economy and IB, to other literatures in the humanities and social sciences, and to genuinely multi–disciplinary inquiry. The challenge is to make it happen.

THE STATE OF THEORY AND RESEARCH

In his chapter on Trends in International Business Research: the Next 25 Years, Peter Buckley feels it necessary to begin by defending the contribution of economics to the development of international business theory. This defence is frankly unnecessary. Aside from Macharzina and Engelhard (1991), there must be few scholars who would deny the major contribution of economists to international business thought, and especially to the theme of explanations for the emergence and growth of the multinational enterprise. Simmonds in this volume cautions against over reliance on economics paradigms, but this is a different point. Both Peter Buckley and John Dunning in this volume trace the history of economists' contributions to international business theory — from Hymer, Kindleberger, Caves, Vernon and Aliber to Buckley and Casson and Dunning and to Hennart, Kogut, Cantwell and others. Much of this work has focused upon the discrete investment decisions of MNEs within a rationalist, profit–maximising framework.

Attempts are being made to provide explanations for joint ventures, strategic alliances and for other kinds of cross–border relationships between and within firms, and for the choice between greenfield ventures and acquisitions. The even greater challenge is to incorporate globalisation and systems of transactions as opposed to individual transactions within the analysis, where strategic variables have a major influence (Dunning 1993). Whether a uniquely economics–based approach is up to these to challenges is doubtful: for Dunning, the solution is seen in terms of explanations around the concept of 'alliance capitalism'; for Buckley, the central notion of business culture (deriving from social anthropology and social psychology) provides some possibilities. The theoretical approaches have been criticised for their static nature, and there is in consequence a revival of interest in an evolutionary theory of the MNE (Kogut and Zander 1993). In reality, this is bringing back to centre–stage the early work of scholars such as Penrose, Vernon, Burenstam Linder and Aharoni. In terms of the development of these dimensions of international business theory, the field of IB is not a fragmented adhocracy.

Aside from the struggle to keep pace with the rapid changes in the world economy, it has to be questioned whether sufficient attention has been paid by economists to critical questions concerning the implications of multinational enterprises for resource allocation globally and nationally. Policy attitudes to MNEs have oscillated radically over time from the honeymoon period of the 1950s and '60s, through the separation and divorce years of the 1970s and early '80s (with policy efforts directed to controlling MNEs at both national and international levels), to remarriage in the 1990s (or what Dunning p. 63, calls 'the renaissance of the free market system'). Yet the dramatic policy shifts have not really been justified by sound economic analysis. Do we, for example, have a sound theoretical and empirical basis for supporting free markets and unrestrained fdi in developing or indeed developed countries? What are the implications of global oligopoly behaviour (of which international strategic alliances are one component) by MNEs? Interestingly, while coming at this from a different angle, some of the work of Alan Rugman and Alain Verbeke on the distinction between efficiency–based and shelter–based strategies is very relevant to the latter topic. And John Dunning comments that reconciling the advantages of inter–firm cooperation with those of effective inter–firm competition will be the main challenge in developing a core theory of IB in the twenty first century; given a different twist, this could equally be applied to issues of resource allocation. Turning from explanations for multinationality to the management of the MNE, the chapters by Yip, Rugman and Verbeke, Bartlett and Ghoshal and Adler and Izraeli provide a wide range of insights. Topics covered in the wide span of literature on managing across borders include global strategic planning, organising strategy (organisation design and structure) and functional management strategies in production, marketing, human resource management and finance. In reviewing the development of theories, models and frameworks (mostly the latter) in international management, what is apparent is that very little of the early work provides insights which still have applicability today: this is very different to studies on the theory of the MNE as discussed above. One conceptual framework from the early days which is still widely cited is Perlmutter's (1969) typology of management orientations. Perlmutter advocated geocentrism, meaning a global approach in both headquarters and subsidiaries, as the ideal for MNEs. The Perlmutter model was based on the prevailing culture of the company and its chief executives. While this would be regarded as only one of a series of determinants of MNEs' strategic approach today, Perlmutter's thinking was undoubtedly a precursor to the work of Bartlett (1986) on the 'transnational' and that of Hedlund (1986) on the heterarchical MNE (see also Nonaka's 1990, multiple headquarters system).

It is arguable that the most consistent themes in the international management literature have related to the strategy and structure of the multinational enterprise. Evolving from Chandler's (1962) classic environment–structure–strategy paradigm, there have been a series of theoretical and empirical contributions concerning the organisation of the MNE. Bartlett and Ghoshal's (1989) conceptualisation of the 'transnational organisation' as opposed to the 'international', 'multinational' or 'global' categories has aroused some attention, at least as a future prospect. And in this volume, Christopher Bartlett and Sumantra Ghoshal, have extended the model of the transnational company to incorporate new thinking on the organisational processes of this emerging corporation. Rejecting conventional organisation structures, Bartlett and Ghoshal suggest a new management approach in terms of three core processes entrepreneurial, integration and renewal processes — which mean very different roles and tasks for front–line, middle and top–level managers. It has to be said that the required mind–set changes and implementation problems may prove an insuperable barrier to the adoption of such a radically new approach in many companies. The fashion for leaner, flatter structures is already causing significant problems because of the loss of management capacities; and the authors themselves admit to the problems caused by radical decentralisation without a centrally managed strategic framework. What is important, however, is the recognition of the requirement to face up to 'the ever increasing pace of globalisation of markets and the rising cost, complexity and convergence of technologies' and, therefore, the need for managers 'to consolidate and integrate their diverse organisational capabilities' (p. 130). International business teaching and training which is fundamentally concerned with the management of diversity and complexity should have a major role to play in this new era

The chapter by George Yip continues the global management theme by addressing issues and evidence on global strategies. What is interesting is that Yip does not attempt a formal definition of global strategies, restricting himself to reproducing the fairly anodyne description of others that a 'global strategy can be defined as a globally coordinated and integrated approach to operating multinational'. This is disappointing especially since the author provides a useful contingency model of global strategy in which industry globalisation factors and company characteristics (size, history and extent of internationalisation, competitive position, etc.) are major drivers, moderated by organisational factors (structure, processes, people and culture), and nationality. These multiple causal and moderating factors will in turn influence performance in some indeterminate ways. Yip's excellent review of the various dimensions of the literature on global strategies highlights the contributions to date and the gaps, especially the need for research applying more complex modelling, and for the investigation of the consequences of global strategy for performance. What is apparent too is the relative dearth of both theory and empirical evidence in many aspects of this highly topical area of international business. Until this further inquiry is undertaken, there will continue to be ambiguity about what a global strategy actually is: not only is clarification required on the coordination and integration dimensions when applied to the range of value added activities; but there are added complexities pertaining to the roles of corporate and regional headquarters and indeed national subsidiaries, to the nature and extent of market focus and to methods of supplying markets.

Yip acknowledges the contributions of Prahalad and Doz (1987), Bartlett and Ghoshal (1989) and Porter (1986) in the search for models of global strategy. The extent of the contribution of Porter to the international business field is a contentious one. His work on competitive advantage and competitive strategy in a domestic context (Porter 1980, 1985) is rightly praised. At least from a Western perspective, the model of the forces driving industry competition, the concepts of the value chain and of generic competitive strategies are powerful and have been extremely influential (even though one of the most famous propositions from his model of generic strategies, that is 'not to be stuck in the middle', is now widely discredited). There are question marks, however, over those aspects of Porter's work which encompass or impinge upon international business and the activities of multinational enterprises. Alan Rugman and Alain Verbeke in this volume are highly critical of most of Porter's work, alleging that it is 30 years out of date when applied to the analysis of MNEs. Certainly Porter (1990) argues strongly for the role of the home country, with MNEs using their domestic base as a launching pad for globalisation; whereas there is growing evidence of multiple centres and not simply a single home centre, as multinational enterprises seek to exploit competitive advantages wherever they occur. The result is that there may not be one national 'diamond' of competitive advantage but many.

John Dunning (1992) has also been critical of the diamond model because of its omission of the role of multinational business activity which is crucial in linking national diamonds of competitive advantage to each other. He argues rightly that inward and outward investment are likely to influence the diamond of competitive advantage and hence the multinational business variable should be considered as a separate factor in the model. Rugman disputes the validity both of Porter's generic strategy model when applied in an international context and of his configuration/coordination framework of global strategies; and, more interestingly, presents ideas for a new organising framework to analyse the role of multinational networks in global competition.

There are two issues worth picking up from the above debates which are highly relevant to this volume. The first is to note a growing self–confidence in the international business field and the real value which IB scholars can add to conventional thinking which may be myopically domestically oriented. The second, however, is to reinforce earlier observations concerning uncertainties over the boundaries of the IB field inquiry. Is, for example, the area of strategic management part of the international business field of inquiry (or vice–versa)? Certainly the two are converging as Casson et al. point out in this volume.

Aside from the topics discussed above, a recent *Reader on International Management* (Ghauri and Prasad 1995) suggests three other main themes in the literature viz. cooperative international competition, understanding non–Western structures and developing global managers. Strategic alliances have, without question become a major feature of global competition in the world economy. Definitional advances have primarily come from international business economists, as have the limited attempts at modelling alliances and collaborations (Buckley and Casson 1988; Parkhe 1991; see also Sheth and Parvatiyar 1992); but there have been efforts to incorporate collaboration within the context of global strategy formulation (Hamel, Doz and Prahalad 1989) and the management of inter–organisational networks with multiple actors (Westney 1993). As Ghauri and Prasad (1995) point out, following the emphasis in the 1960s and 1970s on comparative management studies using the US context as a norm, in the 1980s Japanese management and an understanding of non–Western structures became a major focus for comparative research.

The above work developed separately from that on cross–cultural management; and the common core, namely that of culture, has not been utilised to provide a unifying framework in the international management field. Hofstede (1994) claimed in a recent article that: 'The business of international business is culture', and his own work on the dimensions of national cultural differences has had an important impact (Hofstede 1980, 1991). However, because of the fact that it concerned organisational cultures and derived from anthropological roots, it perhaps has not stimulated the wider discussion and research which it undoubtedly deserves. With the growing interest of well known writers in the area of culture, perhaps this will change. The Casson et al. chapter reviews different perspectives on the importance of national and corporate culture to competitive advantage. Empirical evidence is then provided on the relationship between human resource management (HRM) practice and the stances adopted by senior management towards other strategic issues. The authors' results support other evidence that HRM is more likely to be shaped by business strategy.

Nancy Adler has made a significant contribution with her work on international dimensions of organisational behaviour, and in this volume has provided a stimulating chapter on women managers in the world economy. Despite the undoubted barriers which still remain for women in the workforce, the major contributions which they can make at executive level is undisputed. These barriers are even greater at expatriate management level, and, therefore, Adler and Izraeli's chapter, empirically rejecting some of the myths about women managing across borders, is very welcome. Women do want to be international managers and they do succeed internationally, but companies remain hesitant or often completely unwilling to send women managers abroad.

THE STATE OF THE FUTURE

As befits an exciting and innovative subject, the contributions in this volume provide a range of stimulating insights into many of the current issues in international business. Topics such as globalisation, the growth of international alliances, and regional and multilateral trade and investment liberalisation, provide a challenging agenda for those studying explanations for international production, the management of international enterprises or the societal dimensions of international business.

From a European perspective, at least, international business inquiry does not face the problems identified by Contractor for the USA, namely an influx of scholars from a range of subject areas who threaten 'to reduce the core competencies and distinctiveness of IB studies' (p. 210). Accepting the need to set some boundaries to international business (as a subject theme rather than discipline), the aim should rather be to actively promote contributions from a range of related subjects. Tom Brewer's suggestions for international business–international political economy interdisciplinary studies is a model in this regard. Instead of threatening core competencies, this approach could actually increase the intellectual rigour of international business and its impact as a subject area.

The time is, therefore, ripe for international business journals and conferences to encourage contributions of a review nature, which specifically seek to explore the international dimensions of related subjects. This will both further promote interdisciplinary and multi–disciplinary research and highlight more clearly the boundaries of international business. An approach that would not be helpful would be to analyse solely the interdisciplinary articles which have appeared in core international business journals. Further contributions investigating what we have learned and where we go from here should also be supported, along the lines of the chapter by George Yip (which identifies the next frontier in global strategy research) and indeed others in this timely book. Finally, recognising that International Business must continue to develop as an academic subject, vocational elements mustn't be forgotten. It is important, therefore, to get closer to practitioners and the writings of managers and consultants, to ensure that IB research does not get isolated from the work of the international executive. The differing, sometimes opposing views expressed in this book are a necessary part of the intellectual development of the subject. Let us have more such debates (Boddewyn and Iyer 1996).

REFERENCES

Arpan, J., Folks, W. and Kwok, C. 1993. *International Business Education in the 1990s: A Global Survey,* Columbiam, SC: The American Assembly of Collegiate School of Business.

Bartlett, C.A. 1986. Building and Managing the Transnational: The New Organisational Challenge. In M.E. Porter (ed.), *Competition in Global Industries,* Boston, Mass.: Harvard Business School Press, 367–404.

Bartlett, C.A. and Ghoshal, S. 1989. *Managing Across Borders,* Boston, Mass.: Harvard Business School Press.

Boddewyn, J.J. and Iyer, G.R. 1996. *International Business Research: Assorted Lacunae and Remedies.* Paper presented at the Annual Meeting of the Academy of International Business, Banff Springs, Canada, September.

Buckley, P.J. and Casson, M. 1988. A Theory of Cooperation in International Business. In F.J. Contractor and P. Lorange (eds), *Cooperative Strategies in International Business*, New York: Lexington Books.

Chandler, A.D. Jr. 1962. *Strategy and Structure,* Boston, Mass.: MIT Press.

Dunning, J.H. 1993. *Multinational Enterprises and the Global Economy,* Wokingham, Berks: Addison–Wesley.

Dunning, J.H. 1992, The Competitive Advantage of Countries and the Activities of Transnational Corporations, *Transnational Corporations,* 1(1): 135–68.

Ghauri, P.N. and Prasad, S.B. 1995. *International Management. A Reader*, London: The Dryden Press.

Hamel, G., Doz, Y.L. and Prahalad, C.K. 1989. Collaborate with your Competitors — and Win. *Harvard Business Review,* (January–February), 133–9.

Hedlund, G 1986. The Hypermodern MNC — A Heterarchy? *Human Resource Management*, 25(1): 9–35.

Hofstede, G. 1994. The Business of International Business is Culture. *International Business Review,* 3(1): 1–14.

Hofstede, G. 1980. *Culture's Consequences: International Differences in Work Related Values,* Beverly Hills: Sage Publications.

Hofstede, G. 1991. *Cultures and Organizations: Software of the Mind*, London: McGraw Hill.

Kogut, B. and Zander, U. 1993. Knowledge of the Firm and the Evolutionary Theory of the Multinational Corporation. *Journal of International Business Studies,* 24(4): 625–5.

Macharzina, K. and Engelhard, Johann 1991. Paradigm shift in international business research: from partist and eclectic approaches to the GAINS paradigm. *Management International Review,* 31 (Special Issue): 23–43.

Nonaka, I. 1990. Managing Globalisation as a Self–Renewal Process: Experiences of Japanese MNCs. In C.A. Bartlett, Y.L. Doz and G. Hedlund (eds), *Managing the Global Firm*, London: Routledge, 69–94.

Parkhe, A. 1991. Interfirm Diversity, Organizational Learning and Longevity in Global Strategic Alliances. *Journal of International Business Studies*, 22(4): 579–601.

Perlmutter, H.V. 1969. The Tortuous Evolution of the Multinational Corporation. *Columbia Journal of World Business*, 4: 9–18.

Porter, M.E. 1980. *Competitive Strategy*, New York: The Free Press.

Porter, M.E. 1985. *Competitive Advantage*, New York: The Free Press.

Porter, M.E. 1986. *Competition in Global Industries*, Boston, Mass.: Harvard Business School Press.

Porter, M.E. 1990. *The Competitive Advantage of Nations*, New York: The Free Press.

Prahalad C.K. and Doz, Y.L. 1987. *The Multinational Mission: Balancing Local Demands and Global Vision*, New York: The Free Press.

Sheth, J.N. and Parvatiyar, A. 1992. Towards a Theory of Business Alliance Formation. *Scandinavian International Business Review*, 1(3): 3–8.

Toyne, B. and Nigh, D. 1996. *International Business: An Emerging Vision*, Columbia, SC: University of South Carolina Press.

Westney, D.E. 1993. Institutionalisation Theory and the Multinational Corporation. In S. Ghoshal and D.E. Westney (eds), *Organisation Theory and the Multinational Corporation*, New York and London: St Martin Press, 237–255.

Index